The European Right to Confrontation in Criminal Proceedings

Europa Law Publishing, Groningen 2006

The European Right to Confrontation in Criminal Proceedings

Absent, Anonymous and Vulnerable Witnesses

Dr. Stefano Maffei

Europa Law Publishing is a publishing company specializing in European Union law, international trade law, public international law, environmental law and comparative national law.
For further information please contact Europa Law Publishing via email: info@europalawpublishing.com or visit our website at: www.europalawpublishing.com.

Typeset in Scala and Scala Sans, Graphic design by G2K Designers, Groningen/Amsterdam

NUR 828
ISBN-10: 90-76871-64-7
ISBN-13: 978-90-76871-64-6

European and International Criminal Law Series (1)
Series Editor: Dr. Olaoluwa Olusanya (University of Wales, Aberystwyth)

British Library Cataloguing-in-Publication Data
A catalogue record for this book is available from the British Library

Acknowledgements

On the Italian front, this work has greatly benefited from the comments on early drafts by Professor Piermaria Corso of the University of Parma. Professor Corso is leading me through the academic career and I am mostly grateful to him for his continuous help and support. On the English front, my greatest debt of gratitude is to Professor Andrew Ashworth of All Souls College. His indispensable advice and guidance were a continuous source of inspiration not only for this work, but also for my personal education and my career as a teacher and jurist. Thanks also to the Law Librarians at the Bodleian Library and to the "Special Collection" Department of the Harvard Law School for their help throughout. My gratitude goes also to Prof. Spyridon Flogaitis, director of the European Public Law Center, for his teachings while I was working as a researcher in Greece. Last, but by no means least, thanks must go to my parents Pino and Luciana, my brother Roberto, my fiancée Maria and all my friends scattered around the world, from which I derived limitless support.

CONTENTS

Introduction

Since criminal proceedings are the epitome of the power of the State, steps must be taken to contrast abuses of public authorities and to entrench safeguards against legal incursions into fundamental rights. Although the vision embedded in this rather simple statement may be said to be shared among all European Member States, the level of protection of the fundamental rights of an accused person varies significantly. This is because – across contemporary Europe – criminal policy still remains, with minor exceptions – a matter for the domestic realm. Criminal law, procedure and evidence do not fully participate of the movement towards a unified European legal area as Members States seem almost stubbornly attached to their own way of prosecuting, judging and punishing those who have allegedly committed a criminal offence. While each national order has its own set of constitutional rights and guarantees, it is inevitable that national variants emerge with regard to almost all phases and features of criminal proceedings. This also affects the attitude of lawyers and scientists engaged in the study and research of criminal matters. A Belgian criminal jurist probably knows very little of the landmark amendments to the English rule against hearsay of Criminal Justice Act 2003, while Swedish criminal lawyers probably ignore that an Italian defendant is allowed to negotiate a criminal sanction directly with the prosecutor. A few Italians are aware that Greece is about to overturn its codes of criminal code and criminal procedures, while few Polish know that in Ireland a Governmental Committee is currently engaged in the drafting of a codification for criminal justice. It is true that national systems communicate occasionally – as in the cases of transnational arrest warrants or rogatory letters – but it is also true that no comparative effort has yet broken national barriers and led to the establishment of a common European 'vision' on criminal justice.

Yet, fundamental rights cannot tolerate national barriers and variants in an integrated area of peace, security and justice, as European authorities are proud to describe the old Continent. If the concept of a fundamental right is to have any meaning, it must surely sound in the protection which the law affords to it. With this principle in mind, this book shall attempt to establish a European discourse on the right of any accused person to confront his accusers. This will be based on principles of constitutional theory and natural justice, the parameters outlined by ECHR law and the rules of evidence of Italy, France and England and Wales. So far, comparative scholars have shown little, if any, interest in drawing a detailed map of the contours of the Right to Confrontation and still lack a precise sense of its far-reaching potential. The reason can be easily explained: while the Right to Confrontation is declared in almost identical terms in several national and international jurisdictions, its implementation depends upon the technicalities of their laws of criminal procedure and evidence. These subjects differ significantly across European countries and are often regarded as bastions of nationhood. It is true that a growing tendency towards 'harmonisation' may be found in Europe due to the meta-principles established by the Human Rights institutions and the independent commitment of certain legislators responsive to foreign legal solutions. Nevertheless, national laws of evidence are based upon independent concepts and conflicting legal traditions, which directly affect the rules of admissibility, collection and evaluation of the testimony of witnesses.

Were the Right to Confrontation an absolute right, each and every prosecution witness would be challenged under oath, face-to-face with the defendant in accordance with the ultimate confrontational paradigm of a public cross-examination. History shows that no criminal justice system – neither adversarial nor inquisitorial – has ever agreed to strike out all other 'testimonial' evidence adverse to the defendant. Even in the United States of America, the birthplace of the constitutional Right to Confrontation, intrusions are tolerated in the form of exceptions to the rules against hearsay. This is because a number of values have been – and still are – commonly invoked to justify even the most penetrating intrusions into the Right to Confrontation. Some of these values can be effectively described as 'public interest' concerns: in essence, the claim is that protection of confrontation has an adverse effect on the 'efficiency of the proceeding' and the process of 'accurate adjudication'. Other values include the protection of the fundamental rights of the intimidated or vulnerable accuser.

This work argues that, once acknowledged by a national or international legal order, the Right to Confrontation must be taken seriously, and intrusions should be construed to minimise the impact against the defendant.

Discussion is in six chapters. Chapter 1 establishes a theoretical concept of confrontation as a fundamental Human Right. It also discusses the history and developments of the Right to Confrontation in an international perspective, with some brief reference to the law of the U.S., where this right was announced for the first time in a constitutional text. Further, Chapter 1 defines the 'confrontational paradigm', the 'testimonial' statements to which it applies and a number of 'departures' from the confrontation paradigm and their correspondent counterbalances. In Chapter 2, three categories of problematic witnesses, common to criminal systems of both the adversarial and the inquisitorial traditions, are outlined: the absent, anonymous and vulnerable witnesses. Chapter 3 explores the ECHR version of the Right to Confrontation, stemming from the case law on Article 6(3)(d) of the European Convention. Although this case law sets certain minimum standards for the admissibility, collection and evaluation of unchallenged testimonial evidence, major inconsistencies may be found in the Strasbourg bodies' approach to the subject. Chapter 4 serves as an introduction to the subsequent cross-national discussion of matters of confrontation. France, Italy and England and Wales are chosen as model European countries in light of their peculiar legal traditions (adversarial in England, inquisitorial in France, *mixte* in Italy, where an adversarial Code has been transplanted in 1988 into an inquisitorial legal culture). Something will have to be said about the sources of the law and the general principles of criminal procedure and evidence of the model Countries, in a comparative fashion. Chapter 5 investigates the ordinary course of testimony in the model countries and argues that a host of differences derive from the inquisitorial or adversarial inspiration of the respective proceedings. Chapter 6 finally explores the evidence of absent, anonymous and vulnerable witnesses in the model jurisdictions. Although none of them yet fully complies with the Confrontation Clause of the European Convention and the guarantees established by the European Court of Human Rights, certain domestic rules and practices may bring an additional meaningful contribution to a general European policy on the Right to Confrontation.

CHAPTER I

Confrontation of Adverse Witnesses as a Fundamental Right of the Accused Person

1 Preliminaries

1.1 Outline

Whilst the right to confront unfavourable witnesses emerged as a fundamental right of the defendant in adversarial systems of criminal justice, Human Rights discourse has more recently accredited it as a universal feature of a fair criminal trial. References to the Right to Confrontation can now be found in the European Convention for the Protection of Human Rights and Fundamental Freedoms,[1] the International Covenant on Civil and Political Rights,[2] the Statutes of the International Criminal Tribunals for the Former Yugoslavia,[3] Rwanda[4] and Sierra Leone,[5] the Rome Statute of the International Criminal Court,[6] and the Constitutions of the United States,[7] Italy[8] and Albania.[9]

The fact that several jurisdictions declare their open commitment to confrontation should not lead the reader to believe that a consensus exists around the world on the administration of the evidence of witnesses adverse to the defendant. The enforcement of this fundamental right greatly depends upon the technicalities of the laws of procedure and evidence, and these vary significantly in national as well as international orders. In this Chapter, an attempt is made to establish a theoretical discourse on the Right to Confrontation: this will be based upon the interests that the right is meant to ensure and the values that are commonly invoked to curtail it. It is anticipated that criminal justice systems face great pressure to allow incursions into fundamental rights for reasons of public interest, or for the protection of other competing rights.

The main goal of this chapter is to define what the Right of Confrontation entails according to principles of constitutional theory and natural justice. A meaningful theory of confrontation must provide criminal defendants with an enforceable opportunity to challenge the rules of evidence and procedure of the jurisdiction in which they are being prosecuted. It is also necessary to establish in abstract terms when a *witness* is fairly *confronted* with the accused person and which intrusions into this right can be tolerated. Research will show that

---

1 Art. 6(3)(d), Rome, 4 November 1950; T.S. 71 (1953); Cmd. 8969.

2 Art. 14(3)(e), New York, 19 December 1966; T.S. 6 (1977); Cmd. 6702.

3 Art. 21(4)(e) Statute I.C.T.Y., U.N. Sec. Council Res. No. 827 (May, 25 1993); (1993) 47 U.N. Ybk. 440.

4 Art. 20(4)(e), Statute I.C.T.R., U.N. Sec. Council Res. No. 955 (November, 8 1994); (1994) 48 U.N. Ybk. 299.

5 Art. 17(4)(e) Statute Sierra Leone, established in accordance with U.N. Sec. Council Res. No. 1315 (August 14, 2000), (2000) 54 U.N. Ybk. 205.

6 Art. 67(1)(e) Statute I.C.C., adopted on July 17, 1998.

7 Sixth Amendment to the United States Federal Constitution.

8 Art. 111(3) Italian Constitution.

9 Art. 31(e) Albanian Constitution.

departures from a confrontational process of adjudication are numerous in the practice of criminal litigation, since an array of highly respected interests clash with the right in question. In the following chapter, special attention will be paid to three categories of declarants (termed *absent*, *anonymous* and *vulnerable* witnesses) whose evidence is not gathered in a confrontational manner, yet is often admissible in both adversarial and inquisitorial proceedings.

1.2 Terminology

Three problems of terminology must be resolved at the outset. Firstly, as the Right to Confrontation is not treated here as an object of unconditional devotion,[10] I shall avoid making reference to it as a Human Right, given the symbolism that contemporary discourse attaches to the expression. The adjective 'Human' may be easily replaced by 'fundamental', or 'constitutional', in the light of the standing of the right in the sources of law of the jurisdictions of the Western World.

Secondly, the word *confrontation* may generate some confusion, as it is employed with independent meanings by national laws. In England, confrontation is a procedure for the identification of the accused, to be used in the last resort when a parade or group identification is not possible.[11] In Italy[12] and France,[13] confrontations are trial procedures whereby the accused and a witness, or two witnesses, sit in front of each other and challenge the conflicting accounts they have previously given in evidence. Instead, in this work the term 'confrontation' describes the procedure of an open examination of the witness in the courtroom, in line with the requirements of the paradigm described in section 3.2.

Thirdly, readers may wonder why the phrase *right to confrontation* is preferred to *right to cross-examine*. I can give three arguments at this regard. At first, *cross-examination* is a procedure for the questioning of witnesses unknown to the inquisitorial tradition of Continental Europe. In addition, in the adversarial trial a right to cross-examine the adverse witness is also granted to the representatives of the prosecution (as well as the civil party), with regard to those who are summoned by the defence. The prosecution's 'procedural' right to cross-examine, however, cannot by any means be equated to the *fundamental* right to cross-examine of the accused person, since only the latter finds its ulti-

---

10 The alleged temptation of human rights lawyers to treat human rights 'as an object of devotion rather than calculation' is 'part of the problem' of the contemporary human rights movement, in the words of D. Kennedy, *The International Human Rights Movement: Part of the Problem?*, [2001] European Human Right Law Review 245, 246.

11 Cf. §2.10-2.11, *Code of Practice for the identification of persons by police officers (Code D)*.

12 Arts. 211, 212 Italian Code of Criminal Procedure.

13 Arts. 114 to 121 French Code of Criminal Procedure.

mate foundation in constitutional texts and treaties for the protection of fundamental rights and freedoms. Furthermore, not only does the concept of *confrontation* embrace the feature of adverse questioning, but also the publicity of the examination, disclosure of the real identity of the declarant and the obligation of sincerity.

1.3 Fundamental Rights, Public Interest and Intrusions into Confrontation

Rights theories are acutely controversial and cannot be extensively discussed here. At a very minimum level, it is acknowledged that when a right is fundamental it cannot be taken away simply by showing that a majority of people would be better off if it were not applied in a given situation.[14] Fundamental rights are essentially counter-majoritarian[15] and place straitjackets on the policies that may be established by the law. Once a fundamental right is announced, an 'added value'[16] is attached to it; such right must be then taken seriously and some preference must be given to it when related policies are implemented.

In his theory of rights, Ronald Dworkin challenges the idea that clashes between interests and values ought to be resolved by striking a 'balance' between the rights of the individual and the demands of society at large. A right would hardly be worthy of description as 'fundamental' if it could be curtailed by a simple reference to the public interest. In comparison, he argues that:

> It cannot be an argument for curtailing a right simply that society would pay a further price for extending it. There must be something special about that further cost, or there must be some other feature of the case, that makes it sensible to say that although great social cost is warranted to protect the original right, this particular cost is not necessary. Otherwise the Government failure to extend the right will show that its recognition of the right in the original case is a sham.[17]

Dworkin's view has constructive implications for this work. Firstly, it suggests that protection of fundamental rights is an expensive business for society. In the case of the Right to Confrontation the social 'cost' is the exclusion of a great deal of unchallenged testimonies from admissible evidence. Secondly, it specifies

---

14 See the approach taken by A. Ashworth, *Human Rights, Serious Crime and Criminal Procedure*, Sweet & Maxwell, London, 2002, 70-76.

15 This approach echoes the famous say that 'I am not the more disposed to pass beneath the yoke because it is held out to me by the arms of a million men', A. De Tocqueville, *De la Démocratie en Amérique*, 17th edn., Lévy, Paris, 1888, vol. III, 21.

16 *Allie Mohammed Appellant v. The State Respondent* [1999] 2 A.C. 111 (P.C.) at 123.

17 R.M. Dworkin, *Taking Rights Seriously*, Duckworth, London, 1977, 200.

that case-by-case scrutiny is essential to determine what specific value – if any at all – was referred to by the law, in order to justify the intrusion into a fundamental right. Careful legal analysis is needed to disclose whether a given intrusion into confrontation was really necessary, or rather excessive or inadequate, to serve the interests which purportedly occasioned it.

Dworkin also outlines three grounds on which intrusions into fundamental rights can be tolerated:

> First, the government might show that the values protected by the original right are not really at stake in the marginal case, or at stake only in some attenuated form. Second, it might show that if the right is defined to include the marginal case, then some competing [and equally fundamental] right [...] would be abridged. Third, it might show that if the right were so defined, then the cost to society would not simply be incremental, but would be of a degree far beyond the cost paid to grant the original right, a degree great enough to justify whatever assault on dignity or equality might be involved.[18]

Even at this very early stage, these principles can be straightforwardly applied to the Right to Confrontation. When Mr. A does not take the stand at trial, but a confrontational examination was staged at a dedicated pre-trial hearing, the intrusion into the right is minimal, and the evidence should be admissible. When Mr. A is sick at the time of the trial, attendance at the hearing may arguably impair his right to medical treatment. Imagine also that Mr. A, summoned as a witness in Country Alpha, is detained in Country Beta. If Country Beta refuses to collect his evidence on commission, Country Alpha cannot certainly move war against country Beta, for the sole purpose of ensuring the attendance of Mr. A at the concerned trial. The cost of a war far exceeds what country Alpha is prepared to pay to protect the Right to Confrontation. More discussion on the legitimacy of the incursions into this right and on the counterbalances available to minimise them is provided later in this Chapter.

2 The Origins and Development of the Right to Confrontation

2.1 Ancient Laws

The notion of a face-to face confrontation between the defendant and his accusers is a recurrent feature of criminal proceedings over the centuries. Historical research on the theory and practice of criminal trials shows

[18] R.M. Dworkin, *Taking Rights...*, *supra* note 17, at 200.

that witnesses testifying under oath, in an open proceeding and *face-to-face* with the accused has always existed as an underlying idea. This was the practice of the Greeks,[19] the Hebrews[20] and the Romans[21]. Nonetheless, the fact that witnesses were often heard in open court does not mean that the accused could claim a 'right' to obtain their presence and challenge their testimony. Instead, open confrontation was only one of several possible ways in which depositions could be tendered before a criminal court.

2.2 Adversarial Origins (England, United States of America)

When Sir Walter Raleigh was charged with conspiracy against King James in 1603, he could hardly have imagined that he would have made history as the first champion of confrontation. The prosecution argued that Sir Walter was raising money abroad to distribute among malcontents in England in order to support Arabella Stuart's claim to the throne. The most powerful evidence against him was a statement by purported conspirator Lord Cobham. Under pressure – if not torture – by officers of the Crown, Cobham had named Raleigh as the instigator and had claimed that he went abroad to garner support for an insurrection. The statements were introduced in evidence. Raleigh vigorously denied the charges and offered explanations for his loans. He urged the court to call his accuser so he might stand face to face with him. He conceded that a witness need not be called where he 'is not to be had conveniently', but pointed out that Lord Cobham was 'alive and in the house'. He begged the court in vain: 'let him be produced'.[22] Raleigh was sentenced to death in 1603 and, fifteen years later, executed.

The anecdote suggests that the common law courts were still reluctant to afford to the defendant the right to cross-examine adverse witnesses in trials for treason, in spite of the acknowledgement of this right by Statute as early as

---

19 F. Helie, *Traité de l'instruction Criminelle*, Hingray, Paris, 1845, vol. I, 25.

20 L.H. Shiffman, *Sectarian Law in the Dead Sea Scrolls: Courts, Testimony and the Penal Code*, Chico Scholars, California, 1983, 55-65.

21 In Acts 25:16 (King James), Roman Governor Festus is reported to say: 'It is not the manner of the Romans to deliver any man to die, before that he which is accused, have the accusers face to face, and have licence to answer for himself concerning the crime laid against him'. Similarly, the Roman Emperor Trajan, when asked by the younger Pliny how to treat the 'new sect known as Christians', replied: 'anonymous accusations must not be admitted in evidence as against any one, as it is introducing a dangerous precedent, and out of accord with the spirit of our times'; this episode is reported by J.L. O'Brian, *National Security and Individual Freedom*, Harvard Univ. Press, Cambridge, 1955, 62.

22 The passages quoted in the text are reported in T.B. Howell, *A Complete Collection of State Trials and Proceedings for High Treason and Other Crimes and Misdemeanors from the Earliest Period to the Year 1783*, London, 1816, vol. II, 15-22.

1547.[23] The provision in question did not spare the life of Sir Walter Raleigh, although Sir Edward Coke later affirmed that cross-examination had by then already been established as a principle of common law.[24] At that time, the continental inquisitorial style was also making its way to England and Wales. Some equity courts and the Star Chamber[25] adhered to the secret procedures of the Inquisition. These courts, however, proved so unpopular with English culture that most of them were abolished in the seventeenth century. No criminal jurisdiction was left to the ones that survived. Moreover, common law courts were required to disregard equity procedures when it turned out that a witness was unavailable to testify at trial. The process of recognition of the 'right to cross-examination' figuratively ends in 1848, when judge Pitt Taylor announces it in his monumental treaty on the law of evidence.[26]

Whilst English law has always been short on public announcements of general principles of law, U.S. law has made such announcements at the earliest possible stage. In 1791, the right to confront witnesses was formally announced in the Bill of Rights, as part of the Sixth Amendment to the Federal Constitution. The history and origins of the confrontation clause have been extensively described elsewhere[27] but still raise debates and controversy among United States evidence scholars. The matter can only be briefly investigated here. In the 18th century, England was constantly seeking to protect its maritime interests abroad: colonial trade with foreigners was forbidden except in cases of necessity,

---

[23] 5 & 6 Edward VI, chap. 11, s. IX: [the] accusers [...] shall be brought in person before the partie soe accused, and avowe and maynteyne that that have to saye against the saide party to prove him guilty of the Treasons. According to H.L. Stephen, *The Trial of Sir Walter Raleigh*, (1919) 2 Trans. Royal Hist. Soc. (4th Series) 172, at 183, 'it is impossible to say how far a right in the accused man to be confronted with the witnesses against him was generally recognised in the 16th century'.

[24] Cf. E. Coke, *Institutes of the Laws of England – Part III*, Clarke, London, 1809, 25.

[25] The Star Chamber was a court of law which evolved from meetings of the King's Royal Council. In 1487, the court became a judicial body separate from the King's council, with a mandate to hear petitions of redress. The power of the court of Star Chamber grew considerably under the Stuarts, and by the time of Charles I it had become a byword for misuse and abuse of power by the King and his circle. James I and his son Charles used the court to suppress opposition to royal policies. Finally, in 1641 the Long Parliament abolished the hated Star Chamber, though its name survives in the public perception to designate arbitrary, secretive proceedings in opposition to protection of personal rights and liberty. For an account of the events that led to the abolition of the Star Chamber cf. J.F. Stephen, *Criminal Procedure from the Thirteen to the Eighteenth Century*, in *Select Essays in Anglo-American Legal History*, Little Brown, Boston, 1908, vol. II, 500-504.

[26] J.P. Taylor, *A Treatise on the Law of Evidence as Administered in England and Ireland: with Illustrations from the American and Other Foreign Laws*, Maxwell & son., London, 1848, vol. II, §1050.

[27] D.H. Pollitt, *The Right of Confrontation: Its History and Modern Dress*, (1959) 8 Journal of Public Law 381. See also R.N. Jonakait, *The Origins of the Confrontation Clause: An Alternative History*, (1995) 27 Rutgers L.J. 77.

and all foreign ships were forbidden to trade with any of the American colonies. Customs laws were not vigorously enforced until Charles Townsend became First Lord of Trade in 1763. Enforcement was achieved, in particular, by promising informers of customs offences a moiety of forfeitures, and the wishes of those who desired their name to remain unknown were also respected.[28] When cases were tried before colonial courts, however, juries often ruled in favour of the alleged offender despite their obvious guilt, in support of the political principle 'no taxation without representation'. For this reason, in 1769, the English government gave jurisdiction over these matters to the Admiralty courts. These courts followed a written procedure: testimonies were replaced by depositions because it was extraordinarily difficult to secure the attendance of a sailor at the hearing. These trials overseas – instituted without a jury, by secret informants, where adverse evidence was by deposition or given in private before the judge – reawakened in the colonist the need to assert what were considered the inalienable rights of Englishmen. In this way, confrontational concerns played a role in the events that led to the American Revolution and the Declaration of Independence. The 1778 U.S. Constitution, however, was silent on the procedure to be followed by the federal judiciary in criminal cases.[29] When the Constitution was put before the States for ratification, objections were raised against the lack of such guarantees,[30] and many States agreed to ratify it on the understanding that the approval of a Bill of Rights would be the first concern of the new Congress. This was done, and on 15 December 1791 the Right to Confrontation became constitutional law in the United States federal system. More will be said on the contemporary state of the U.S. law on confrontation in section 4.

2.3 Transplant in the Continent of Europe

Confrontational concerns were foreign to the practice of the Roman Canonical trial in the Continent of Europe. Established in 1215, this mode of procedure served for centuries the purpose of oppressing religious heresy and political opponents.[31] It was embraced not only by the notorious Tri-

[28] L.A. Harper, *The English Navigation Laws: A Seventeenth-Century Experiment in Social Engineering*, Columbia Univ. Press, New York, 1939, 138.

[29] D.H. Pollitt, *The Right of Confrontation...*, *supra* note 27, at 399.

[30] A famous tirade against the lack of procedural guarantees for the accused in criminal proceedings, with specific mention to the Right to Confrontation as an alienable right of the citizen, was made by Abraham Holmes, in the Massachusetts Convention held in Boston, on January 30, 1788; cf. J. Elliot, *The Debates in the Several State Conventions on the Adoption of the Federal Constitution*, 2nd edn., Lippincott, Philadelphia, 1836, vol. II, 110-111.

[31] The procedure adopted by the tribunals of Inquisition is best illustrated by the ultimate hand-book for examining magistrates committed to witch hunting: H. Institoris and J. Sprenger, *Malleus Maleficarum*, Nuremberg, 1519.

bunal of the Inquisition,[32] but also by the lay judicial institutions of the Ancient Régime. In the inquisitorial style, confession by torture[33] was the preferred method of proof and anonymity of accusations (*diffamationes*) was commonplace. Witnesses were interviewed in secret by zealous examining magistrates. Their depositions were included in the court dossier and could stand as evidence at trial. A fair description is that the trial was conducted by 'learned technocrats'[34] who gave judgments 'based on the dead writings of torture and witness transcripts'.[35] Understandably, no mention of the Right to Confrontation can be found in the two main statutory compilations of this era: the 1532 German *Constitutio Criminalis Carolina*[36] and the 1670 French *Ordonnance Criminelle.*[37]

Anger against this state of affairs was voiced by the philosophers of the Enlightenment. Voltaire, in particular, wondered why the law could leave a matter as important as the open confrontation between the defendant and the witness to the discretion of a judge.[38] The criminal system that came out of the French Revolution, however, left the champions of confrontation disappointed. While the system of legal proof was abolished and torture formally abandoned, prior out-of-court depositions of witnesses counted as evidence and no exclusionary rule on *de relato* testimony was introduced in the 1808 *Code de l'Instruction Criminelle.*

The virtual transplant of the Right to Confrontation in the Continent of Europe took place in 1950, when the European Convention on Human Rights included it among the guarantees of the defendant in criminal cases. In the late 1970s, the first cases on Article 6(3)(d) were considered by the Strasbourg organs while a comprehensive discourse on hearsay and confrontation only began to consolidate a decade later.[39]

---

[32] The denomination *Tribunal of the Inquisition* refers to various judicial institutions. First, to the several medieval European tribunals of Inquisitions, whose chief aim was the fight against the Chatharists. Secondly, to the Spanish Inquisition founded in 1478 by Pope *Sisto IV* at the request of King Ferdinand and Queen Isabela of Spain. Thirdly, to the Roman Inquisition founded in 1542 by Pope *Paolo III* through the bull *Licet ab Initio* and later renamed *Congregazione dell'Inquisizione.*

[33] On confession and torture in the Ancient Régime cf. P. Fiorelli, *La Tortura Giudiziaria nel Diritto Comune*, Giuffrè, Milano, 1953, vol. I; J.H. Langbein *Torture and the Law of Proof: Europe and England in the Ancien Régime*, Chicago Univ. Press, Chicago, 1977.

[34] F. Cordero, *Procedura Penale*, 7th edn., Giuffrè, Milano, 2003, 17.

[35] G. Radbruch, *Zur Einführung in die Carolina*, in Die Peinliche Gerichtsordnung Kaiser Karls V von 1532 (Carolina), 5th edn., Reclam, Stuttgart, 1996, 22.

[36] *Peynliche Hals-Gerichts-Ordnung Ihro Romisch-Käys. und Königl Majestät Caroli V Glorwürdigsten Andenkens*, published in *Jurisprudentia criminalis in judicio castrensi et forensi, seu coprus juris caesarei, in delictis militaribus et criminalibus, opus theoretico-practicum*, 1746, Vienna, 100.

[37] *Ordonnance criminelle du mois d'août 1670*, published in D. Jousse, *Nouveau Commentaire sur l'Ordonnance Criminelle du Mois d'Août 1670*, Paris, 1756.

[38] Voltaire, *Commentario sopra il Libro dei Delitti e delle Pene*, 1767, chapter XXII, 111.

[39] ECHR law on confrontation is extensively discussed in Chapter 3.

In the 1990s, reforms were passed in many European Countries in an attempt to align domestic rules of evidence and procedure with the requirements of ECHR law. By way of illustration, the Netherlands restructured the rules for anonymous witnesses, Italy went so far as to duplicate the Confrontation Clause of the Convention in Article 111 of its Constitution, France introduced a new *article préliminaire* to the *Code de procédure pénale,* under which literally all main features of ECHR jurisprudence are referenced: equality of arms, impartiality of the judiciary, reasonable time requirement and right to an effective remedy against unlawful convictions.

The transplant of the concept of confrontation, however, did not bring about a harmonisation of Continental evidence law in resemblance to the adversarial practice of the common law. Instead, multidirectional changes[40] appear to characterise contemporary criminal procedure.

In this framework, the phrasing of the Right to Confrontation was adjusted to suit the practice of Continental litigation from two different perspectives.

Firstly, while the Sixth Amendment to the United States Constitution employs the term *confront,* Article 6 of the European Convention inaugurated the reference to the *examination* of witnesses.[41] This phrase is now replicated in the Statutes of the International criminal tribunals[42] and, more recently, in the Article 111 of the Italian Constitution. In implying an almost physical challenge to the unfavourable witness, the verb *confront*[43] accords with the adversarial style of adjudication of the United States criminal process and its sporting theory of justice.[44] In comparison, the noun *examination* places more emphasis upon the observation of the declarant's behaviour at the time of the deposition.

Secondly, and more importantly, the European Convention established the equivalence between the right *to examine a witness* and the right *to have that witness examined* by the court.[45] This was clearly meant to protect inquisitorial

---

40 M.R. Damaška, *Negotiated Justice in International Criminal Courts,* (2004) 2 Journal Intl. Crim. Justice 1018.

41 Alternative phrases may be found in some American State Constitutions. A recurrent option is 'right.... to meet the witnesses against him face to face' (Art. 15, pt. I, New Hampshire 1784 Const.; Art. I §18a, Missouri 1945 Const.). For minor variants see Art. 1 §7, Delaware 1897 Const. (right ... to meet the witnesses in their examination face to face) and Art. 21, Maryland 1867 Declaration of Rights (right to be confronted with the witnesses against him; ... to examine the witnesses for and against him on oath).

42 For discussion on the right to confront witnesses in international criminal proceedings see S. Zappalà, *Human Rights in International Criminal Proceedings,* Oxford Univ. Press, Oxford, 2003, 129-138.

43 The word 'confront' derives from the Latin prefix *con* (*contra,* meaning 'against' or 'opposed') and the noun *frons* (forehead).

44 For a critical view of this theory, see the remarks of R. Pound, *The Causes of Popular Dissatisfaction with the Administration of Justice,* (1964) 35 Federal Rules Decisions 273, at 281.

45 Similar concerns also inspire the phrasing of Art. 15(E) of the Law of Administration for the State of Iraq for the Transitional Period (8 March 2004), according to which the accused person has the 'right to summon and examine witnesses or to ask the judge to do so'.

countries from challenges under ECHR law: there, examinations by the judge on behalf of the parties are – and always have been – the norm.

3 Concepts and Formula for a Theory of Confrontation

It is now time to establish the nature and scope of the Right Confrontation. Two are the central elements to this analysis: the method of *confrontation* and the evidence of a *witness*. As a point of departure, confrontation must be perceived as the ultimate paradigm for the collection of the testimony of witnesses and any other evidence that may be said to be equivalent to such testimony.

The following discussion is in four main parts. Firstly, the expression *testimonial evidence* is investigated. Secondly, I will define the *confrontational paradigm* and separate it into its components. Thirdly, some theoretical assumptions are put forward. Finally, attention concentrates on the typology of departures from the confrontational paradigm. Certain combinations of these departures will later lead to the establishment of the three categories of *absent, anonymous* and *vulnerable* witnesses as potential threats to the Right to Confrontation.

3.1 Testimonial Evidence

3.1.1 From the Term 'Witness' to the 'Testimonial' Attribution of a Statement

The Right to Confrontation applies to the evidence of a witness. At it most basic, the word 'witness' describes 'the action or condition of being an observer of an event'.[46] In theory, every fact that a human being may experience through sight, smell, hearing, touch and taste can be witnessed.[47] On closer inspection, however, this consideration has no selective impact: every fact may be *relevant* to a criminal proceeding and *relevance* cannot be inferred from certain features of the fact in question. Also, individuals with no knowledge of any fact in issue may well be summoned as witnesses. This may happen when summons are served by mistake due to homonymy or in certain cases of striking perjury.

For the purposes of this study, an individual will be termed a *witness* whenever his *testimonial statements* are available for consideration by a criminal court.

---

[46] J.A. Simpson and E.S.C. Weiner, *The Oxford English Dictionary*, 2nd edn., Clarendon Oxford, 1989, vol. XX, 464 2b.

[47] According to J.B. Thayer, *A Preliminary Treatise on Evidence at the Common Law*, Sweet and Maxwell, London, 1898, 500, witness is he who speaks 'to the fact that he had seen and heard' and 'to what hath fallen under his senses'.

A witness is adverse to the defendant whenever his statements, if accepted as true by the court, may have an unfavourable impact on the case for the defence.

The main question to be answered here is when a statement is to be deemed testimonial for the purpose of confrontation. This will clarify that confrontational concerns arise not only in relation to the courtroom testimony, but also to several evidentiary equivalents.

3.1.2 Definition in Theory and in Action: Courtroom Testimony and its 'Equivalents'

The universe of statements is vast and human verbal and non-verbal expressions constitute a complex area of analysis for any discourse on evidentiary matters. In the world of common law, the doctrine of hearsay[48] offers an all-inclusive theory for the investigation and assessment of the probative value of any human *assertion*. However, this doctrine cannot be used here because a hearsay approach is unknown to the trials and the legal culture of Continental Europe.

For the purpose of this study a statement is testimonial when (a) it consists of the description of a personal observation and experience of the declarant, and (b) a court of justice may rely upon it in order to prove the truth of the matter therein asserted.[49]

Under the requirement sub (a), a statement is testimonial when the declarant makes an account of a matter of his own knowledge.[50] This happens when Mr. A. declares that he saw the accident, heard the gunshot, or overheard Mr. B.'s speech to a bystander. It is obviously irrelevant whether the account is true or false. Examples of non testimonial statement under requirement (a) are: warnings, expressions of courtesy, contractual offers and acceptances. More broadly, each of the statements that philosophers of language call 'performa-

---

48 Recognised by the end of the 17th and established at the beginning of the 18th century, the rule is one of the cornerstones of the Anglo-American trial, although it has a reputation for being extremely difficult and has puzzled generation of commentators, causing striking disagreement. In a famous case on hearsay, Lord Reid expressed his view that 'it is difficult to make any general statement about the law of hearsay which is entirely accurate' (*Myers v. D.P.P.* [1965] A.C. 1001 (H.L.) at 1019-1020). According to its best-known definition, this exclusionary rule of evidence provides that 'any statement other than one made by a person while giving oral evidence in the proceedings is inadmissible as evidence of any fact or opinion stated'; C. Tapper, *Cross and Tapper on Evidence*, 9th edn., Butterworths, London, 1999, 530.

49 This definition is objective in nature as it places no reliance on the state of mind of the maker of the statement at the time of his assertion. Instead, a 'subjective' parameter is endorsed by *Criminal Justice Act 2003*, s. 115, which govern the admissibility of the out-of.-court depositions of witnesses. According to such provision, one of the questions for the court is to assess whether 'the purpose, or one of the purposes of the maker of the statements was to cause the person to believe the matter'.

50 F. Cordero, *Procedura Penale, supra* note 34, 665.

tive'[51] are in principle not testimonial, as their function is 'to do' something, rather than 'to describe it'. These statements may be relevant to a criminal proceeding as any other fact, for the reason that they have been made (or not); when this is the case, these statements are the object of a testimony, although they are not in themselves 'testimonial'.

As to the requirement sub (b) the very same statement may or may not be testimonial according to rules of evidence of the jurisdiction under scrutiny. Hearsay logic shows that a statement may be tendered in evidence for different purposes. Sometimes, it may be tendered as evidence of the matter asserted while sometimes as evidence that such a statement had in fact been made.[52] When the courts are allowed to treat the statement as evidence of the matter asserted the statement is *testimonial* and its author is a witness. When the statement is tendered into evidence to prove other matters (*e.g.* that the author was alive, that he could speak at the time the statement was made, that the statement is inconsistent with what the author has said at a later stage) the statement is not testimonial, and no confrontational problems arise.

The typical testimonial evidence is a courtroom testimony, in which individuals are asked to give an account of their prior experience, upon request of the judge or the parties. Nonetheless, it is crucial to understand that at least three functional *equivalents* to courtroom testimony may come to relevance when discussing matters of confrontation: indirect testimony, readings of out-of-court depositions, and documentary evidence.[53]

Let us consider a hypothetical case. Mr. Brown is inside a bank at the time of a robbery. He takes notice of the firearm and the peculiar accent of the offender. We might expect Mr. Brown to be interviewed on the scene a few moments later by a police officer. Alternatively, Mr. Brown could just go home and tell what happened to his wife, or write what he saw in his personal diary. At the time of the trial, Mr. Brown may be summoned as a witness and testify against Mr. Black. In accordance with the rules of evidence of each jurisdiction, his statements to the police or his writings in the diary could also be tendered into evidence. In certain jurisdictions, his wife could also be summoned to report what she was told at the time of the offence. The vehicles through which the experience of Mr. Brown may be brought to the attention of a court are different, but the legitimate expectation of Mr. Black remains the same: to challenge Mr. Brown's account. For instance, the defence may wish to argue that he has no experience of gun models and no understanding of foreign accents so that the court should place no reliance on his evidence. Only in the case of courtroom

---

[51] J.L. Austin, *How to Do Things with Words*, Oxford Univ. Press, Oxford, 1962, 6.

[52] The very same statement 'may or may not be hearsay': *Subramaniam v. Public Prosecutor* [1956] 1 W.L.R. 965 (P.C. Ceylon).

[53] These are described as means of 'derivative proof' by M.R. Damaška, *Of Hearsay and its Analogues*, (1992) 76 Minnesota Law Rev. 425.

testimony, however, does Mr. Black enjoy his fundamental right to be confronted with the accuser.

Testimonial statements may take on various forms. If the person is questioned in open court, statements are given *orally* to the judge or jury. As anticipated, the law of evidence may also allow the introduction in evidence of *written* statements collected out of court by the prosecutor, police or counsel. Even expressive non-verbal behaviour (such as nodding or shaking of the head) may fall in the category of testimonial statement, especially if made in the context of formalised procedures of evidence collection.

The declarant may anticipate in some way his (or her) intention to make a statement available for the judicial proceeding concerning a given offence. This happens when the statement is addressed to one of the authorities that are legally responsible for the investigation, prosecution or judgement of the offence.[54] Sometimes, such an intention may be inferred from the content and the circumstances in which the statements are made, as in the case of a dying declaration to a bystander. For the purposes of this work, however, the category of witnesses cannot be restricted to people who have consciously fed information into the criminal justice system.[55] Even when the declarant had no intention of reporting his (or her) experience in a court of justice his or her diary may be found and introduced in evidence or somebody may give away his (or her) story. When the law of a given jurisdiction allows the criminal court to rely upon such a document or indirect testimony – as may be the case when no rule against hearsay applies – this poses an immediate threat to the Right to Confrontation.

Defining the boundaries of the category of testimonial evidence can prove complex. All legal definitions have grey zones at their margins. This does not necessarily affect their value, as long as they help in conducting selective legal discourse. With regard to hearsay matters, for instance, doubts exceed certainties and commentators agree that even under the jurisdictions most accustomed to hearsay logic, the hearsay quality of a good deal of evidence still goes

---

54 For example, police agents and officers, prosecutors, judges, counsel and private investigators, when acting in these capacities.

55 A definition of this kind has been subscribed by some American commentators (such as R.D. Friedman, *Thoughts from across the Water on Hearsay and Confrontation*, [1998] Crim. L.R. 697, at 706 and A.R. Amar, *Confrontation Clause First Principles: A Reply to Professor Friedman*, (1998) 86 Geo. Law Journal 1045, in the attempt to broaden the definition of witness endorsed by the Supreme Court while interpreting the Confrontation Clause (for more discussion see Chapter 3). Supreme Court judges, however, have once openly dismissed this attempted by suggesting that 'attempts to draw a line between statements made in contemplation of legal proceedings and those not so made would entangle the courts in a multitude of difficulties', *White v. Illinois*, 502 U.S. 346, 112 S. Ct. 736 (1992) (concurring opinion by Justices Scalia and Thomas) at 364; 747.

unnoticed.[56] Yet no American or English scholar would seriously argue that the theory of hearsay serves no legal purpose.

3.1.3 Exception: The Evidence of the Accused Person

The definition provided in the previous section is subject to a major exception. Save for the restrictions mentioned below, I will not include among the category of *testimonial statements* any of the depositions given in evidence by the person who allegedly perpetrated the offence that is being prosecuted.

The reasons for excluding the defendant's evidence from this book's analysis are twofold. Firstly, all western jurisdictions grant to the defendant a peculiar status and a variety of protective measures. Pending judicial investigation, he or she is treated as a suspect. At trial stage and subsequent appellate proceedings, he or she falls under the greater protective shield consistent with an accused person's status. As a result, the defendant's depositions, whether given in or out of court, whether consisting of an admission or a denial of the related charges, are governed by a tailor made legal regime. Secondly, the present study only concentrates on the right to challenge witnesses providing adverse evidence. No confrontational issues derive from the employment in evidence of the defendant's depositions, when they refer to his or her own liability.

Nevertheless, statements of the accused may be deemed testimonial when they refer to the responsibility of others, jointly or separately charged of the same or related offences. In this case, the use of non confronted statements of the *accused* may well jeopardises a *co-accused*'s Right to Confrontation.[57] Drawing an exact distinction between a declaration concerning one's own or someone else's responsibility may be difficult in practice, but its abstract value remains central to this work.

---

56 A.L.T. Choo, *Hearsay and Confrontation in Criminal Trials*, Clarendon, Oxford, 1996, 163. Theory of hearsay has been pushed to its paradoxical limits by E.M. Morgan, *Hearsay and Non–Hearsay*, (1935) 48 Harvard L.R. 1138, 1145. In the author's view, nothing is more common than to allow a witness to rely upon a timepiece in stating the time of day when an event happened. If he should testify that he looked at a Western Union clock and noted the time, he would be considered as giving particularly accurate testimony, but would it not be anonymous hearsay upon anonymous hearsay? Certainly the person in charge of the master mechanism which regulated the clock consulted by the witness did not make the astronomical observations in accordance with which that clock was made to indicate the hour and minute of the day. Yet just as certainly an objection upon the ground of hearsay would receive scant attention.

57 See Chapter 2, section 1.4.

3.2 The Confrontational Paradigm

It is now time to outline a theoretical model for a fair collection of testimonial evidence in criminal cases, based upon principles of natural justice drawn from evidence law and jurisprudence. A testimony is collected in accordance with the 'confrontational paradigm' when the declarant, whose real identity is known to the defence, gives evidence in open court, facing the accused and the trier of fact, under the obligation of truth-telling, and the defence has a chance to challenge the statements through contemporaneous adverse-questioning. In the following sections, the six components of the *confrontational paradigm* are described and reasons are given for their inclusion in it.

3.2.1 Publicity

Roman law suggests that a criminal trial should be a *res publica*, conducted transparently before the people.[58] While English law has been devoted to publicity since its origin,[59] the intellectual movement of the Enlightenment has restored it in the Continent of Europe, in response to the secret and obscure practice of the Inquisition.[60]

At present, public scrutiny is commonly believed to enhance the quality and safeguard the integrity of the fact-finding process, with benefits for both concerned parties and society. Moreover, public access to the criminal trial fosters an appearance of fairness, thereby heightening respect for the judicial process. While trials are often held *in camera* in undemocratic nations, open access to courtrooms serves as a check upon the way justice is delivered and 'a medium of communication with the public at large'.[61] Publicity also plays a role in the field of witnesses' testimony. First, it has been argued that it may encourage the declarant's truthfulness.[62] Secondly, it ensures some form of 'social control', since any informed person may bring missing information to the attention of the court and challenge what he believes to be false or inaccurate.[63]

---

58 T. Mommsen, *Römisches Strafrecht*, Duncker & Humblot, Leipzig, 1899, 148.

59 With the limited exception of the jurisdiction of the *Star Chamber* (*supra* note 25).

60 For a famous tirade against the practice of the criminal trials of the Inquisition cf. C. Beccaria, *Dei Delitti e delle Pene, con Commentari di Varii Insigni Scrittori*, Masi, Livorno, 1824, chapter XIV, 67.

61 Cf. I.H. Dennis, *The Law of Evidence*, 2nd edn., Sweet & Maxwell, London, 2002, 43. An ECHR authority on matters of publicity can be found in *Riepan v. Austria*, [2000-XII] RJD 1.

62 J. Bentham, *Traité des Preuves Judiciaires*, 2nd edn., Paris, 1830, vol. I, 148; E. Florian, *Delle Prove Penali*, Vallardi, Milano, 1924, vol. II, 65.

63 K.J.A. Mittermaier, *Teoria della Prova nel Processo Penale*, F. Ambrosoli Italian Translation, Sanvito, Milano, 1858, 357.

For the purposes of this work, a deposition is public not only when the people are entitled to enter the room in which the deposition is given, but also when access to its content is ensured through press coverage or other means.[64] Further, public examinations do not necessarily have to take place in the courtroom. Even tailor-made pre-trial hearings may be equally effective in this regard, provided that no further adverse evidence is submitted in secrecy by the same witness at a later stage of the proceedings.

3.2.2 Presence of the Accused

Confrontation evokes an eyeball-to-eyeball dispute between the defendant and his accuser. For centuries, this has been a function of the engrained but unsupported belief that 'it is always more difficult to tell a lie about a person "to his face" than "behind his back"'.[65] However, in the context of the common law, Wigmore has stated that 'the opponent demands confrontation not for the idle purpose of gazing upon the witness, or of being gazed upon him, but for the purpose of cross-examination'.[66]

In contemporary trials, however, defendants seldom[67] participate in the interviewing of witnesses. In certain countries (*e.g.* France), the law does not even allow the accused directly to question the witness. Elsewhere, tactical reasons may dictate that the examination be performed by counsel: the defendant may lack the indispensable training, and his antagonistic conduct may cast a bad light upon him, especially in trials by jury.

Still, the presence of the accused is an essential component of the confrontational paradigm, since it alone gives the opportunity of physically identifying the witness. This may be crucial whenever the defendant is unable to recognise who the accuser really is (and, for instance, whether any prior contacts between the two may have occurred), despite the disclosure of his legal identity.

---

[64] Most hearings before the International Criminal Tribunal for the Former Yugoslavia, for instance, are broadcasted live in electronic format via a link in the Tribunal's website: <www.un.org/icty>.

[65] *Coy v. Iowa*, 487 U.S. 1012, 108 S. Ct. 2798 (1988) at 1019. In the same line, United States Supreme Court judges have also suggested that personal confrontation 'undoubtedly makes it more 'difficult to lie against someone, particularly if that person is an accused and present at trial'; cf. *Ohio v. Roberts*, 448 U.S. 56, 100 S. Ct. 2531 (1980) at 64.

[66] J.H. Wigmore, *Evidence in Trials at Common Law*, J.H. Chadbourn Rev., Little Brown, Boston, 1974, §1395.

[67] An isolated exception is the trial against the former Yugoslav President before the I.C.T.Y. (ICTY-02-54), in which the defendant availed himself of his right to pro se representation and directly questioned all witnesses. Examination in person by the accuser in English, Italian and French law is summarised in Chapter 5, section 3.3.1.

3.2.3 Presence of the Fact-finder

The assumption that the observation of the body language of the maker of a statement – the so called *demeanour evidence*[68] – would provide a reliable indication of his trustworthiness has a steadfast reputation. In 1949, Jerome Frank suggested that

> All of us know that, in every day life, the way a man behaves when he tells a story -his intonations, his fidgetings or composure, his yawns, the use of his eyes, his air of candor of evasiveness- may furnish valuable clues to his reliability. Such clues are by no means impeccable guides but they are often immensely helpful.[69]

The practice of litigation demonstrates that a wide range of approaches has been espoused by lawyers and prosecutors for capitalizing on aspects of body language that may indicate whether or not someone is being deceptive. Such approaches have included paying close attention to a prospective witness's demeanour at a pre-trial deposition in order to plan a more or less aggressive examination at trial, encouraging friendly witnesses to exhibit supposedly 'favourable' demeanours through appropriate coaching, and exploiting an adverse witness's nervousness or discomfort in order to elicit certain behavioural reactions. Sometimes the law of evidence explicitly encourages jurors and judges to employ demeanour evidence in the assessment of a witness's credibility.[70]

Frank's point, however, reflects only one side of the ongoing debate on the multifaceted links between demeanour[71] and a statement's reliability. Empirical

---

[68] Cf. J.A. Blumenthal, *A Wipe of the Hands, a Lick of the Lips; the Validity of Demeanor Evidence in Assessing Witness Credibility*, (1993) 72 Nebraska L.R. 1157.

[69] J. Frank, *Courts on Trial. Myth and Reality in American Justice*, Princeton Univ. Press., Princeton, 1949, 21.

[70] For the relevant instruction to the jury in U.S. federal cases see K.F. O'Malley, J.E. Grenig and W.C. Lee, *Federal Jury Practice and Instructions – Criminal*, 5th edn., West, St. Paul, 2000, 1A, 350: 'In making that assessment of that witness you should (...) consider (...) the manner while on the witness stand'. In England, conduct of witnesses is 'real' evidence. According to C. Tapper, *Cross and Tapper on Evidence*, *supra* note 48, 49, demeanour is 'analogous to the answers given by a witness who is being cross-examined as to credit, and may rightly be regarded as evidence in the case'.

[71] The word 'demeanour' refers to every visible or audible form of self-expression manifested by a witness, whether voluntary or involuntary, as suggested by M. Stone, *Instant Lie Detection? Demeanour and Credibility in Criminal Trials*, [1991] Crim. L.R. 822. According to J.A. Blumenthal, *A Wipe of the Hands...*, *supra* note 68, 1164, the term encompasses 'the tone of voice in which a witness' statement is made, the hesitation or readiness with which his answers are given, the look of the witness, his carriage, his evidences of surprise, his gestures, his zeal, his bearing, his expression, his yawns, the use of his eyes, his furtive or meaning glances, or his shrugs, the pitch of his voice, his self-possession or embarrassment, his air of candor or seeming levity'.

research[72] has shown that non-verbal communication is of little help to non-professionals in assessing whether a person is truthful. More specifically, it was designed to assess whether it is possible to detect in a speaker's behaviour indications of attempted deception and concluded that 'the capacity of ordinary people to detect unreliability by observing demeanour is simply a myth'.[73] Experimental findings, in fact, demonstrate that the behavioural clues used by observers to perceive and measure deceptive discourse are 'more strongly associated with judgments of deception than with actual deception'.[74] Moreover, there is no known physiological connection between the brain processes of a lying person and any bodily or vocal signs. Anxiety or relaxation might be detected but, even if detected correctly, cannot be automatically seized upon to indicate veracity, or insincerity.

While it is recommended that fact finders refrain from *instant lie-detection* based on behavioural clues, nevertheless their attendance at the time of the examination is an essential component of the confrontational paradigm. The reliability of a testimonial statement depends upon several parameters other than the sincerity of its author; fault of memory, perception or verbal communication may result in ambiguity and misrepresentation of reality. As a result, the role of the fact finder is by no means confined to lie-detection. Judges and jurors attend court hearings to listen to the witness's accounts and, in all jurisdictions, they are entitled to ask for clarifications and pose their own questions, during or after the parties' examinations.[75]

3.2.4 Obligation of Sincerity

Although every testimonial statement might be a lie, only certain lies are punishable as criminal offences under the law. For centuries, witnesses have been required to swear on oath to testify truthfully. At common law, witnesses were incompetent unless they were prepared to swear on the Gospel or the Bible.[76] Similar rules governed continental criminal procedure.[77] The underlying idea was that the oath's religious importance would somehow compel the person to state the truth and, more broadly, to reduce the number of lies in court.

---

72 O.G. Wellborn, *Demeanor*, (1991) 76 Cornell L.R. 1075.

73 Same work, at 1104.

74 M. Zuckerman, B.M. Depaulo and R. Rosenthal, *Verbal and Nonverbal Communication of Deception*, (1981) 14 Advanced Exper. Soc. Psychol. 1, at 16. The studies showed that some of our favourite cultural stereotypes about liars (such as their furtive glances or nervous blinking) simply do not withstand the test provided by the existing empirical data.

75 The role of the court as interviewer in the examination of witnesses in England, Italy and France is discussed in Chapter 5, section 3.3.1.

76 *R. v. Tew*, (1855) Dears 429 (C.C.A.).

A progressive relaxation of the religious implications of sworn testimony characterises contemporary law. The reasons are twofold. On the one hand, discrimination between different religious beliefs, or between religious people and atheists, are no longer tolerated. On the other hand, the cultural framework of Western nations makes it doubtful that the moral implications of an act may play a decisive part in influencing human conduct.[78] Consequently, legal systems have begun to accept solemn affirmations as adequate alternatives to oaths.

Here, no attention is paid to the diverse formulation of oath and affirmation in national law. Instead, it is argued that this component is complied with whenever the concerned statements were given by a subject under the threat of a criminal sanction[79] for perjury or false testimony.

In this regard, a further distinction should be made. In legal orders that establish the offence of perjury (such as England or the United States), a criminal sanction applies if, and only if, the statements of the author were given under oath. Elsewhere, where the relevant offence is *false testimony* (as is the case in Italy and France), punishment may also be served upon individuals who never took an oath, although the principle of *mens rea* requires that they be duly informed of the legal consequences of a false deposition.

3.2.5 Disclosure of Personal Identity

Although anonymity may encourage human communication, knowledge of the identity of the author raises its value for the recipient.[80] This assumption applies to ordinary life as much as to evidence law; in the latter, rumours do not qualify as court testimonies.

The reason why the disclosure of a witness's identity is crucial for the defence is clear. The credibility of a witness may be challenged mainly upon prior episodes of perjury or other discreditable conduct. For this reason, counsel is entitled to access the criminal records of witnesses under some restrictions

---

77 Art. V, Tit. XV, *Ordonnance Criminelle du mois d'août 1670* (*supra* note 37).

78 In discussing the cultural and social changes occurred in last decades in western societies, it seems acceptable to imply that the overall role of religious beliefs have increasingly turned from a *public* to a more *private* – and thus relativist – dimension. Undoubtedly, the religious condemnation of a given behaviour and of the related sinner is at present less capable to affect in concrete his personal freedom.

79 This study does not endorse the argument that the taking of a formal promise and the 'gravity of the occasion' alone may persuade the witness to state the truth, even when no criminal sanction applies; cf. M.L. Seigel, *Rationalising Hearsay: A Proposal for a Best Evidence Hearsay Rule*, (1992) 72 Boston Univ. L.R. 907, at footnote 44. However, it also been argued in the United States that fear of perjury is close to non-existent because such cases are rarely prosecuted R.O. Lempert and S.A. Saltzburg, *A Modern Approach to Evidence. Text, Problems, Transcripts and Cases*, 2nd edn., West, St. Paul, 1982, 352 at footnote 11.

80 Cf. S. Levmore, *Law, Economics, & Norms: The Anonymity Tool*, (1996) 144 Univ. Penn. L.R. 2191.

specified under national law. Furthermore, counsel often argues that unfavourable witnesses are prejudiced against the defendant. If well supported, a claim that the accusations are malicious may seriously affect the case for the prosecution. Obviously, such a claim may only be put forward when the defence is duly informed of the identity of the witness. It may also be argued that such information should be given in advance. An investigation might be necessary, for instance, to prove that the accuser was the defendant's secret companion or that the corporation of the latter had once dismissed a job application from the former.

The term *identity* must be construed with reference to the *real* identity. In comparison, legal identities are subject to changes and modifications, under the conditions specified by the law. Pseudonyms or virtual (even false) identities may also be relevant, if at all capable of establishing past occurrences of the witness's life.

3.2.6 Adverse-questioning

The concept of adverse-questioning refers to an oral challenge to unfavourable testimonial evidence at the time of its collection, intended to cast doubts on its reliability and on the credibility of the declarant. Of all the components, this is certainly the most difficult to define.

The cross-examination of the Anglo-American trial is the adverse-questioning method that attracts the most supporting rhetoric within evidence jurisprudence. In the past, it has been described in turn as 'beyond any doubt the greatest legal engine ever invented for the discovery of truth',[81] 'a powerful and valuable weapon for the purpose of testing the veracity of a witness and the accuracy and completeness of his story'[82] and, even, 'the best security agent against incomplete, distorted or false evidence'.[83] At this stage, it is not my intention to

---

81 *Wigmore's Evidence*, *supra* note 66, at §1367.

82 *Lehwess v. Austin* [1935] A.C. 346 (H.L.) 359. In recent years, however, scholars have claimed that the value of cross-examination has been exaggerated; see J. McEwan, *Evidence and the Adversarial Process*, 2nd edn., Hart, Oxford, 1998, 13-17, 124-165. In particular, sceptics have wondered whether the stressful experience of a cross-examination, instead of leading to a reduction of lies in court, should turn into a truth-distorting weapon in the hands of 'gladiator' counsel (Same work, at 106-107). This would be extremely dangerous whenever the individuals examined are unable to face tough adverse-questioning and interact effectively with the examiner, as the mechanics of the cross-examination requires. This is why the real ability of a skilful cross-examiner has been once described as 'to make an honest witness appear at best confused and at worst a liar', D. Birch, *The Criminal Justice Act 1988-The Evidence Provisions*, [1989] Crim. L.R. 15, at 17.

83 F.J. Wrottesley, *The Examination of Witnesses in Court*, 3rd edn., Sweet and Maxwell, London, 1961, 58. Compare also J.P. Taylor, *A Treatise on the Law of Evidence*, *supra* note 26, vol. II, §1050; in the author's view, 'for however artful the fabrication of falsehood may be, it cannot embrace all the circumstances, to which a cross-examination may be extended'.

provide a comprehensive description of the sophisticated features of the cross-examination. It is enough to recall that it is conducted by the opposing side with the deliberate intention of destroying or diminishing the effect of the witness's evidence-in-chief and, if possible, extracting evidence in support of the cross-examiner's case. Technically, it is not limited to the scope of the examination-in-chief and allows leading questions. In broad terms, cross-examination can be directed to both (i) the facts upon which the testimony-in-chief was given and (ii) the credibility of the witness.[84] As to the cross-examination on facts, its aims are twofold. The first is to complete and correct the account provided under the examination-in-chief, obtaining from the witness missing elements that would potentially be favourable to the accused. The second is to test the hostile content of the testimony-in-chief, hoping to get the witness to modify, specify or even to admit that it was a mistake or a lie. By contrast, cross-examination as to credit aims to attack adverse testimony indirectly, by persuading the fact-finder that it is not safe to place reliance on his account of events.

As anticipated, methods other than cross-examination may satisfy the adverse-questioning requirement. For a start, the phrasing of the Right to Confrontation in international legal treaties leaves some room for flexibility: the accused enjoys a right to examine witnesses or, alternatively, to *have them examined.* Such expression gives full legitimacy to the continental style of evidence collection whereby counsel are prevented from directly addressing the witness and the judge has an intermediary role. The European Court of Human Rights has also once stated that frequent interruptions by the judge in counsel's examination of an adverse witness did not amount to a violation of the accused's Right to Confrontation.[85]

Case-by-case scrutiny of the interviewing procedure is essential to verify whether the concerned witness has been subject to adverse-questioning for the purposes of this work. As a guideline, I will consider the adverse questioning requirement complied with only if the same minimum conditions are met.

Firstly, counsel must be granted the opportunity to introduce to the witness damaging facts which are inconsistent with the evidence of the witness, or alternatively, to insinuate a new story, consistent with the evidence, but more favourable to the accused. The mere chance to present the courts with a set of previously drafted written questions to be posed to the witness is inadequate, as the party would have no means to adjust its conduct to the unpredictable developments of the interrogation.[86] Secondly, leave must be given to attack the

---

84 An alternative terminology distinguishes between cross-examination on issue(s) and cross-examination on credibility. The topic will be discussed extensively in Chapter 5.

85 *C. G. v U.K.*, App. No. 43373/98 (19 December 2001), (2002) 34 EHRR 789, for which some discussion is provided in Chapter 5.

86 In exploring the disadvantages of a 'chain of written interrogatories', Jeremy Bentham argued that 'in such a state of darkness to know what, for the purposes of giving completeness as well as correctness to

witness's credibility by raising matters of character or bias, and to appreciate the declarant's reaction. Thirdly, counsel must be in a position to observe the declarant's body language and demeanour in the witness-box, in order to comment upon it and later report to the judge or jury.

Further, this component cannot be said to be complied with when the courts are free to discard the court testimony in favour of any prior inconsistent statements, made by the same person at an earlier stage of the proceedings. If this were the case, a defendant could be convicted even when his accuser had explicitly withdrawn his prior allegations. Use of prior inconsistent statement must therefore be regarded as a 'departure' from the confrontational paradigm.

3.3 Theoretical Assumptions

Now that both the expressions *testimonial evidence* and *confrontational paradigm* have been defined, I will now put forward three fundamental assumptions upon which my research stands.

The first assumption is that testimonial evidence collected in a confrontational manner poses no threat to the fairness of a criminal trial. No complaint is legitimate if the testimonial sources employed in the determination of the accused's responsibility have been gathered in accordance with the aforementioned six procedural safeguards. It is implied that the manner in which these statements are collected is a preliminary guarantee against the dangers of legal testimony.

The second assumption is that the Right of Confrontation is not an absolute right and therefore may be subject to derogation. No jurisdiction has ever excluded all non-confronted testimonial evidence from the trial process and I am not prepared to argue that this would be the only fair system of adjudication. As anticipated, the inquisitorial tradition largely approved the use of depositions taken in secret hearings. Also, the everlasting respect paid to the principle of orality never precluded common law courts from admitting unchallenged statements into evidence, under certain exceptions to the hearsay rule. Contemporary European jurisdictions are no different, as the evidence of absent, anonymous and vulnerable witnesses may also be admissible. Confrontation being a fundamental right, however, intrusions into it are legitimate only when they can be based upon on of the reasons outlined above, in section 1.3.

The third assumption is that the defendant may legitimately waive certain or even all components with regard to one or more witnesses. For instance, the accused may well insist upon the collection of a testimony *in camera*, as well as

---

the testimony, the next question ought to be, will frequently be no less impossible, than, in a game of chess or draughts, to know what your next move ought to be, without knowing what you're antagonist's last preceding move has been'; J. Bentham, *Rationale of Judicial Evidence, Specially Applied to English Practice*, Hunt and Clarke, London, 1827, book III, chapter I.

refusing a face-to-face encounter. Under these circumstances, no later confrontational claims would be legitimate.

In addition, when the witness undertakes questioning at several stages of the same proceedings, it is required that evidence collection take place *at least* once in accordance with the confrontational paradigm. Under normal circumstances, the confrontational examination will be the last one, so that the accused is aware of the whole range of accounts provided by that declarant and may effectively challenge it. In short, a confrontational examination should follow, not precede, the submission of relevant adverse evidence. That said, early confrontations are acceptable when later depositions are favourable to the defendant.

3.4 Departures and Counterbalances

For the purposes of this study, any rule of law that allows criminal courts to place reliance upon testimonial evidence other than that collected in accordance with the requirements set forth in section 3.2 shall be termed a 'departure' from the confrontational paradigm. It is convenient to group departures according to their respective standing in the sources of the law and content.

Departures may be established by the Constitution,[87] statute,[88] case law[89] or practice of the courts. I will refer to them respectively as 'constitutional', 'statutory', 'judicial' and 'customary' departures. Given the constitutional standing of the Right to Confrontation, the reader may believe that only constitutionally-established departures are legitimate. This argument is not sustainable. It is one thing to say that all departures should be directly or indirectly based upon values and principles of constitutional standing. It is quite another thing to require constitutional law to lay down such procedural technicalities.

Departures from confrontation may also be grouped according to the components of the paradigm to which they specifically refer: publicity, presence of the accused or fact-finder, oath, disclosure of the witness's identity, performance of adverse-questioning, or a combination of these. In theory, each departure or combination of departures has a specific impact on the confrontational paradigm. However, no ranking of the aforementioned component is established here since compliance with confrontation is only achieved when adverse statements are collected in accordance with the six requirements described above.

---

87 *E.g.* Art. 111(5) Italian Constitution pursuant to which the process of adjudication may deviate from adversarial assumptions (1) when the defendant consents to such a deviation, (2) in the case of misconduct (violence or threats against a witness to keep him or her out of the way), or (3) when 'objective impossibility' prevents the collection of oral evidence.

88 Arts. 706-58 to 706-63 of the French Code of Criminal Procedure, concerning the evidence of anonymous witnesses.

89 Cf. certain common law exceptions to the hearsay rule ('dying declarations', *res gestae*).

Further, I do not consider it useful to investigate each and every departure or group of departures separately. The reason is twofold. Firstly, such an approach would lead to an excessive fragmentation of the topic.[90] Secondly, it would fail to convey the importance of certain 'combinations of departures' that are central to the practice of criminal litigation and upon which a comparative discourse can be profitably established.

The challenge has now been thrown down: each departure from the paradigm raises the question of the legitimacy of the related intrusion into the Right to Confrontation. In theory, intrusions into fundamental rights can only be tolerated for the reasons outlined in section 1.3. In practice, it is expected that broad claims over the legitimacy of these intrusions will be made by the champions of the 'public interest'.

The alternative between compliance and departure from the confrontational paradigm, however, is not inflexible: the effects of departures may sometimes be compensated for by counterbalances favourable to the accused. The scope and nature of such countermeasures will now be discussed.

In principle, counterbalances should accord with the extent of the departure. The more profound the departure, the more effective the compensation for the accused. In this respect, separate and independent approaches are taken by different jurisdiction, on the basis of the principles and technicalities of their laws of procedure and evidence. Even the jurisprudence of the European Human Rights organs is reluctant to enforce a strict policy in this area of the law, for the reasons exposed in Chapter 3. At this point, I will not enumerate the whole panoply of counterbalances available to legislators or courts of justice; instead, it is anticipated that such counterbalances may operate in two different ways. On the one hand, they may establish some procedural safeguards favourable to the defendant in the taking of evidence through 'protected examinations'. On the other hand, they may reduce the probative value of certain unchallenged depositions.

4 The Right to Confrontation in Contemporary U.S. Law

Earlier it was argued that, since the Right to Confrontation is a constitutional right, a theory of confrontation must be construed as a challenge to criminal evidence law, insofar as it may conflict with a more highly ranked right. In asserting this position, one would expect support from the United States law of confrontation,[91] given the constitutional standing of the Sixth

---

[90] In total, sixty-three categories could be established in this way (a, a-b, a-b-c, a-b-c-d, etc...).

[91] Most of what American legal scholars call the law of confrontation stems from Supreme Court decisions handed down after 1965. For an introduction to the topic in a constitutional perspective see A.R. Amar, *The Constitution and Criminal Procedure: First Principles*, Yale Univ. Press, New Haven, 1997, 125.

Amendment in the sources of the law. This expectation is frustrated by the fact that modern Sixth Amendment scholarship and case law treat confrontation as a redundant rule of evidence that serves very limited purposes. In addition, legal scholarship still fails to draw a distinction between confrontational features and the doctrine of hearsay.[92]

In theory, many Supreme Court rulings express the commitment of American society to the values embedded in the Right to Confrontation. This right is perceived as the best guarantee against the fabrication of testimony[93] and as 'an essential and fundamental requirement for the kind of fair trial which is [the United States'] constitutional goal'.[94] Beyond declarations of principles, however, lie legal technicalities.

The Confrontation clause obviously bears on the problem of using hearsay against a defendant. If the term 'witnesses against' includes anyone who makes an out-of-court statement that may be proved by a third party or reading of a document, all statements to the police and prosecutor submitted by those who do not testify at trial would be inadmissible. In this way, the Clause would abrogate virtually all the exceptions to the hearsay rule, a result long rejected as contrary to the present state of United States legal affairs. In the past, some commentators simply aligned the content of the Confrontation clause with the law of hearsay.[95] The supporting argument was that the Right to Confrontation, though evidently a constitutional right, found its origin not just in the fundamental charter but in the spirit of the common law of evidence. The Supreme Court has once argued against the idea that the Confrontation clause is a mere codification of the law of hearsay,[96] but still struggles to carve out a role for the clause which is independent of it.

One of the few points of certainty is that the Confrontation Clause entitles the accused to be there when witnesses testify against him.[97] In the 1990s, however, protective measures for victims of sexual assaults were approved on the assumption that children would be traumatised if forced to sit in court.[98]

---

92 Most United States evidence textbooks discuss confrontation as an ancillary section of the law of hearsay: cf. C.B. Mueller and L.C. Kirkpatrick, *Evidence under the Rules*, 4th edn., Aspen Law & Business, Gaithersburg, 2000, 423-453; J.W. Strong *McCormick on Evidence*, 5th edn. West, St. Paul, 1999, 386; I. Younger, M. Goldsmith and D.A. Sonenshein, *Principles of Evidence*, 4th edn., Anderson, Cincinnati, 2000, 722.

93 *Coy v. Iowa*, 487 U.S. 1012, 108 S. Ct. 2798 (1988) at 1019.

94 *Pointer v. Texas*, 380 U.S. 400, 85 S. Ct. 1065 (1965) at 405.

95 For an extensive account of this debate cf. R.D. Friedman, *Confrontation: The Search for Basic Principles*, (1998) 86 Geo L.J. 1011, at 1014.

96 *California v. Green*, 399 U.S. 149, 90 S. Ct. 1930 (1970).

97 *Coy v. Iowa*, *supra* note 93, at 1012.

98 *Maryland v. Craig*, 497 U.S. 836, 110 S. Ct. 3157 (1990).

Evidence via a live video-link, therefore, is now constitutionally admissible. On the other hand, anonymity of courtroom witnesses violates the Right to Confrontation.[99]

In contrast, the Confrontation Clause does not apply to hearsay statements from courtroom declarants since the term 'witness' in the Sixth Amendment means only 'people who testify in open court'. In such cases, matters of admissibility of hearsay are resolved by reference to the Federal Rules of Evidence (F.R.E.).[100] Wigmore endorsed this position long ago,[101] and Supreme Court Justices adopted it in a number of leading cases.[102]

Further, the Confrontation clause is of little use in excluding out-of-court depositions made by persons who are 'unavailable'[103] to take the stand. It is not contested that the Confrontation clause requires prosecuting authorities to produce a person *in preference* to offering his prior statements. The question is to address cases in which live testimony is not offered. The Supreme Court reading of the Confrontation Clause is that it operates in two ways to restrict the range of admissible hearsay. First, the prosecution must show that the declarant was unavailable (the so called *rule of necessity*). Secondly, a minimum standard of trustworthiness for the concerned hearsay statements must be met (*rule of reliability*). Something will be said about these two prongs in turn.

The landmark case on constitutional unavailability is *Barber v. Page.*[104] This was a case in which everyone knew where the witness was. Nevertheless, bringing him to court from a federal prison in a different State would have proved difficult for procedural reasons. Still, attendance *could* have been ensured and the Court held that the prosecutor had made 'absolutely no effort'[105] to secure it. The judgment of the Court of Appeals was therefore reversed and the case was

---

99 Cf. R. Iraola, *The Sixth Amendment Right to Confrontation a Witness in Federal Criminal Trials About his True Name, Address, and Place of Employment,* (2002) 38 Crim. L.B. 396; M. Leigh, *Witness Anonymity Is Inconsistent with Due Process,* (1997) 91 American Journal Intl. Law 80.

100 F.R.E. contain two separate lists of exceptions to the hearsay rule. While F.R.E. 804 only applies when the declarant does not testify in court, F.R.E. 803 sets provisions which are independent of the declarant's availability. In addition, under F.R.E. 807, a further exception to both lists (catchall exception) renders admissible any other hearsay, subject to five conditions. The main ones refer to matters of trustworthiness and probativeness of the concerned statements.

101 J.H. Wigmore, *Evidence in Trials at Common Law,* J.H. Chadbourn Rev., Little Brown, Boston, 1974, §1397.

102 *Dutton v. Evans,* 400 U.S. 74, 91 S. Ct. 210 (1970) (concurring opinion by Harlan); *White v. Illinois,* 502 U.S. 346, 112 S. Ct. 736 (1992) (concurring opinion by Thomas and Scalia).

103 Not only does it include situations in which the declarant is unable to be present because of death or inability of the parties to secure his attendance, but also when he testifies to a lack of memory or is exempted on the ground of privilege.

104 390 U.S. 719, 88 S. Ct. 1318 (1968).

105 *Barber v. Page,* 390 U.S. 719, 88 S. Ct. 1318 (1968), at 723.

remanded for further proceedings. In *Ohio v. Roberts,*[106] the potential witness left the State in question and severed contact with his family. The prosecution tried to trace his various movements but could not finally locate him. The concept of *good faith effort* was then established to allow the prosecution to use out-of-court statements in compliance with the Confrontational Clause. Under the good faith effort theory, for instance, prosecutors are not expected to produce witnesses living permanently abroad,[107] due to substantial difficulties in the process of international rendition of witnesses.

The Supreme Court also attempted to define the reliability prong. It stated that only hearsay marked with such trustworthiness that admitting it does not represent 'a material departure from the rationale of the general rule'[108] against it may be brought before the court. It framed the requirement so that indicia of reliability must be found in order to admit the evidence. Case law shows that indicia may be inferred by both previous tests as to the veracity of the hearsay and also by intrinsic or circumstantial factors, which have nothing to do with questioning or testing the speaker.

Judicial reasoning could have proceeded towards a sophisticated articulation of the aforementioned requirements, so that they could work independently of the hearsay doctrine. Instead, the recent authority of *White v. Illinois*[109] shows that both requirements have very little bite. In a trial for sexual assault, the four-year-old victim twice came to court but failed to testify because of emotional difficulties. The trial judge admitted several statements given by the victim to her mother, babysitter, and investigating officer prior to trial. Statements were introduced under specified exceptions to the hearsay rule, namely the 'spontaneous declaration'[110] and 'medical examination'[111] exceptions. The Supreme Court unanimously rejected the defendant's argument that his Right to Confrontation had been violated. The Court accepted, on the one hand, that statements that fit the spontaneous utterance and medical statements exceptions are free from a constitutional unavailability requirement. On the other hand, it also affirmed that the reliability standard *is* automatically satisfied when the concerned statements fall within a *firmly rooted* hearsay exception.

---

[106] 448 U.S. 56, 100 S. Ct. 2531 (1980).

[107] *Mancusi v. Stubb,* 408 U.S. 204, 92 S. Ct. 2308 (1972).

[108] *Ohio v. Roberts, supra* note 106, at 65.

[109] Reference to this leading case is provided above, note 102. For extensive comments cf. H.M. Harlan, *White v. Illinois and the "Hearsay Clause" of the Sixth Amendment,* (1993) 54 Luisiana L.R. 177; N.H. Baughan, *The Confrontation Clause and the Supreme Court's Preference for Out-of-Court Statements,* (1993) 46 Vanderbilt L.R. 235; P.W. Bennet, *After White v. Illinois: Fundamental Guarantees to a Hollow Right to Confront Witnesses,* (1993) 40 Wayne L.R. 159.

[110] F.R.E. 803(2). British lawyers refer to this exception to the hearsay rule as *res gestae.*

[111] F.R.E. 803(4).

The underlying argument is that evidence admissible under an entrenched exception to the hearsay rule is so trustworthy that adversarial testing can be expected to add little to its reliability. The court's finding of compliance with a long-standing hearsay exception simply *replaces* and *bypasses* any test of confrontation. It must also be understood that in the United States confrontation claims follow on the heels of unsuccessful hearsay objections. Issues of confrontation are discussed after the court has already determined that hearsay is admissible under evidence rules. That determination stems from at least an implicit finding that the evidence is reliable, precisely because hearsay exceptions are supposed to administer the admissibility of reliable hearsay. Hence, the 'confrontation challenge begins with a strike against it'.[112] This is the reason why the hearsay exceptions have ended up swallowing up the very spirit of the Confrontation clause. Modern United States confrontation-hearsay opinion ends precisely when the process of confrontation ought to begin. If the court admits the statement in evidence, the case typically proceeds without exploring means of testing the accuracy or credibility of that statement. In other words, once the hearsay statement is in evidence the Confrontation clause serves no further purpose since, under these circumstances, 'the Confrontation clause *is satisfied*'.[113] Treatment of the Clause as a constitutional test for reliable evidence has produced a constitutional rule that excludes 'a slice of hearsay so thin that the application of the rule seems little more than a theoretical possibility'[114] and has rendered this part of the Sixth Amendment a 'minor adjunct of evidence law'.[115]

It must also be noted, however, that in the recent leading case of *Crawford v. Washington*[116], the Supreme Court has decided that some hearsay evidence – that which contains *testimonial* statements – is inadmissible in criminal prosecutions unless the declarant (the person making the out-of-court statement) either testifies or, if not, the prosecution demonstrates both a constitutionally acceptable reason for not producing the declarant as a witness, and, more importantly, that the defendant had an opportunity to confront and cross-examine the declarant

---

[112] J.G. Douglas, *Beyond Admissibility: Real Confrontation, Virtual Cross-Examination and the Right to Confront Hearsay*, (1999) 67 Geo. Wash. L.R. 191, at 220.

[113] *White v. Illinois, supra* note 102, at 356; §743 (*emphasis added*).

[114] J.G. Douglas, *Beyond Admissibility..., supra* note 112, at 195.

[115] R.N. Jonakait, *Restoring the Confrontation Clause to the Sixth Amendment*, (1988) 35 U.C.L.A. L.R. 557, at 622. It must be acknowledged, however, that the present state of affairs leaves several United States commentators perplexed. The problem of identifying hearsay that may properly be excluded under the constitutional right to confrontation is still regarded as one of the unsolved dilemmas of constitutional criminal law. An alternative interpretation of the confrontation Clause is put forward by J.G. Douglas, *Beyond Admissibility, supra* note 67, 191-272.

[116] 124 S. Ct. 1354 (2004). For a comment see J. F. Yetter, *Wrestling with Crawford v. Washington And The New Constitutional Law of Confrontation*, (2004) 28 Florida Bar Journal 26 and R.D. Friedman, *Adjusting To Crawford: High Court Decision Restores Confrontation Clause* Protection, (2004) 19 Criminal Justice 4.

at an earlier proceeding. Many commentators have argued that *Crawford* has eventually transformed the doctrine of the Confrontation Clause, although it left many open questions that are, and will continue to be, the subject of a great deal of litigation and academic commentary.

As to what qualifies as a testimonial statement, for instance, the Court left the interpreters with no answer:

> We leave for another day any effort to spell out a comprehensive definition of "testimonial." Whatever else the term covers, it applies at a minimum to prior testimony at a preliminary hearing, before a grand jury, or at a former trial; and to police interrogations. These are the modern practices with closest kinship to the abuses at which the Confrontation Clause was directed.[117]

The ruling of *Crawford* is certainly innovative insofar as it finally affirms that the presence of the aforementioned *indicia reliability* is not itself a reason for curtailing the constitutional Right to Confrontation. On the other hand, the most problematic aspect of *Crawford* is its failure to describe the general defining criteria for defining what is a *testimonial* statement.[118] For this reason, this work cannot place a direct reliance on the United States law of confrontation as a whole. Nonetheless, some references to United States legal discourse may occasionally be found in the subsequent pages, since the contribution made by American jurisprudence to the conceptualisation of confrontation as a *fundamental inalienable right* remains extremely significant.

In *Crawford*, for instance, the Supreme Court also acknowledged a Confrontation Clause exception to its new rule on the inadmissibility of testimonial statements of unavailable witnesses when the hearsay exception of 'forfeiture by wrongdoing' applies.[119] As the Court explains, 'the rule of forfeiture by wrongdoing (which we accept) extinguishes confrontation on essentially equitable

---

[117] *Crawford v. Washington, supra* note 116, at 1374.

[118] After the ruling of *Crawford*, the theory of the 'mental anticipation' (described earlier in note 55) in the mind of the declarant over the possible use in future criminal proceedings has regained momentum as the crucial element to define what is a testimonial statement. Specifically, the topic re-emerged with regard to 9-1-1 calls (*i.e.* emergency calls addressed to operators by individuals requiring assistance or reporting emergencies, possibly during the occurrence of the crime). Whether a 9-1-1 call is testimonial or not, however, is still very much open to debate: contrast *People v. Moscat*, 2004 W.L. 615113 (Crim. Ct. Bronx Co., 2004) – according to which the woman stabbed was not contemplating being a 'witness' in future legal proceedings; she was usually trying simply to save her own life' – with U.S. v. Arnold, 410 F.3d 895 (6th Cir. 2005) – in which the call of a woman reporting the threat with a gun was excluded from evidence as it was deemed 'testimonial'.

[119] According to FRE 804(b)(6) the 'forfeiture by wrongdoing' exception to the hearsay rule refers to statements 'offered against a party that has engaged or acquiesced in wrongdoing that was intended to, and did, procure the unavailability of the declarant as a witness'.

grounds...'[120]. The Confrontation Clause, in other words, grants the accused person the privilege of being confronted with the witnesses against him; but if he voluntarily keeps the witnesses away, he cannot insist on his privilege. This basic principle of judicial fairness – so clearly exposed by the U.S. Supreme Court – will by greatly valuable to the discourse on 'absent witnesses', carried out in Chapter 2.

5 Preliminary Foundations for a Law on Confrontation

This chapter has defined the foundational features of the Right of Confrontation according to principles of constitutional theory and natural justice. Since the Right to Confrontation is a constitutional right, a theory of confrontation is being construed as a means for the challenge to domestic evidence law. In the framework of the tension between fundamental rights and public interest in the criminal process, however, it was acknowledged that the Right of Confrontation is not an absolute right and therefore may be subject to multiple derogations. Yet, the right must be taken seriously by any jurisdiction that announces it. In essence, this means that incursions into the Right may be only justified by competing fundamental *invidivual* rights or reasons of strict necessity, in line with Ronald Dworkin's and Andrew Ashworth's rights theories.

Analysis has focused on two elements: the method of *confrontation* (which was termed 'confrontational paradigm') and the evidence of a *witness*. Evidence is collected in accordance with the confrontational paradigm when the declarant, whose real identity is known to the defence, gives evidence in open court, facing the accused and the trier of fact, under the obligation of truth-telling, and the defence has a chance to challenge the statements through contemporaneous adverse-questioning. It has also been argued that the Right to Confrontation has an impact not only upon the admissibility of courtroom testimonies, but also upon any other evidence that may be said to be *testimonial* in nature (such as prior statements to police, prosecutor, counsel, etc...).

Something was said about the historical origins of the Right to Confrontation in the Anglo American world and his early champions (Sir. Walter Raleigh in England, Abraham Holmes in the United States). The transplant of the right in the Continent of Europe took place in 1950, when the European Convention on Human Rights included it in its 'fair trial' provision (Article 6).

For the establishment of a supra-national European approach to confrontation, unfortunately, only few lessons can be learned from the United States. There, in fact, modern Sixth Amendment scholarship and case law treat confrontation as a redundant rule of evidence that serves very limited purposes, while the issues concerning the relation between the accused person and his

---

[120] *Crawford v. Washington, supra* note 116, at 1370.

accusers mostly depend upon the law of hearsay. Hearsay logic, instead, is practically unknown to the Continental tradition and – as it will be shown later in this work – is losing importance also in the United Kingdom, following the entry into force of the *Criminal Justice Act 2003*.

Discussion now moves on to the establishment of three categories of problematic witnesses, common to criminal orders of both the adversarial and the inquisitorial traditions: the *absent, anonymous* and *vulnerable witnesses*. These categories will serve as a theoretical foundation for the critical analysis of ECHR law – carried out in Chapter 3 – and the comparison of the rules of procedure and evidence of three model European Counties – carried out in Chapters 4 to 6.

CHAPTER 2

Absent, Anonymous and Vulnerable Witnesses

In this Chapter, departures from the confrontational paradigm established in Chapter 1 are grouped so as to establish three categories of *problematic* witnesses. Readers must be aware that these categories are not construed to cover each and every departure, and that they are not exclusive in respect of each other. Certain departures may not be independently discussed in this work, while certain declarants may fall at once into two or even three of the classes.

1 Absent Witnesses

1.1 Definition

For the purpose of the present study, a witness will be termed *absent* if his or her out-of-court statements may be employed as evidence of the matter stated, despite the fact that he or she has not taken the stand at trial.[1] The impact on confrontation is self-evident. Out-of-court statements are often offered unsworn and behind closed doors to the investigating authorities, not the fact-finder. Further, no opportunity of attendance, let alone of adverse questioning, may have been afforded to the defendant or counsel at the time of the pre-trial interview. There are numerous circumstances under which criminal litigation proceeds on the basis of a loud voice from an empty chair. The most significant and recurrent ones are briefly discussed in the following sections.

1.2 Death and Poor Health

Death and poor health are obvious obstacles against trial testimony. Sometimes, it might be difficult to ascertain whether the declarant is dead or alive (as in the case of missing persons), or how serious the concerned illness is, but these matters are quite peripheral to this work.

In principle, the death and serious illness of a potential adverse witness can constitute legitimate reasons for curtailing the Right to Confrontation. In the case of death, the 'cost' of making all prior testimonial evidence inadmissible would be entirely on the prosecution, despite the fact that it bears no responsibility for such an inevitable occurrence. In broader terms, the cost may be said to exceed what the Right to Confrontation is meant to ensure; namely, the live challenge of those accusers that could – at least in theory – be brought inside a courtroom. In the case of illness, the justification for the curtailment of the

---

1 A similar approach in defining the *absent witness* has been adopted by J.R. Spencer, *Orality and the Evidence of Absent Witnesses*, [1994] Crim. L.R. 628 and T.J. Murray, *Videotaped Depositions: Putting Absent Witnesses in Court*, (1982) 68 A.B.A.J. 1402. Other commentators use the phrase 'missing witnesses', *e.g.* R.H. Stier, *Revisiting the Missing Witness Inference. Quieting the Loud Voice from the Empty Chair*, (1985) 44 Maryland L.R. 137.

Right to Confrontation lie in the competing right of the declarant to adequate health care.

More complicated questions arise when the death, or illness, results from the failure of the Government to comply with the positive obligation to protect the safety and life of the declarant (e.g. in the case of persons under arrest or detainees).[2] In such cases, the use in evidence of prior statements would be the consequence of illegal conduct on the part of public authorities and a claim stands that no effort was in effect made to ensure a live confrontation. Alternatively, when the cause of the death, or illness, is a criminal offence by the defendant or an associate, this obviously amounts to a waiver to the Right to Confrontation, since the accused expresses with such conduct his (or her) intention to avoid confrontation with the concerned witness. This is a plain reminder to the concept of 'forfeiture for wrongdoing' of F.R.E. 804 (b)(6), which was briefly described in Chapter 1, section 4.

1.3 Non-compellable Witnesses

Criminal jurisdictions grant to certain individuals the privilege to refuse to take the stand as witnesses. Prestige and deference for public offices is one reason: Her Majesty the Queen of the United Kingdom and the French President of the Republic, by way of illustration, cannot be compelled to testify.[3]

The privilege is also granted to the spouse,[4] the close relatives[5] and, occasionally, the fiancée[6] of the accused. The rationale is steeped in the protection of family unity,[7] to ease the moral dilemma of either testifying against the accused or committing perjury.[8] Confrontational concerns arise when these persons make some allegations against the accused at the investigation stage, and later decide to claim the said privilege. National laws often allow the use in evidence

---

2 For discussion see *Reeves Respondent v. Commissioner of Police of the Metropolis Appellant*, [2000] 1 A.C. 360 (H.L.); *Ribitsch v. Austria*, Series A No. 336, (1996) 21 EHRR 573, §31; *Edwards v U.K.*, App. No. 46477/99 (14 March 2002), §56.

3 (F) Cass. ass. plén, 10 oct. 2001, *Bull. crim.* n°11, published in [2003] Arch. Nuova Proc. Pen. 87, with a comment by S. Maffei; see also G. Delaloy, *La Cour de Cassation et la Statut Pénal du President de la République*, [2002-1] Droit Pénal 1. Instead, in Italy, the President of the Republic and the Prime Minister may be called as witnesses, although their testimony is normally be collected at their respective offices, not the office of the prosecution (Art. 205 I-CPP).

4 *Police and Criminal Evidence Act 1984*, s. 80; in the United States cf. *Hawkins v. U.S.*, 358 U.S. 74, 79 S. Ct. 136 (1958).

5 Cf. Art. 199 I-CPP, Art. 416 Spanish Code of criminal procedure.

6 In Germany, cf. §52 St.P.O.

7 See G.M. Baccari, *La Testimonianza del Prossimo Congiunto dell'Imputato*, Cedam, Padova, 2003, 33.

8 Arguments in favour and against a general principle of non-compellability are broadly discussed in I.H. Dennis, *The Law of Evidence*, 2nd edn., Sweet & Maxwell, London, 2002, 447-448.

of their prior depositions. On close inspection, however, no competing fundamental rights may be invoked to justify their treatment as *absent witnesses*, since family harmony has obviously been broken at the earlier stage in which prior allegations were made. To comply with the Right to Confrontation, national rules of evidence face the alternative of compelling these declarants to submit to a court examination or else, of excluding their unchallenged depositions from admissible evidence.

1.4 The Accuser Co-defendant

Separate discussion is needed for the accuser co-defendant. In the practice of criminal litigation, multiple co-defendants may be tried jointly, or in separate but somehow related proceedings, for the same or related offences. Confrontational concerns arise when a co-defendant who previously submitted an allegation *contra alios*, refuses to take the stand at trail or avails himself of his right to silence. Protection of the accused person often includes the privilege not to give evidence at trial, even when prior charges were brought against others.

The question to be answered here, once again, is whether these subjects may be treated as *absent witnesses* by the law. For the purposes of this work, the difference between a co-defendant and a 'non-compellable witness' lies in the fact that a fundamental right to silence is acknowledged worldwide as a basic principle of law. The Right to Silence and the Right to Confrontation, however, should not be regarded as competing and irreconcilable rights. For a start, it is the job of the prosecution to ensure the collaboration with justice of a co-accused throughout the proceedings. It would be unjust if a capricious decision of the defendant suddenly to interrupt such collaboration automatically converted his or her out-of-court statements into 'evidence'. In addition, national procedures could also compel a co-accused to face an examination on the prior allegations, while ensuring that such oral evidence would still be inadmissible against him or her.[9]

1.5 The Absconding Witness

Sometimes a summons is served on a prosecution witness but he or she simply does not come to court to testify. An investigation of the reasons that led to such behaviour is essential for the study of the Right to Confrontation.

The concerned person might not even be aware of his or her duty to testify, following disruption in the serving of a summons. Here, the 'absconding' condition is the disgraceful consequence of a poor administration of justice. Else-

9 This is the approach taken by Italian law with regard to certain co-defendants who are being tried in separate proceedings for a related offence.

where, the courts or prosecution may have made little effort to secure attendance. While witnesses can be compelled to come to court in most jurisdictions, enforceable orders are only rarely served, due to the financial constraints on criminal justice systems. Clearly, these scenarios do not allow any intrusion into the Right to Confrontation.

Instead, the question to be addressed here is whether proof that the courts made any reasonable effort to call a witness is *per se* sufficient in order to use prior depositions as evidence. The answer is in the negative, with some qualification. Earlier, it was argued that the acknowledgment of the Right to Confrontation, as with any other fundamental right, places extra costs on the society that announces it. No 'extra cost' would be suffered if the public authorities could employ prior statements as evidence when the 'standard' procedures for tracking a missing person have failed. We must face the fact that individuals with a positive interest in avoiding confrontation can escape summons with relative little difficulty, for instance by changing their residence or flying abroad at the time of trial. The 'extra cost' attached to the Right to Confrontation is precisely that prior statements are in these circumstances inadmissible evidence. In addition, some consideration must be given to the failure of the prosecution to monitor the witness' availability prior to trial: the prosecution cannot claim to be taken by surprise by an absence of which they should have been aware.

Different conclusions apply when the court, or prosecutor, demonstrates that a specific reason made it *impossible* to obtain the attendance of a certain witness. For example, the person may be living abroad, in a country that does not allow the collection of testimony on commission. In such a case, an intrusion into Confrontation could be grounded upon the fact that any damage to the diplomatic relations with the country in question (which would likely result from any attempt to apprehend the informant) far exceeds the values that the Right to Confrontation is meant to ensure.

Also, the prosecution may show that a prior declarant was kept away from proceedings against his or her will, for fear of reprisals. If such claims are sustained by adequate evidence of misbehaviour on the part of the accused, prior statements could certainly be used in evidence. In the case of intimidation, as well as in the case of violence against the declarant, it does not 'lie in the mouth of the accused to protest that the witness is not available for cross-examination'.[10]

1.6 Counterbalances

It has been argued that intrusions into the Right to Confrontation are acceptable in the case of death or illness of the declarant, and also when the prosecution proves that it is truly impossible to secure a courtroom examina-

[10] *R. v. Harvey*, (1998) 10 Archbold News 2 (C.A.).

tion. These conditions may arise in proceedings of any kind, regardless of the nature and seriousness of the concerned offence.

Something must now be said about the counterbalances that ought to be granted to the accused person who faces an absent accuser. Since no evidence is given at trial, it could be argued that the only compensation available is the diminution of the probative value of the prior statements. This is in fact the approach taken by ECHR law.[11] Nonetheless, it should be acknowledged that out-of-court depositions can also be challenged in some of the usual ways by which one may challenge court testimony.[12] These options must be left available to the defendant, regardless of the presence of the declarant at the trial hearing. The absence of a witness, for instance, does not preclude the defendant from raising the question of the inconsistencies among his multiple out-of-court statements. Nor does it prevent the report of his earlier convictions or episodes of discreditable conduct. The problem is that national provisions are often phrased in such a manner that the pursuance of certain challenges to testimonial evidence is limited to live witnesses alone.

An example may clarify this point. While counsel are normally entitled to access the criminal record of witnesses, procedural rules may restrict such access only to the records of those who are summoned to testify (e.g. in Italy, Art. 236(2) I-CPP). If interpreted literary, such a rule would obviously prevent the collection of the record of a *dead* absent witness, and thus prevent the challenge of his or her credit, in violation of the confrontational aspiration of the defendant.

2 Anonymous Witnesses

2.1 Definition

For the purpose of the present study, a witness will be termed 'anonymous' if his *real* identity is concealed from the accused and counsel. By definition, anonymous testimonial statements fall short of the requirement mentioned in Chapter 1, section 3.2.5. In practice, this category entails far more extensive departures from the confrontational paradigm.

For obvious reasons, anonymity is commonly accompanied by the screening of the witness's physical appearance. Modern techniques of image manipulation may allow the broadcasting of portions of the witness's body, presenting the defence at least with a limited chance to check upon the declarant's demeanour.

---

[11] See Chapter 3.

[12] The idea of a *virtual* cross-examination to impeach a hearsay declarant who never testifies at trial is endorsed by J.G. Douglas, *Beyond Admissibility: Real Confrontation, Virtual Cross-Examination and the Right to Confront Hearsay*, (1999) 67 Geo. Wash. L.R. 191, at 231. Also, of the same author, *Virtual Cross-Examination: The Art of Impeaching Hearsay*, (2003) 34 Journal Mar. Law & Com. 149.

Similar considerations can be made with regard to sound manipulation, whenever clues to identity may be drawn from someone's accent or way of speaking. The public and press may also be excluded from examination in the courtroom. Further, anonymity arguably has an impact on the adverse-questioning requirement of the confrontational paradigm, since some restrictions must be established on the range of admissible questions that can be put to the witness (such as those concerning prior relationship with the accused, or prior misconducts).

The following sections explore three scenarios in which criminal jurisdictions often consider the employment of the anonymity tool, in order to persuade witnesses to take the stand. It is commonly agreed that the granting of anonymity is legitimate only under very exceptional circumstances.

2.2 Witness Intimidation

The expression '*witness intimidation*' refers to threats made or actions taken by defendants, or others acting on their behalf or independently, to prevent someone from reporting information to the judicial authorities. Arguably, witness intimidation is a pervasive phenomenon of contemporary societies and its consequences are extremely harmful to the administration of justice.[13] Nonetheless, claims of witness intimidation must be carefully investigated since giving evidence against a suspect invariably involves some degree of discomfort and inconvenience for the declarant.

Inconvenience cannot be claimed by those who bear a specific obligation to bring charges against offenders, such as police agents or officers. Further, it must be assumed that, under ordinary circumstances, other means of social control are in principle sufficient to ensure due protection to the life and security of informants. The traditional answers to intimidation are the pre-trial detention of the defendant and tailor-made criminal offences.[14] More recently, specific Witnesses and Victims Protection Programs have been established worldwide in an effort to enhance the quality of the support to witnesses, especially in the aftermath of their public deposition.

In the last decade however, scholars[15] and prestigious international institutions[16] have put forward the view that measures of this kind may sometimes

---

[13] For discussion see M.H. Graham, *Witness Intimidation. The Law's Response*, Quorum Books, Westport, 1985.

[14] In England, intimidation of witnesses (*C.J.P.A. 2001*, s. 39); in the United States, *subornation of perjury* (18 *United States Code* §1622); in Italy *subornazione* (Art. 377 Italian Criminal Code).

[15] Resolution No. 6 on Criminal procedure, adopted at the XVIth International Congress of Penal Law (Budapest 5-11 1999) justifies anonymity, provided that certain conditions are envisaged and regulated by national law. The said Resolution is published in (1999) 70 R.I.D.P. 904.

[16] Cf. *Recommendation No. 13/1997 of the Committee of Ministers of the Council of Europe*, concerning intimidation of witnesses and the rights of the defence. For a comment of this document cf. J.F. Nijboer, *Children and Young Persons in the Criminal Justice System: The Council of Europe Recommendation on Witness Protection and Rights of the Defence*, (1999) 10 Criminal Law Forum 443-65.

be ineffective and, therefore, that witness anonymity should be justified as a legitimate tool to counter intimidation. In many European countries[17] the evidence of anonymous witnesses is now admissible and such practice appears to be tolerated by ECHR law.[18] Typically the tool of anonymity is praised in the fight against organised crime,[19] because abundant empirical evidence suggests that criminal organisations make systematic use of intimidation to protect their interests and maintain their local power.[20] Anonymity is also granted to court witnesses by the International criminal Tribunals:[21] these jurisdictions have no means of providing social control, since they have no police or other law-enforcement agencies at their disposal.

At this stage, a further distinction must be made. Anonymity is primarily a measure of *prevention* against possible intimidation, not a *remedy* against ongoing menaces. When a person is threatened by the defendant (or an associate) it is precisely because the latter foresees what the former may report in court, and the informer would arguably be recognisable from the substance of such evidence. Persons subject to actual intimidation would rather abscond or, in the case of co-defendants, remain silent in the courtroom. Their pre-trial depositions must be treated here as 'absent testimonial statements'. Alternatively, they may take the stand and lie, withdrawing prior allegations: in such case, a question would arise as to the use in evidence of their prior inconsistent statements.

Within the theoretical framework followed in this study, the intrusion into the right to confrontation in case of serious risk of intimidation finds its justification in the competing fundamental rights to life and security of the concerned declarants.

---

17 Such as The Netherlands (Arts. 226 to 226f, Code of criminal procedure), Norway (§130a, Code of criminal procedure, as inserted by Statute 98/2001), Belgium (Arts. 86bis to 86quinquies, *Code d'instruction* as inserted by *Loi relatif à l'anonymat des témoins*, 8 April 2002, *Mon. Belge*, 31 May 2002.) and France. Rules for anonymous witnesses may also be found in common law jurisdictions, such as New Zealand. There, the *Evidence (Witness Anonymity) Amendment Act 1997* inserted ss. 13B to 13J into the *Evidence Act 1908*.

18 See Chapter 3.

19 M.H. Graham, *Witness Intimidation, supra* note 13, at 5.

20 For a comprehensive study on the organised crime and the strategies available to criminal jurisdictions to fight against cf. *Criminal Justice Systems Facing the Challenge of Organised Crime* (1998-1999) 68-69-70 R.I.D.P.

21 Anonymous evidence was first admitted before the I.C.T.Y. in the case *Prosecutor v. Tadic* (IT-94-1-T). For comments cf. M. Leigh, *The Yugoslav Tribunal: Use of Unnamed Witnesses against Accused,* (1996) 90 American Journal International Law 235; M. Momeni, *Balancing the Procedural Rights of the Accused against a Mandate to Protect Victims and Witnesses: An Examination of the Anonymity Rules of the International Criminal Tribunal for the Former Yugoslavia,* (1997) 41 Howard L.J. 155.

2.3 Victims

The anonymity of victims as a means of avoiding intimidation requires separate discussion: their situation is often so peculiar as to render the tool absolutely ineffective. It is arguably easy to detect when a deposition is submitted by the victim of the offence. Depositions could include details that no external observers would be able to perceive and recall. Often, the offender is familiar with the identity of the victim: the majority of offences are committed against certain individuals precisely because they are *who they are*. Even when the legal identity of a victim is concealed from the offender, he or she may easily discover it. In a case of burglary, for instance, the suspect would obviously have immediate access to the address of the victim. This being said, concealment of a victim's identity might be useful only when he or she is 'indistinguishable' from the offender's point of view. Mass terrorist attacks are good examples, since those who suffer their consequences are not likely to be selected on an individual basis.

2.4 Undercover Agents

The establishment of efficient investigation and intelligence services is a priority of any legal order. Traditional methods of investigation are ineffectual when a well-insulated and mutually protective environment surrounds offenders and their endeavours. The lack of complainants, witnesses and tangible evidence of wrongdoing, together with consideration of the viciousness of these offences, renders necessary the employment of strategies of infiltration and deception.[22]

Conventionally regarded as an essential resource in the repression of terrorism and drug trafficking, undercover agents may also prove useful in disclosing gambling offences or corruption in political circles. Their task is to approach suspects, establish ties with certain offenders and, possibly become insiders of criminal organisations, in an attempt to gather as much valuable intelligence as possible. The activity of undercover agents poses several challenges to criminal law for both substantive and procedural reasons. Here, it is sufficient to highlight that the intelligence gathered by undercover agents is frequently employed as a preliminary input for investigation while it is only seldom tendered in evidence.

Intricate problems arise when an undercover agent is summoned as a prosecution witness. Certainly, disclosure of his or her identity entails immediate danger for his or her personal safety. Anonymity cannot be granted on this basis alone, since it is the primary obligation of undercover agents to put their life and

---

[22] The justification and legitimacy of undercover operations have been recently discussed in S. Bronitt, *Entrapment, Human Rights and Criminal Justice: A Licence to Deviate?*, (1999) 29 Hong Kong L.J. 216.

security at stake. Granting of anonymity is essential for quite a different reason. The disclosure of the identity of an undercover agent will make it impossible to deploy him or her in the same or similar environments and, in the long run, would affect the ability of the police to perform secret investigations. This effect qualifies as a 'cost that greatly exceeds what the society was prepared to pay when it acknowledge the Right to Confrontation',[23] and an intrusion into it may thus be considered legitimate.

2.5 Counterbalances

The evidence of an anonymous witness may only be admissible in the aforementioned – and rather exceptional – instances of 'serious witness intimidation', 'indistinguishable victims' and 'undercover investigations'. When the law lists the criminal offences in the prosecution of which anonymity is permissible, such a list ought in principle to be limited to specified and widely acknowledged criminal 'emergencies' (*i.e.* organised crime for Italian law, terrorist activities in Northern Ireland for English law).

Given the pervasive impact of anonymity into the confrontational paradigm, each of the two types of counterbalances described in Chapter 1 section 3.4 must be applied to the evidence of the anonymous witness. On the one hand, the need for supportive evidence is imperative due to the restrictions to which the challenge to reliability is subjected. On the other hand, procedural guarantees must be established to ensure the participation of the defence at the time of the collection of the evidence, either in or out of court. These are, in essence, the principles put forward by ECHR law. Disclosure of information on the declarant is also essential. In this regard, the recent statutory reform of Queensland (Australia) in relation to the evidence of undercover agents is especially interesting. There, the police must now maintain a register in which all undercover agents and operations are listed. For each agent, a 'witness anonymity certificate' may be sent upon request to the defence, including the name used by the agent in the concerned operation, all prior convictions, prior episodes of discreditable conduct of the agent, and any other information that may be relevant to his or her credit.[24]

An anonymous witness might occasionally also be an *absent witness*. This happens when a person who submitted out-of-court *anonymous* evidence fails to take the stand. In such a case, the departure from the confrontational paradigm reaches its peak, as none of its components are complied with. It is hard to find a scenario in which such evidence would not cause a violation of the Right to Confrontation. At any rate, strict reasoning suggests that admissibility of 'absent

---

[23] This is one of the reason for which a curtailment of fundamental rights is admissible according to the theoretical approach followed in this work, cf. above, Chapter 1.

[24] See *Evidence Act 1977*, §21B to 21K, as amended by *Evidence (Witness Anonymity) Amendment Act 2000*.

and anonymous testimonial evidence' might be acceptable only if the grounds supporting the granting of anonymity are accompanied by a separate independent reason for the absence, from among those described earlier in section 1.

3 Vulnerable Witnesses

3.1 Definition

For the purpose of the present study, a witness will be termed *vulnerable* when adverse-questioning is ruled out as a method of collection of his/her evidence at any stage of the proceeding.

As with absent and anonymous witnesses, the category in question is established upon a *departure* from the confrontational paradigm. Contrary to these, nevertheless, this particular class does not take its name from the content of such a departure. The term 'vulnerability' anticipates the findings of the following sections, where it is shown that jurisdictions exclude adverse questioning precisely when the individuals are fragile and/or incapable of facing an antagonistic interviewer.

By definition, the vulnerable are exempted from undertaking adverse-questioning. Further infringement of the confrontational paradigm may result from the screening of the witness from the accused, waiving of the oath or affirmation and the setting up of *in camera* hearings, even in venues other than the courtroom.

Screening of the physical appearance of the vulnerable is especially problematic. Many jurisdictions set up visual barriers between the accused and the vulnerable at the time of the examination. In the United States, where similar provisions have been in effect in many State jurisdictions for some time, there have been in fact some successful constitutional challenges based on their alleged contrast with the Sixth Amendment.[25] It must be understood that measures of this kind serve purposes different to those mentioned in relation to anonymous witnesses. There, concealment of physical appearance is meant to protect the real identity of the declarant: more simply, the accused should not *see the witness*. Here, the aim is the opposite: the witnesses should not see *the accused*, since such a vision could cause distress and affect the quality of the evidence. As a matter of fact, in most offences involving vulnerable children or adults the identity of the witness is familiar to the defendant and everybody knows the identity of the person on the other side of the screen: there is no reason to prevent the defendant and counsel from checking the witness's

[25] *Coy v. Iowa*, 487 U.S. 1012, 108 S. Ct. 2798 (1988), at 1012. For discussion see A.W. Hasselbach, *Placing a Child Victim of Sexual Abuse Behind a Screen During Courtroom Testimony as Violation of Sixth Amendment Confrontation Clause*, (1989) 57 Univ. Cincinnati L.R. 1537.

demeanour while giving testimony. In this respect, appropriate one-way mirrors would suit both the witness's needs and the accused's call for confrontation.

It is now time briefly to outline the legal discourse that surrounds a few groups of individuals for which non-antagonistic examinations are normally established by national laws of evidence.

3.2 Children

Protection of the juvenile is a firmly rooted value of western societies. Safeguards are established for their benefit in almost every field of the law, under the assumption of the existence of very special needs. In evidentiary matters, it is agreed that they pose a real challenge[26] for the parties and courts. In the 1990s, the problems involved in the administration of their testimony have been investigated by both legal and psychological scholars.[27] Empirical research shifted from the strategies of interviewing children to the analysis of potential mutual language comprehension difficulties, from the peculiarity of children's memory to the trauma of testifying in court, especially for victims of the offence under prosecution.[28] It is neither my intention nor my task to review the far-reaching, although sometimes contrasting conclusions, reached by research concerning the child witness. Only a few remarks are essential to a discourse on confrontation.

On the one hand, a process of revision has characterised the traditional *dogma* of the suggestibility of children[29] that, by implication, would invariably render them less reliable than adults. In broad terms, experts now agree that young age does not make evidence *per se* unreliable.[30] On the contrary, children are capable of reporting the events they have observed or experienced with great accuracy if both the method and the setting of the interview take account of their psychophysical needs.[31] It is accepted, for instance, that they are

---

26 J.E.B. Myers, K.J. Saywitz and G.S. Goodman, *Psychological Research on Children as Witnesses: Practical Implications for Forensic Interviews and Courtroom Testimony*, (1996) 28 Pacific L.J. 3, 76.

27 Among the vast literature on child witnesses see M.S. Zaragoza, *Memory and Testimony in the Child Witness*, Sage, Thousand Oaks, 1995; H. Dent and R. Flin, *Children as Witnesses*, Wiley, Chichester, 1992; J.R. Spencer and R Flin, *The Evidence of Children: the Law and the Psychology*, 2nd edn., Blackstone, London, 1993.

28 G.S. Goodman and others, *Testifying in Criminal Court*, Chicago Univ. Press, Chicago, 1992: this much cited study examined the emotional effects of court testimony on a sample of 218 children victims of sexual abuse.

29 M.E. Pipe and G.S. Goodman, *Elements of Secrecy: Implications for Children's Testimony*, (1991) 9 Behav. Science & Law 33, at 39.

30 R. Flin, *Children's Testimony. Psychology on Trial*, in M.S. Zaragoza, *Memory and Testimony*, *supra* note 27, at 240-254.

31 K.J. Saywitz, *Improving Children's Testimony: the Question, the Answer and the Environment*, in M.S. Zaragoza, *Memory and Testimony*, *supra* note 27, at 113-140.

intimidated and confused by the appearance of court personnel in unfamiliar costumes, distressed by the presence of the public and particularly fearful of confronting the accused face-to-face. The very size and layout of the courtroom may be a source of anxiety for both the child defendant[32] and the child witness.

On the other hand, it is settled that the ability of children to recollect past events is more easily distorted. As the long-term memory of children deteriorates more rapidly than that of adults,[33] their evidence suffers from the negative effects of delay. In particular, their memories can be overlaid or over-written by information acquired after the event, especially through misleading questioning.[34] The quality of the evidence deteriorates even more greatly when they are required to review their story at different, and temporarily distant, stages of a judicial proceeding.

In recent years legislation has been passed worldwide in order to tackle the problems associated with courtroom stress and procedural delays. While certain protective measures are neutral to concerns of procedural fairness for the defendant (*e.g.* rules that allow parents or other trusted persons to sit near the child and provide support at the time of interview, use of anatomical dolls, drawings or other tools to overcome verbal inhibitions) others have a direct impact on the Right to Confrontation. In principle, however, such intrusions are justified by the competing fundamental rights of the juvenile.

3.3 Victims of Sexual Offences

The dramatic increase in reports of sexual abuse in the last decade[35] has contributed to a growing concern for an effective prosecution of the

---

32 Cf. *V. v. U.K.*, [1999-IX] RJD 111, (2000) 30 EHRR 121. In discussing the arrangements of a trial of two young defendants charged with homicide, the European Court of Human Rights held that 'the formality and ritual of the (...) Court must at times have seemed incomprehensible and intimidating for a child of eleven, and there is evidence that certain of the modifications to the courtroom, in particular the raised dock which was designed to enable the defendants to see what was going on, had the effect of increasing the applicant's sense of discomfort during the trial, since he felt exposed to the scrutiny of the press and public'. As to the procedure to be followed at English trials, see the practice direction issued by Lord Bingham C.J. on February 16, 2002: cf. *Practice Direction (Crown Court. Trial of children and young persons)*, [2000] 1 Cr. App. R. 483.

33 J.E.B. Myers and others, *Psychological Research..., supra* note 26, at 14.

34 Multiple testing sessions reduce the stability of the related narration of facts and tend to increase the risk of induced inconsistencies; cf. D.A. Poole and L.T. White, *Tell Me Again and Again-Stability and Change in the Repeated Testimonies*, in M.S. Zaragoza, *Memory and Testimony, supra* note 27, 24-43.

35 R.G. Nuce, *Child Sexual Abuse: A New Decade for the Protection of Our Children?*, (1990) 39 Emory L.J. 581.

offender. Not only are the victims frequently women,[36] but very often children[37] and disabled persons. Prosecuting sexual offences can be arguably an intricate task. There are usually no witnesses available other than the victims themselves and, most often, their accounts are often plainly contradicted by the defendant.

In these proceedings, court testimony can easily turn into a dramatic and negative experience, even into a process of 're-victimisation' of the abused. Virtually all commentators, judges, prosecutors and support professionals who deal with sexual offences acknowledge that the pre-existing trauma of the assault is only exacerbated by the emotional demands put upon the witness during testimony. Studies show that victims of sex crimes are particularly prone to suffering emotional distress from giving evidence in the presence of their alleged abuser.[38] It is also reasonable to expect feelings of shame and guilt to play a crucial part in influencing their demeanour. Such factors make these categories of victims extremely reluctant to sit in the witness box and may even lead, in the worst scenarios, to a sudden withdrawal of prior allegations.

It has also been argued that if testimony was to be given under ordinary procedures, the mechanics of adverse-questioning could become a truth-distorting weapon[39] in the hands of counsel. While incidents of confusion, panic or contradiction are very frequent when victims are required to focus on the details of the alleged assault, their character may also be maliciously questioned.

Attention must also be paid to the victim's condition in the aftermath of the public testimony. Research shows that child victims who testified in open trials suffered significantly more behavioural difficulties than those who experienced no exposure to the criminal justice system.[40] Moreover, it has also been suggested that recovery is significantly affected for those who were subjected on multiple occasions to procedures of evidence collection.[41]

---

36 A comparative approach to sexual offences against women is provided in I. Bacik, C. Maunsell and S. Gogan, *The Legal Process and Victims of Rape*, Dublin Rape Crisis Centre, Dublin, 1998. For a focus on the woman victim's behaviour at trial see J.A. Allison and L.S. Wrightsman, *Rape-The Misunderstood Crime*, Sage, Newbury Park, 1993, 171-193.

37 For a recent completed study on child abuse cf. C. Bagley and K. Mallick (eds), *Child Sexual Abuse and Adult Offenders: New Theory and Research*, Ashgate, Aldershot, 1999.

38 In particular, in case of child victims of sexual abuse the trauma induced by having to face the accused have displayed by 'noticeable signs of nervousness, fear and anxiety' during the adjudication of the testimony in court: cf. L.C. Brannon, *The Trauma of Testifying in Court for Child Victims of Sexual Assault v. the Accused's Right to Confrontation*, (1994) 18 Law & Psychol. Rev. 442.

39 On this respect, with regard to the Anglo-American cross-examination, see J.R. Spencer and R. Flin, *The Evidence of Children..., supra* note 27, at 273-274.

40 R.G. Nuce, *Child Sexual Abuse..., supra* note 35, at 608.

41 G.S. Goodman and others, *Testifying in Criminal Court..., supra* note 28, at 117.

3.4 Adults with Learning Disabilities

The term encompasses a variety of conditions and manifestations.[42] Sometimes, the disability is the direct consequence of an organic pathology. At other times, it is the result of lack of education or social segregation. Some people lack the mental ability and verbal skills to present coherent testimony. Others may simply be unable to understand and respond to questions. Others may be susceptible to dramatic memory deterioration. In all these circumstances adverse questioning is unsuitable to elicit their testimonial account. Once again, it is for the behavioural sciences engaged in the scrutiny of human demeanour to suggest alternative manners of conducting examinations and interviews.

For confrontational purposes, the category of the vulnerable adult must be kept separate from that of the *seriously ill witness*, described in the context of absent witnesses. In the case of a *seriously ill absent witnesses*, health conditions prevent their attendance at trial but, in principle, do not affect their previous contribution to the case. At the time of giving their pre-trial depositions, their state of mind is presumably normal. On the contrary, the features of the vulnerable adult (in particular, his or her deficit of communication skills) are not necessarily incompatible with attendance to trial or tailor-made interviewing sessions. Nevertheless, such status affects the entire spectrum of his or her testimonial contributions. While vulnerability is a 'permanent' condition, absence is the consequence of 'supervening' circumstances. The implications of this distinction will emerge in the discussion of ECHR law.

3.5 Counterbalances

Adverse questioning is ruled out when the physical and/or psychological conditions of the individual make him or her incapable of facing a hostile process of evidence collection. The decision to pursue alternative methods of examination may be based upon considerations concerning both the witness's personal qualities and the nature of the offence under prosecution.

The need for *ad hoc* techniques of examination is engrained in considerations relating to the special needs of juveniles, the mentally impaired or the mentally distressed. In all these cases, departures from confrontation are intended as a concession to uncommon communication difficulties. Since the only certain outcome of antagonistic interviewing sessions would be a further harm to the present and future health conditions of the vulnerable, some precautions are in principle legitimate.

---

[42] Some 200 causes of learning disabilities have been located by Home Office, *Speaking Up for Justice: Report of the Interdepartmental Working Group on the Treatment of Vulnerable or Intimidated Witnesses in the Criminal Justice System*, London, Stationery Office, 1998, Annex A.

In any case, counterbalances favourable to the accused must also be established to tackle confrontational concerns. At this point a further distinction should be put forward. When the vulnerable person undertakes a 'protected' examination before the parties and the court, either before or at the trial hearing, counterbalances would consist of certain procedural guarantees to ensure the participation of the defence. For example, the defence could be allowed to appoint its own expert or intermediary[43] to perform or supervise the examination, when the prosecution is also allowed to do so.

Sometimes, national rules may allow the vulnerable to remain *absent* and avoid judicial examination. In such cases, parents, social workers, doctors, third parties or police officers would normally report the allegation made by the vulnerable prior to trial. In the perspective taken in this work, absence should only be allowed upon one of the independent causes mentioned in section 1. When the witness is absent and vulnerable, corroborative evidence will also be imperative.

4 Moving Forward: From Theory to Practice

An original approach for the investigation of confrontational matters has now been fully established. In Chapter 1, the ultimate fair paradigm for the collection of testimonial statements in criminal proceedings has been described, together with the most recurrent and significant departures from it. It has been proved that public and oral confrontation, although desirable, is not always possible, for a variety reasons. The absent, anonymous and vulnerable witnesses are the most significant threats to the Right to Confrontation since the use of their evidence, although sometimes justified, should not be employed beyond the threshold of absolute necessity. These theoretical assumptions need know to be tested against the practice of domestic criminal justice. In the following chapters, discussion will then move onto the implementation of confrontation on European soil. The strength of the theory must be judged in the light of the diversity of national laws of procedure and evidence. In Chapter 3, something will be said about the ECHR law on confrontation, developed over 30 years on the basis of claims submitted by the criminal defendants of more than forty European States. In Chapters 4, research will become comparative in nature. Italy, France and the United Kingdom will be chosen as model Countries and the principles of their law of evidence will be briefly exposed. In Chapter 5 and 6, some lessons on confrontation will be learned from the analysis of the

[43] In the United States, for instance, 18 U.S.C. §3509(i) states that a child testifying shall have the right to be accompanied by an adult attendant but it also specifies that he 'shall not provide the child with an answer to any question directed to the child during the course of the child testimony or otherwise prompt the child'.

manner in which Italian, French and English law treat courtroom declarants and the evidence of absent anonymous and vulnerable witnesses. Finally, certain common European trends and some considerations valuable to a common European policy will emerge.

CHAPTER 3

The Right To Confrontation In European Human Rights Law

1 Preliminaries

Article 6(3)(d) of the Convention for the Protection of Human Rights and Fundamental Freedoms (the Convention)[1] lists in its first clause the Right to Confrontation among the guarantees of any person subject to the criminal process. The Right to Confrontation stands out as one of the most controversial features of the fair trial theory,[2] which represents the greatest achievement in forty years of interpretation of the Convention by the Court of Human Rights (the Court).[3] It is established that the main purpose of the Convention is the protection of individual rights from infringement by public authorities. The Convention seeks to achieve this purpose through the promotion of the 'ideas and values of a democratic society',[4] such as 'pluralism, tolerance and broadmindedness'[5] and the 'rule of law'.[6] Democratic values also call for the acknowledgment of the importance of the rights of the defence in the criminal process, since the fair trial 'holds a prominent place in a democratic society'.[7] This Chapter begins with the discussion of some general features of ECHR jurisprudence which are essential for the understanding of the judgments and decisions on the law of evidence. It then moves on to concentrate on testimonial evidence. Later, the categories of *absent, anonymous and vulnerable witnesses* / as defined earlier in this work – will be explored separately. It will be shown that, although ECHR law openly announces its commitment to confrontation, it has not yet been able to minimise the array of national incursions into it.

---

1 Rome, 4 November 1950; T.S. 71 (1953); Cmd. 8969.

2 For an overall approach on the Convention see D.J. Harris, M. O'Boyle and C. Warbrick, *Law of the European Convention on Human Rights*, Butterworths, London, 1995; P. Van Dijk and G.J.H. Van Hoof, *Theory and Practice of the European Convention on Human Rights*, 3rd edn., Kluwer, The Hague, 1998; C. Ovey and R.C.A. White, *European Convention on Human Rights*, 3rd edn. Oxford univ. Press, Oxford, 2002; F. Sudre *Droit International et Européen des Droits de l'Homme*, 5th edn., P.U.F., Paris, 2001; E. Lambert, *Les Effects des Arrêts de la Cour Européenne des Droits de l'Homme: Contribution à une Approche Pluraliste du Droit Européen des Droits de l'Homme*, Bruylant, Bruxelles, 1999; J.A. Frowein and W.P. Peukert, *EMRK-Kommentar*, 2nd edn., Engel, Kehl, 1996.

3 In 1998, Protocol 11 to the Convention abolished the European Commission on Human Rights (the Commission). As a result, the Convention is now administered by two bodies, the new permanent Court and the Committee of Ministers of the Council of Europe. Reorganisation was prompted by the increasing number of Member States and applications to the Strasbourg organs.

4 *Kjeldsen and others v. Denmark*, Series A No. 23, (1979-80) 1 EHRR 711, at §53.

5 *Handyside v. U.K.*, Series A No. 24, (1979-80) 1 EHRR 737, at §49.

6 *Golder v. U.K.*, Series A No. 18, (1979-80) 1 EHRR 525, at §34.

7 *De Cubber v. Belgium*, Series A No. 86, (1985) 7 EHRR 236, at §30.

2 The Interpretation of the European Convention

While the interpretation of the Convention is in principle governed by established rules of international law,[8] the Strasbourg organs have also developed some tailor-made interpretative techniques.[9] These deserve some discussion, as they also have an influence upon the rulings on criminal evidence.

2.1 Evolutive Interpretation

The Strasbourg bodies adopt an evolutive and dynamic, rather than a static and historical, approach to interpreting the Convention. The Convention is to be interpreted in the light of present day conditions, as opposed to those prevailing when it was drafted, the main concern being that it is to be a 'living instrument',[10] capable of adjusting to the social changes which have occurred in the Member States throughout the last decades. As a general rule, the older a decision of the Court, the less reliable it is as a guide. In *Stafford*, it was held that:

> While the Court is not formally bound to follow any of its previous judgments, it is in the interests of legal certainty, foreseeability and equality before the law that it should not depart, without cogent reason, from precedents laid down in previous cases. Since the Convention is first and foremost a system for the protection of human rights, the Court must however have regard to the changing conditions in Contracting States and respond, for example, to any emerging consensus as to the standards to be achieved ... It is of crucial importance that the Convention is interpreted and applied in a manner which renders its rights practical and effective, not theoretical and illusory. A failure by the Court to maintain a dynamic and evolutive approach would risk rendering it a bar to reform or improvement.[11]

In pursuing its aim of updating the degree of protection afforded to individuals, the Court has not only modified its case law but has also sometimes completely reviewed it. By way of illustration, the solution provided for the rights of transsexuals has been reversed on three occasions within a twelve-year-period, due to subsequent scientific and cultural developments.[12] Changes and improvements

---

8 Cf. Arts. 31 to 33 of the Vienna Convention on the Law of Treaties (May 23, 1969), which codify customary rules of international law.

9 Cf. F. Sudre (ed.), *L'Interprétation de la Convention Européenne des Droits de l'Homme*, Bruylant, Bruxelles, 1998.

10 *Tyrer v. U.K.*, Series A No. 26, (1979-80) 2 EHRR 1.

11 *Stafford v. U.K.*, App. No. 46295/99 (8 May 2002) at §68.

12 Transsexual rights were first considered in *Rees v. U.K.*, Series A No. 106, (1987) 9 EHRR 56, then reviewed in *Cossey v. U.K.*, Series A No. 184, (1991) 13 EHRR 622 and finally in *Sheffield and Horsham v. U.K.*, [1998-V] RJD 2011, (1999) 27 EHRR 163.

also characterise the fair trial doctrine, chiefly in criminal cases, a field in which the Court has raised the standards of protection required of national systems in order to upgrade the quality of justice across Europe.

Evolutive interpretation is closely linked to the presence of common standards in the domestic law of the Member States and is only applied when certain values appear to have achieved widespread acceptance. Assessing whether a clear European trend exists, however, is complex and may result in a nebulous distinction between evolutive interpretation and judicial revision of the Convention. Unsurprisingly, the major differences in the domestic rules of criminal procedure and evidence have led the Court to minimise evolutive interpretation in this area of the law; in the last fifteen years, little has changed in the essence of the rulings on criminal testimony.

2.2 Autonomous Meaning

Legal concepts that are employed by domestic laws are also referred to in the Convention. The terms of the Convention, however, are considered to have an autonomous meaning, independent of and not necessarily corresponding to that of identical or similar terms in the legislation of Member States. In order to guarantee a common approach for the analysis of national laws, the Strasbourg organs' rulings often offer a re-interpretation of such terms.

For example, the autonomous meaning theory applies to the concepts of Article 6: *civil rights and obligations, criminal charge* and, of particular relevance to this work, *witnesses*. In fact, if national definitions were allowed to prevail, classification of a certain offence as 'disciplinary' or 'administrative' could circumvent the guarantees established by the Convention to the detriment of the accused.

The Court considers its task to be one of applying 'substantive' rather than 'formal' concepts.[13] This tendency can also be seen on occasions when the Convention itself refers back to national legislation, as in the case of expressions such as 'in accordance with the law', under Article 8(2), or 'lawful arrest or detention', under Article 5. The Court is not satisfied with the mere existence of a provision of national law, but requires that the legal source which is the basis for restricting rights and freedom meet certain requirements, such as accessibility, clarity and lack of arbitrariness. The autonomous meaning applied by the Court to the term *witness* will be investigated in details as the discussion unfolds, in Chapter 5.

---

[13] *Deweer v. Belgium*, Series A No. 35, (1979-80) 2 EHRR 439, at §44.

2.3 Principle of Proportionality

It is frequently suggested that inherent in the Convention system is the search for a fair balance between the protection of individual rights and the interest of the community at large.[14] The principle of proportionality is purportedly concerned with defining such a balance. The matter requires some consideration because references to the principle of proportionality may easily be abused to surrender individual rights to arguments of *public interest* and *social defence*. Balancing tests can operate to undermine the protection of Human Rights, since those disposed to rule against them will often simply put ample weight on the other side of the balance.

Although the word *proportionality* does not appear in the Convention or its Protocols, commentators nevertheless consider it to be the decisive Strasbourg approach to Human Rights discourse.[15] This claim is not entirely persuasive. For a start, the principle of proportionality does not apply to the rights mentioned in Article 15, for which not even a state of emergency justifies a derogation.[16] By contrast, the principle applies to the rights under Articles 8-11 (privacy, religion, expression, assembly), whose phrasings explicitly admit incursions when they are 'necessary in a democratic society'.

The question to be answered here is whether a proportionality discourse also applies to Article 6 (and Article 5), for which the letter of the Convention provides no qualification at all. The goal of fairness in the criminal process often clashes with other valuable interests protected by the Convention[17] and it is open to debate whether reference to proportionality can help in solving such clashes. In favour of proportionality one could invoke a ruling on Article 6, in which the Court suggested that the 'fair balance' between the protection of the individual's procedural rights and the interests of the community can only be achieved if restrictions on these rights are *strictly proportionate* to the aim they pursue.[18] One could also argue that the very concept of fairness, entrenched in Article 6, implies the need to solve tensions between competing values, through a pattern of checks and balances. Nevertheless, a closer look to the ECHR case law suggests that there may well be a more structured and demanding approach than simple proportionality, or balancing, in an effort to protect Human

---

[14] *Sporrong and Lonnroth v. Sweden*, Series A No. 52, (1983) 5 EHRR 35, at §69.

[15] P. Van Dijk and G.J.H. Van Hoof, *Theory and Practice, supra* note 2, 80-82; F. Sudre *Droit international, supra* note 2, 167-169. See also S. Van Drooghenbroeck, *La Proportionnalité dans le Droit de la Convention Européenne des Droits de l'Homme: Prendre l'Idée Simple au Sérieux*, Bruylant, Bruxelles, 2001.

[16] Art. 15 refers to Art. 2 (right to life), Art. 3 (prohibition of torture), Art. 4 (prohibition of slavery and forced labour) and Art. 7 (*nulla poena sine lege*).

[17] See *Doorson v. The Netherlands*, [1996-II] RJD 446, (1996) 22 EHRR 330 (interests of victims and witnesses as opposed to the rights of the defendant).

[18] Cf. *Ashingdane v. U.K.*, Series A No. 93, (1985) 7 EHRR 528, at §57.

Rights.[19] In *Rowe and Davis* it was stated that the entitlement to disclosure of evidence is not an absolute right. Any criminal proceedings may involve competing interests (*e.g.* the efficiency of prosecutions, the protection of society, the personal security of intimidated witnesses, the secrecy of investigations), which could be weighed against the rights of the accused. Despite these considerations, the Court came to the conclusion that 'only such measures restricting the rights of the defence which are *strictly necessary* are permissible under Article 6(1)'.[20] Moreover, in order to ensure that the accused receives a fair trial, any difficulties caused to the defence by a limitation on its rights must be 'sufficiently counterbalanced by the procedures followed by the judicial authorities'.[21]

This reasoning is convincing insofar as it conveys that there is a difference between allowing certain limited restrictions on a right in case of necessity and holding that all restrictions that can be said to be proportionate to considerations of 'public interest' should be tolerated.[22] This accords with the unambiguous, but regrettably isolated, statement that 'the general requirements of fairness embodied in Article 6 apply to proceedings concerning all types of criminal offence, from the most straightforward to the most complex'.[23] This approach gives some kind priority to the fundamental right of the citizens over the interests of the 'majority'. It is useful to recall the argument made earlier on that incursions into fundamental rights are to be tolerated only if grounded upon certain compelling reasons (which are mentioned in Chapter 1, section 1.4) but not simply upon a purported call for protecting 'society' as a whole.

A further corollary of this approach is that incursions into a right violate the Convention system where a less infringing, yet equally effective alternative, exists. Even when there is a valid reason for suppressing a Convention right, Member States must show that the actual restriction employed does not go beyond what is strictly indispensable to achieve the intended purpose.

---

19 The tension between fundamental rights and the public interest in ECHR discourse is investigated by A. Ashworth, *Human Rights, Serious Crime and Criminal Procedure*, Sweet & Maxwell, London, 2002, 78 s. The author argues that 'although the Court does use the term balance (or counterbalancing) it also sets out some distinct parameters for such reasoning'. These parameters should be followed 'as a template for some of the public interest cases'; there, it is not so much a wide public interest but rather the rights of other individuals (*i.e.* victims, or witnesses) that may conflict with the fundamental rights of the defendant.

20 *Rowe and Davis v. U.K.*, [2000-II] RJD 287, (2000) 30 EHRR 1, at §61 (*emphasis added*).

21 Ibid, at §61.

22 Cf A. Ashworth, *Human Rights, Serious Crime*, *supra* note 19, at 61. The author also suggests that 'there must be an assessment of the potential threat to rights in each case ... it cannot be sufficient to regard a whole category of cases as presenting dangers (*e.g.* organised crime, drug trafficking), in a way that fails to recognise the need for each case to be assessed individually'.

23 *Teixeira de Castro v. Portugal*, [1998-IV] RJD 1451, (1999) 28 EHRR 101, at §36.

2.4 Margin of Appreciation

The depth of ECHR judicial review ranges from extreme deference to national law to severe criticism of certain domestic policies. For several provisions, including the right to a fair trial, the Strasbourg organs recognise that a variable measure of discretion[24] must be left to the State, since there exists a distinction between the roles and responsibilities of the Court and domestic judiciary. The guiding principle is stated in *Handyside*:

> The machinery of protection established by the Convention is subsidiary to the national systems safeguarding Human Rights ... the Convention leaves to each Contracting State, in the first place, the task of securing the rights and the liberties it enshrines ... By reason of their direct and continuous contact with the vital forces of their countries, States' authorities are in principle in a better position than the international judges to give an opinion on the exact content of these requirements as well as on the necessity of [restrictions] intended to meet them.[25]

Respect for fundamental rights does not necessarily call for the implementation of identical legal rules in each Member State, and the Court is in fact quite reluctant to challenge the technicalities of national laws.[26] In fact, the margin of appreciation doctrine comes into play whenever controversial issues of social, moral or economic policy are involved.[27] Unfortunately, there is no universal formula for determining when and how such a discretion should be granted.[28] As a matter of fact, the width of discretion conceded to Member States varies according to parameters such as the importance of the allegedly infringed right, the extent of the interference and the nature of the State's justification. In general, the Court is unwilling[29] to accord a significant margin of appreciation on issues upon which a European consensus is established.

It comes as no surprise that the field of criminal evidence is one in which national discretion reaches a peak, given the profound differences between

---

24 On the margin of appreciation doctrine see H.C. Yourov, *The Margin of Appreciation Doctrine in the Dynamics of European Human Rights Jurisprudence*, Kluwer, The Hague, 1996.

25 *Handyside v. U.K., supra* note 5, at §48.

26 The typical formulas of the margin of appreciation doctrine (such as '[the concerned provision] leaves it to the competent authorities to decide upon the relevance of ...' or 'it is for the national courts to ...') may be easily found in the Strasbourg rulings concerning the law of evidence.

27 B. Emmerson and A. Ashworth, *Human Rights and Criminal Justice*, Sweet & Maxwell, London, 2001, 100.

28 R. Bernhardt, *Thoughts on the Interpretation of Human Rights Treaties*, in F. Matscher and H. Petzold (eds), *Protecting Human Rights: The European Dimension*, Heymanns, Köln, 1988, 65, at 68.

29 *Rasmussen v. Denmark*, Series A No. 87, (1985) 7 EHRR 352, at §40; *The Sunday Times v. U.K.*, Series A No. 30, (1979-80) 2 EHRR 245, at §59.

national laws. Evidence of character is an example. Criminal records are routinely disclosed to continental judges, as they provide uncontested information on the prior incidents in which the defendant has been involved. The assumption within the Anglo-American tradition, in comparison, is that evidence of character is prejudicial and, therefore, inadmissible. A few attempts have been made to stigmatise the continental practice at Strasbourg, but the question of the admissibility of similar fact evidence has been left entirely to the discretion of Member States.[30]

In broader perspective, the margin of appreciation doctrine also reflects the deliberate strategy of avoiding hard-edged reviews in unsettled and controversial matters, in order to retain confidence in the Convention system. In the example of character evidence, a judgement of non compliance with the Convention would have presumably been met with hostility from continental legislators. This interpretative technique, however, could also be regarded as a silent – and arguably illegitimate – abdication of the Strasbourg bodies' responsibilities from the due challenge of domestic evidence rules.

3 The Fairness of Criminal Trials

3.1 The Standard of Fairness

It is now time to discuss the link between the right to a fair hearing[31] set forth in Article 6(1)[32] and the minimum rights to which every person charged with a criminal offence is entitled, which are enumerated in Article 6(3). In ECHR law, an examination for compatibility with the third paragraph does not make an examination for compatibility with the first paragraph superfluous: Article 6(3) 'merely exemplifies the minimum guarantees which must be accorded to the accused in the context of the fair trial referred to in Article 6(1)'.[33] Although these guarantees have been complied with, the proceedings as a whole may nevertheless result in unfairness. In this way, further elements have been added to the theory of a fair proceeding beyond the letter of the Convention. Among them a mention is due to the principle of equality of arms,

---

30 *X. v. Denmark*, (1966) 18 C.D. 44, at 45.

31 The notion of 'fair hearing' is arguably equivalent to that of 'fair trial' or 'fair trial proceedings' cf. P. Van Dijk and G.J.H. Van Hoof, *Theory and Practice*, *supra* note 2, at 428. See also J. Pradel, *La Notion de Procés Equitable en Droit Pénal Européen*, (1997) 27 Revue Général de Droit 505-523.

32 On the ECHR theory of a fair criminal trial cf. S. Stavros, *The Guarantees for Accused Persons under Article 6 of the European Convention on Human Rights: an Analysis of the Application of the Convention and a Comparison with Other Instruments*, Martinus Nijhoff, London, 1993 and G. Ubertis, *Principi di Procedura Penale Europea*, Cortina, Milano, 2000.

33 *Adolf v. Austria*, (1983) Series B No. 43 (Commission Report), at §64.

whose implications are discussed in the following section. As to the guarantees set forth in Article 6(3), it was also said that:

> They exemplify the notion of fair trial ... but their intrinsic aim is always to ensure or contribute to ensuring the fairness of the criminal proceedings as a whole. The guarantees enshrined in Article 6(3) are therefore not an aim in themselves, and they must accordingly be interpreted in the light of the function which they have in the overall context of the proceedings.[34]

Judgments and decisions on criminal proceedings sometimes refer to Article 6(1) *and* the relevant specific right in Article 6(3), sometimes to Article 6(1) alone and, occasionally, to Article 6 as such.

When an alleged breach of the right to confront or obtain the attendance of witnesses is in question, the Court and Commission have always treated the related complaint under Article 6(1) and 6(3)(d) taken together.[35] As a result, no clear distinction has been drawn between the 'overall' concept of a fair trial and the specific provisions concerning the taking and assessment of testimonial evidence. This is why it is so difficult to ascertain whether the ECHR rulings are specifically grounded upon evidentiary arguments or upon a rather nebulous assessment of judicial fairness.

3.2 Equality of Arms

Equality of arms implies 'that each party must be afforded a reasonable opportunity to present his or her case – including the presentation of evidence – under conditions that do not place him or her at a substantial disadvantage vis-à-vis the opponent'.[36] In criminal proceedings, this principle has even greater importance than in civil proceedings, owing to the inherent difference between the parties: the State, represented by the investigating authorities, on one side, and the defendant and counsel, on the other. ECHR law acknowledges that 'the prosecution has at its disposal, to back the accusation, facilities deriving from its powers of investigation supported by judicial and police machinery with considerable technical resources and means of coercion'.[37]

The principle of equality of arms plays a part at all stages of the proceedings and exerts an influence over an array of evidentiary and procedural matters. For instance, it is the equality of arms theory that requires that the parties have

---

34 *Can v. Austria*, (1990) Series B No. 79 (Commission Report), at §48.

35 See, *e.g. Kostovski v. The Netherlands*, Series A No. 166, (1990) 12 EHRR 434, at §39; *Isgrò v. Italy*, Series A No. 194-a, at §31.

36 *Dombo Beheer BV v. The Netherlands*, Series A No. 274, at §33. A recent authority is provided by *F. R. v. Switzerland*, App. No. 37292/97 (28 June 2001), at §34.

37 *Jespers v. Belgium*, (1981) 27 DR 61 (Commission Report), at §55.

the same access to records and documents,[38] and that they be afforded the same opportunity to summon witnesses and experts.[39]

It is admitted that an absolute equality of arms is not always achievable. Certain limitations necessary to the investigation, for instance, are not automatically incompatible with the fairness of trials. While in theory the validation of such limitations requires that they be minimised and open to judicial review, the Court seems reluctant to take any firm stand *in abstracto*. Instead, it discusses such limitations only on a case-by-case basis. This approach inevitably leads to inconsistencies, and these are numerous in the discourse on absent, anonymous and vulnerable witnesses.

4 Principles of Criminal Evidence in ECHR Law

This section illustrates the established approach of the Strasbourg bodies in the scrutiny of domestic laws of evidence.[40] To begin with some point of certainty, the Court and Commission are not inclined to substitute their own views on issues of fact to those adopted by domestic tribunals, provided they are impartial and independent. With specific reference to the testimony of witnesses, it was held that:

> The national judge ... has had the benefit of listening to the witnesses at first hand and assessing the credibility and probative value of their testimony after careful consideration. Accordingly, in the absence of any new evidence having been brought before the Commission and of any indication that the trial judge incorrectly evaluated the evidence before him, the commission must base its examination of the Convention issues before it on the facts as established by the national courts.[41]

When faced with a dispute on facts, therefore, the Court turns to the facts as assessed by domestic authorities,[42] unless new evidence is produced before it,[43] or there are serious reasons to believe that grossly arbitrary conclusions had been drawn at national level. Applications that call for a mere reconsideration of the evidence presented to national courts are thus clear candidates for immediate rejection.[44]

---

38 Cf. *Rowe and Davis v. U.K., supra* note 20.

39 *Bonisch v. Austria*, Series A No. 92, (1987) 9 EHRR 191.

40 See generally M. Van de Kerchove, *La Preuve en Matière Pénale dans la Jurisprudence de la Cour et de la Commission Européennes des Droits de l'Homme*, [1992] R.S.C. 1-14.

41 *Stewart v. U.K.*, (1984) 39 DR 162, at 168.

42 *I.J.L., G.M.R. and A.K.P. v. U.K.*, App. No. 29522/95 (19 September 2000).

43 Cf. Rule 42 (Measures for taking evidence) of the Rules of Court.

44 *X v. U.K.*, App. No. 6208/73 (29 September 1975), 2 Digest Strasbourg 389; *Sofri v. Italy*, App. No. 37235/97 (4 March 2003).

Criminal evidence issues are also influenced by the presumption of innocence,[45] enshrined in Article 6(2) of the Convention. This principle entails that 'the burden of proof is on the prosecution, and any doubt should benefit the accused'.[46] Further, national courts are expected to proceed with no prejudices against the accused person and may sentence him or her only on the basis of lawfully collected evidence. It is also for the prosecution to inform the defendants of the case that will be mounted against them – so that they may prepare and present their defence accordingly – and to adduce sufficient evidence for a conviction. Article 6(2) has also been invoked by those who argue that certain means of proof are *per se* prejudicial to the defence. ECHR law is not prepared to endorse such a claim. In England, for instance, exclusionary rules prevent the disclosure of the criminal record of the accused to the jury while in Continental Europe, records are routinely acquired ex officio. As anticipated, this practice does not conflict with the Convention.[47]

It must also be said that neither Article 6(2) nor any other provision of the Convention requires Member States to adopt certain specific rules concerning the admissibility, collection and evaluation of evidence:

> The admissibility of evidence is primarily a matter for regulation by national rules, and, in principle, it is for the national courts to assess the evidence before them. Accordingly, the Court's task under the Convention is to ascertain whether the proceedings considered as a whole, including the way in which evidence was taken, were fair.[48]

It is thus not for the Strasbourg bodies to decide whether certain evidence should be admitted or not, how the evidence should be presented to the court and what should be its weight. Given the profound diversity of national laws[49], such an approach is for many commentators 'inevitable'.[50] It also aligns with the idea that the Court's task is not to review domestic law and practice *in abstracto*, but instead to determine whether the proceedings brought to its attention had in effect been unfair.[51] Nevertheless, certain parameters within which State

45 The implications of the presumption of innocence are discussed at length in P. Van Dijk and G.J.H. Van Hoof, *Theory and Practice*, *supra* note 2, at 458; D.J. Harris, M. O'Boyle and C. Warbrick, *Law of the European Convention*, *supra* note 2, at 241, C. Ovey and R.C.A. White, *European Convention on Human Rights*, *supra* note 2, at 174.

46 *Barbera, Messegue and Jabardo v. Spain*, Series A No. 146, (1989) 11 EHRR 360, at §77.

47 *X. v. Austria*, App. No. 2742/66, (1966) 9 Y.B. 550, at 554.

48 Cf., *inter alia*, *Windisch v. Austria*, Series A No. 186, (1991) 13 EHRR 281, at §25.

49 Broadly speaking, common law systems control the admissibility of evidence very tightly while civil law systems set traditionally very few restrictions.

50 As suggested by D.J. Harris, M. O'Boyle and C. Warbrick, *supra* note 2, at 210.

51 *Hauschildt v. Denmark*, Series A No. 154, (1990) 12 EHRR 266, at §45; *Padovani v. Italy*, Series A No. 257-b, at §24.

authorities must operate have been established and certain rules of evidence, which may invariably cause the accused's rights to be infringed, have been found. ECHR rulings on criminal evidence may be seen as a list of 'obligations of result', with national courts being allowed to follow their own rules so long as the end result ensures fairness to the defendant.

A basic aspect of fairness is that parties must enjoy equal opportunities to oppose the arguments advanced by their counterparts and to comment upon the evidence presented to the courts.[52] The oft-quoted assumption is that 'all the evidence must in principle be produced in the presence of the accused at a public hearing with a view to adversarial argument',[53] while it is understood that the 'lack of any confrontation'[54] on adverse evidence deprives the accused of a fair trial. The term *adversarial*, employed in ECHR rulings, however, does not refer to the proof-taking style of the common law tradition. In fact, ECHR law does not consider the opposing inquisitorial style[55] – which is applied by the vast majority of Member States – as contrary to the text and spirit of the Convention. For example, an examination of witnesses by the judge on behalf of the parties[56] satisfies the requirements of ECHR law. Further, the right of the accused to *pro se representation* is not acknowledged while all references to a party examination of witnesses refer to the examination by counsel, not by the defendant in person.[57]

This work proceeds on the assumption that the concept of an adversarial proceeding, to which ECHR jurisprudence so frequently refers with no further elaboration, is best described in relation to testimony by the confrontational paradigm outlined in Chapter 1, section 3.2. It will be shown that EHCR law tolerates numerous *departures* from such a paradigm. Discussion of the categories of absent, anonymous and vulnerable witnesses will also clarify the extent to which the Right to Confrontation is open to amendment across Europe and, more broadly, what reasons may be legitimately invoked by domestic courts and law-makers to curtail it.

ECHR law also touches upon some evidentiary matters other than the testimony of witnesses. These matters can only be briefly mentioned here and may be referred to later when essential to the purpose of this work. Despite the silence of the Convention, the fundamental right of the accused to remain silent

---

52 *Feldbrugge v. The Netherlands*, Series A No. 99, at §44; *Ruiz–Mateos v. Spain*, Series A No. 262, at §67; *Lobo Machado v. Portugal* [1996-I] RJD 196, at §31.

53 Among many others see *Kostovski*, *supra* note 35, at §41, *Windisch*, *supra* note 48, at §26.

54 *Saïdi v France*, Series A No. 261-c, (1994) 17 EHRR 251, at §44.

55 The contrast between adversarial and inquisitorial style is extensively described in Chapter 4.

56 This is suggested by the phrase 'right to examine or *have examined* witnesses...' in Article 6(3)(d) of the Convention.

57 More discussion on the right to cross-examine in person is provided in Chapter 5 with regard to Italian, French and English law.

pending proceedings against him is acknowledged. The Court has considered both the limits to compulsory questioning[58] and the drawing of adverse inferences from the failure to explain certain forms of suspicious conduct.[59] Fairness to the defendant under Article 6 is the legal parameter for the assessment of the admissibility of evidence collected by entrapment or other deceptive means. In particular, the roles played by undercover agents posing as purchaser of drugs,[60] accomplices in the delivery of counterfeit notes,[61] or placed in prison to eavesdrop on conversation involving the accused[62] have been repeatedly dealt with by the Strasbourg organs in recent years. Other matters are the admissibility of unlawfully obtained evidence,[63] the value of circumstantial[64] and similar fact evidence,[65] and the timing and extent of disclosure.[66] Instead, the Convention is silent on the issue of criminal investigation and, therefore, only little guidance may be found on the admissibility of evidence from searches, seizures and wiretaps, despite the fact that these are areas of inevitable tension between fundamental rights and public interest concerns. These matters have occasionally been treated as invasions into the privacy of citizens, under Article 8 of the Convention.

5 Testimonial Evidence in ECHR Law

It is now time to focus on Article 6(3)(d), which provides the accused with the right 'to examine or have examined witnesses against him and to obtain the attendance and examination of witnesses on his behalf under the same conditions as witnesses against him'. For convenience, I will hereinafter refer to the two clauses respectively as the 'Confrontation clause' and the 'Attendance clause'.

---

58 Compare *Funke v. France*, Series A No. 256-a, (1993) 16 EHRR 297 with *Saunders v. U.K.*, [1996-VI] RJD 2044, (1997) 23 EHRR 313.

59 *Murray v. U.K.*, [1996-I] RJD 30, (1996) 22 EHRR 29; *Condron v. U.K.*, [2000-V] RJD 1, (2001) 31 EHRR 1; *Averill v. U.K.*, [2000-VI] RJD 203, (2001) 31 EHRR 839. For further discussion see R. Munday, *Inferences from Silence and European Human Rights Law*, [1996] Crim. L.R. 370-385; A. Jennings, A. Ashworth and B. Emmerson, *Silence and Safety: The Impact of Human Rights Law*, [2000] Crim. L.R. 879-894.

60 *Teixeira de Castro v. Portugal*, *supra* note 23.

61 *Radermacher and Pferrer v. F.R.G.*, App. No. 12811/87 (8 December 1988).

62 *A. v. F.R.G.*, App. No. 12127/86 (15 October 1987), (1989) 11 EHRR 84.

63 *Schenk v. Switzerland*, Series A No. 140, (1991) 13 EHRR 242.

64 *Alberti v. Italy*, App. No. 12013/86 (10 March 1989).

65 *X. v. Denmark*, *supra* note 30, at 44.

66 *Jespers*, *supra* note 37, at §55; *Edwards v. U.K.* Series A No. 247-b, (1993) 15 EHRR 417; *Rowe and Davis*, *supra* note 20, at §60.

5.1 The 'Witness'

In *Engel*, the Court argued the case for an autonomous definition of the phrase 'criminal charge'. That argument can be paraphrased as follows with regard to the term *witness*:

> If the Contracting States were able at their discretion to classify an [individual as a witness] the operation of the fundamental clauses of Article 6 would be subordinated to their sovereign will. A latitude extending thus far might lead to results incompatible with the purpose and object of the Convention.[67]

The starting point in the investigation of the term *witness* in ECHR law is that the autonomy of the interpretation is a one-way autonomy: whenever a person is a witness within national law, he or she is unquestionably a witness for the Strasbourg organs. In such cases, Article 6(3)(d) applies without there being room for any further speculation.

The problem is that, in several jurisdictions, the status of witness is restricted to court declarants. In England and Italy, for instance, those who provide information to the police are informed persons or, simply, informants. Earlier in this work, it was shown that United States discourse on the Sixth Amendment is based precisely on the idea that the constitutional clause only refers to witnesses testifying in court. In comparison, the Strasbourg organs are unwilling to subscribe to a formalistic distinction between pre-trial and trial depositions, especially if the former can be used in evidence as the latter. Several ECHR rulings on absent witnesses,[68] in fact, refer to police informants who never appeared in the courtroom to testify. In other words, ECHR law does not consider presence at the public hearing, or before a judge, as an essential element of the status of witness.

Further, it is agreed that testimonial evidence may be brought to the attention of the court through various means other than oral testimony. In *Asch*, first-hand hearsay came into relevance and the Court held that: 'although Mrs. J.L. refused to testify at the hearing, she should ... for the purposes of Article 6(3)(d) be regarded as a witness... because her statements, as taken down by officer B. and then related orally by him at the hearing, were in fact before the court, which took them into account'.[69] Elsewhere, written depositions to the police and prosecutor were considered and it was held that: 'although Mr. D. did not give evidence in person either at first instance or on appeal the Court takes the view that, for the purpose of Article 6(3)(d), he should be regarded as a witness ... because the national courts took account of his statements which *were read*

[67] *Engel v. The Netherlands*, Series A No. 22, (1979-80) 1 EHRR 706, at §81.

[68] See below, section 6.

[69] *Asch v. Austria*, Series A No. 203, (1993) 15 EHRR 597, at §26.

out at the trial'.[70] The process of reading out is not even necessary, so long as the statements are on the court's file[71] and they count as evidence of the matter stated therein.

These considerations should not lead to the conclusion that any *assertion* made by a human being and later included in oral testimony or a written document results in the attribution of the status of witness to its author. All the rulings on the Right to Confrontation concern instead the use in evidence of *depositions* taken by judges, examining magistrates, prosecutors, police or other public officers. Occasionally, statements to private third parties (such as doctors, friends or relatives) have also been dealt with under Article 6, when they had been relied upon as hearsay. In other words, focus is on statements that are *testimonial* in nature, in the sense described in Chapter 1. No cases have so far considered the use of testimonial evidence reported in private documents (*e.g.* letters, diaries) or taken by counsel in a private investigation, yet there is no reason to believe that such evidence would fall outside the scope of Article 6(3)(d).

Peripheral problems arise as to the inclusion of experts and co-defendants in the category of witnesses. Complaints concerning alleged unequal treatment of experts have not normally been discussed under the Confrontation clause, but rather with regard to the principle of equality of arms.[72] Moreover, it has repeatedly been affirmed that 'read literally, Article 6(3)(d) relates to witnesses and not experts'.[73] In comparison, accomplices undoubtedly fall within the category of witnesses, insofar as their evidence is admissible against others co-defendants, whether they be tried jointly or separately.[74]

5.2 Witnesses Favourable to the Accused

The Attendance Clause states that everyone charged with a criminal offence is entitled to 'obtain the attendance and the examination of witnesses on his behalf under the same conditions as witnesses against him'.

---

70 *Isgrò v. Italy*, Series A No. 194-a, at §33 (emphasis added).

71 *Kostovski v. The Netherlands*, Series A No. 166, (1990) 12 EHRR 434, at §40: 'In view of the autonomous interpretation to be given to this term, both authors [of the relevant statements] should be regarded as witnesses for the purpose of Art. 6(3)(d) of the Convention since the statement of both of them, *whether read out at the trial or not*, were in fact before the court and were taken into account by it' (emphasis added).

72 *Bonisch v. Austria*, Series A No. 92, (1987) 9 EHRR 191, and *Brandstetter v. Austria*, Series A No. 211, (1993) 15 EHRR 378.

73 *Bonisch, supra* note 72, at §29; *Brandstetter, supra* note 72, at §42; *Baragiola v. Switzerland*, (1993) 75 DR 76.

74 *Lucà v. Italy*, [2001-II] RJD 145, at §41 with a coment by S. Maffei, *Prova d'Accusa e Dichiarazioni di Testimoni "Assenti" in una Recente Sentenza della Corte Europea dei Diritti dell'Uomo*, [2001] Cass. Pen. 2836-2850.

The phrase *témoins à décharge* in the French version clarifies the ambiguity of the English phrase 'on his behalf' and clearly restricts the scope of this clause to witnesses favourable to the defendant.

It is settled that the Attendance clause does not grant the accused an unlimited right to secure the appearance of witnesses. The recognition of such a right, beyond any control on the testimony's relevance, would lead both to vexatious attempts to prolong trials indefinitely and to excessive costs and lengthy proceedings. It is then settled that 'in respect of the witnesses on behalf of the accused, only exceptional circumstances could lead the Convention organs to conclude that a refusal to hear such witnesses violated Article 6'.[75] Domestic laws may therefore legitimately set conditions and impose restrictions against the summoning of witnesses by the defence, provided that these apply equally to the prosecution. In fact, the fundamental aim of the clause is to fulfil the equality of arms requirement.[76] Protection against arbitrariness is purportedly assured by the fact that reasons must be given whenever a request for the summons of a defence witness is rejected. Regrettably, however, the Court is reluctant to substantially to review the justifications provided by national courts and is normally satisfied with the mere existence of such a justification.[77]

Defendants are expected to require the attendance of any supposedly favourable witness. If they fail to do so, national laws are not compelled to admit their pre-trial depositions in evidence: in other words, there is no obligation under Article 6(3)(d) to open the doors to prior depositions that purport to exonerate the accused;[78] instead, this matter is left to the appreciation of domestic legislation and practice.

5.3 Witnesses against the Accused

ECHR law adopts a two-pronged approach in relation to witnesses adverse to the defendant. Firstly, the Strasbourg bodies assess whether the domestic conviction was based upon testimonial statements collected in accordance with the confrontational paradigm. In the negative, the Court moves

---

75 *M.K. v. Austria*, App. No. 28867/95, (1997) 24 EHRR CD 59.

76 *X. v. Austria*, App. No. 753/60, (1960) 3 Y.B. 310; *X. v. F.R.G.*, (1970) 31 CD 31; *X. v. Austria*, App. No. 4428/70, (1972) 15 Y.B. 265; *X. v. Sweden*, App. No. 10564/83 (10 December 1984), (1986) 8 EHRR 86; *Bricmont v. Belgium*, Series A No. 158, (1990) 12 EHRR 217; *Vidal v. Belgium*, Series A No. 235-b. However, in *Wiechert v. F.R.G.*, App. No. 14040/62, (1964) 7 Y.B. 104 the Commission took the view that the decision to exclude a defence witness, under certain circumstances, may infringe the fair hearing requirement under Art. 6(1).

77 *Bricmont*, *supra* note 76, at §89 and *Vidal*, *supra* note 76, at §34. Contra, the dissenting opinion of Judges Rozakis and Bonello, in *Pisano v. Italy*, App. No. 36732/97 (27 July 2000), (2002) 34 EHRR 705, at 717-718.

78 *Blastland v. U.K.*, (1987) 52 DR 273, (1988) 10 EHRR 528.

on to investigate the extent of the departure from such a paradigm and to locate the counterbalances established at national level to compensate the intrusion into the fundamental right to Confrontation.

One could argue that the right to examine a prosecution witness (or to have him or her examined) necessarily *includes* the instrumental right to obtain his or her attendance in the courtroom. However, these two aspects – attendance and examination – should be distinguished for the purposes of this work. It is certainly true that the departure from the confrontational paradigm is more intense when both examination and attendance of relevant witnesses are missing. Nevertheless, in order to ensure minimum infringement of the Confrontation Clause, the attendance of unfavourable witnesses should be guaranteed *even* when they are not available for a confrontational examination.

The reader should also be aware that, according to the approach followed in this work,[79] restrictions to the rights protected under Article 6 are legitimate only if maintained within the boundaries of strict necessity. This argument calls for the drawing of a clear line between the category of absent witnesses and the categories of anonymous and vulnerable witnesses. With regard to the latter two, it is anticipated that the accused should be afforded at least the opportunity to obtain their attendance for some sort of 'screened' or 'protected' interview.

It must also be highlighted that the Court's reasoning on confrontational matters is driven by 'procedural' rather than 'substantive'[80] concerns. ECHR law does not indulge in an investigation of the content of the evidence. In other words, it makes no difference to the Strasbourg bodies whether it is evidence of facts, hearsay, opinion or character. These conceptualisations are ignored by ECHR law, provided that testimonies are taken in accordance with the confrontational paradigm. The only 'substantive' concern of the Strasbourg organs materialises when the evidence includes other *testimonial statements* given by third persons. In this case, the author of such a statement is himself (or herself) a witness, and Article 6(3)(d) also applies to his or her depositions.

5.4 The Adverse Witness Face-to-face with the Accused

As anticipated, the Strasbourg organs dismiss complaints relating to the evidence of witnesses who were examined in accordance with the confrontational paradigm either before or during trial. It is a general principle of ECHR law that the 'accused should be given an adequate and proper opportunity to challenge and question a witness against him, either at the time the witness made his statements or at some later stage of the proceedings'.[81] Obviously, the

79 See above, Chapter 1.

80 Some exclusionary rules are 'substantive' in nature, while others are merely 'procedural'. This distinction is explored in some detail in Chapter 4.

81 This principle is repeated in each and every judgments concerning adverse witnesses, see *e.g. Windisch v. Austria*, Series A No. 186, (1991) 13 EHRR 281, at §26; *Asch, supra* note 3, at §27.

best chance of confronting a witness arises at trial, while prosecuting authorities collect out-of-court depositions mostly in the absence of the accused and counsel. National jurisdictions, however, may also arrange dedicated pre-trial hearings, with the full participation of the parties and the supervision of a judge. Not for the first time in the present exposition, it is necessary to beware of the danger inherent in the loose use of terminology. In the following sections, any mention of 'out-of-court' or 'previous depositions' refers exclusively to statements collected either in the absence of the accused and counsel or via procedures that prevented any participation of the defence (as in cases where counsel were allowed to observe the examination, but not to pose questions or make comments). By contrast, reference to 'trial examination' will also *lato sensu* include the *ad hoc* hearings in which the examination of witnesses is conducted in accordance with the confrontational paradigm, even if they were held before the formal opening of the trial.

It is crucial to determine whether (and if so, in what specific circumstances) a criminal court ought to be allowed to disregard the outcome of the public confrontation and rely upon what the accuser said during the course of the investigation. This is especially problematic when the courtroom declarant takes back the accusations previously brought against the defendant. When oral testimony is inconsistent with a prior deposition, domestic courts are free to rely upon the account that they deem more persuasive, in the light of all the circumstances of the case, provided that the prior inconsistent statements are put to the witness. The ECHR assumption is that the procedure for challenging a witness with his or her prior statements brings them into the confrontational arena and, thus, makes them admissible not only to impeach the courtroom testimony, but also as evidence of the facts stated.[82] This reasoning suits the judicial practice of Continental Europe, with the sole exception of Italy. In England, tradition will be overruled by the coming into force of the *Criminal Justice Act 2003*, s. 119(1), pursuant to which any prior inconsistent statements are 'admissible as evidence of the matter stated of which oral evidence by [a witness] would be admissible'.

A few unsuccessful attempts have been made to claim a breach of Article 6(3)(d) notwithstanding the performance of a confrontational examination of the witness. In *C.G. v. U.K.* it was the trial judge's conduct that came under scrutiny, as the applicant complained that he made improper interruptions and comments at various stages of the hearing. It was alleged that extreme and undue interventions took place in the course of the cross-examination of the main prosecution witness. Analysis of the official transcript showed that interruptions were 'excessive in number and, on occasion, unduly blunt'.[83] However,

[82] *Camilleri v. Malta*, App. No. 51760/99 (16 March 2000) annotated by S. Maffei, *Un Caso in Tema di Dichiarazioni Testimoniali d'Accusa "Ritrattate" nella Giurisprudenza della Corte Europea dei Diritti dell'Uomo*, [2002] Cass. Pen. 1818-1824.

[83] *C.G. v. U.K.*, App. No. 43373/98 (19 December 2001), (2002) 34 EHRR 789 at §37.

the Court also noted that at no point did the trial judge stop the applicant's counsel from continuing his line of defence. In brief, the Court was not satisfied that the interruptions resulted in a failure to guarantee to the defendant an effective chance of 'adverse-questioning', which is an essential element of the confrontational paradigm as defined in Chapter 1.

National courts also have the responsibility to ensure appropriate management of the trial hearings. The Strasbourg bodies are prepared and willing to assess whether the acoustic[84] and visual standards of the courtroom were satisfactory to ensure the participation of the accused and counsel at the time of the presentation of the evidence.

The defence may challenge adverse depositions only if duly informed of their content. For this reason, Article 6(3)(d) is complied with if the process of confrontation of each and every unfavourable witness takes place *during* or *after* the submission of his or her evidence. For instance, confrontation at trial at first instance does not make confrontation in appeal superfluous if the witness provides new unfavourable evidence at that stage. The wording of the Court's ruling[85] suggests that the performance of early confrontations on a limited amount of evidence fails to meet the requirements of the Confrontation clause.

6 The Evidence of the Absent Witness

The assumptions of ECHR law on absent witnesses are straightforward. The absence of a witness at the public hearing prevents the court 'from observing [his or her] demeanour under questioning and thus forming its own impression of [his or her] reliability'. The reading of prior depositions or the hearsay statements of a third party can 'scarcely be regarded as a proper substitute for direct observation'.[86] Rulings on absent witnesses have been prompted by applications concerning proceedings for a variety of offences, including terrorist acts,[87] kidnapping,[88] murder,[89] drug trafficking,[90] bodily harm[91] as well as forgery of documents,[92] corruption,[93] usury[94], and

84 *Stanford v. U.K.*, Series A No. 282-a.

85 The process of confrontation must occur either *'at the time* the witness made his statements or *at some later stage* of the proceedings' (*emphasis added*).

86 *Kostovski, supra* note 71, at §43.

87 *Hulki Günes v Turkey*, App. No. 28490/95 (19 June 2003).

88 *Isgrò, supra* note 70, at §33.

89 *Ferrantelli and Santangelo v. Italy*, [1996-III] RJD 937, (1997) 23 EHRR 288; *Raniolo v. Italy*, App. No. 62676/00 (21 March 2002). A terrorist murder case was considered in *Barbera, Messegue and Jabardo v. Spain*, Series A No. 146, (1989) 11 EHRR 360.

90 *Doorson v. The Netherlands*, [1996-II] RJD 446, (1996) 22 EHRR 330; *Lucà, supra* note 74.

91 *Unterpertinger v. Austria*, Series A No. 110, (1991) 13 EHRR 175; *Asch, supra* note 69.

92 *Bricmont, supra* note 76.

false accounting.[95] As expected, the rulings are not influenced to any extent by the gravity *in abstracto* of such crimes, or by the penalty served by the national courts.

6.1 Admissibility

The central issue in ECHR discourse on *absent witnesses*[96] is the limited value attached to their out-of-court depositions: a defendant cannot be convicted solely or mainly upon the evidence of an absent witness. In comparison, the Strasbourg organs pay relatively little attention to the question of the admissibility of such evidence. In Chapter 1, it was argued that, in the light of the *fundamental* nature of the Right to Confrontation, the evidence of an absent witness may be employed only in certain cases of necessity. Only *once* the admissibility of such evidence is justified, should the criminal courts consider the question of their evidentiary value. Regrettably, no such distinction inspires the rulings of the Strasbourg organs. The evidence of an absent witness has been considered admissible on numerous occasions, when the declarant was dead, ill, privileged or untraceable. Something must be said about these cases in turn.

National authorities cannot 'be held responsible for'[97] the death of potential witnesses before trial. Their prior evidence is therefore admissible, regardless of the means of its presentation to the court (readings, hearsay statement of third party).

Where there is a consideration of poor health, feasible alternatives should have been pursued to ensure a live collection of testimony outside the courtroom. In *Bricmont*, the Prince of Belgium brought charges of fraud against his former financial adviser and later refused to give evidence at trial on medical grounds. The Court found a breach of the Right to Confrontation and suggested that a confrontational examination could have been set up at the place of residence of the witness.[98] Different considerations prevailed in *Trivedi*,[99] a non-admissibility decision. There, the Commission relied upon the national court's assumption that the health of one Mr. C., an elderly patient of the applicant, had deteriorated so seriously that he would never have been able to testify. The Commission noted that prior to the decision to admit the deposition of Mr. C. in evidence, the trial judge conducted a detailed inquiry into his health. The

---

93 *Pullar v. U.K.*, [1996-III] RJD 937, (1996) 22 EHRR 391.

94 *Artner v. Austria*, Series A No. 242-a.

95 *Trivedi v. U.K.*, (1997) 89a DR 136, [1997] EHRLR 521.

96 M. Bourmanne, *L'Audition des Témoins Lors du Procés Pénal dans la Jurisprudencee des Organes de la Convention Européenne des Droits de l'Homme*, [1995] R.T.D.H. 45-60.

97 *Ferrantelli and Santangelo*, *supra* note 89, at §52.

98 *Bricmont*, *supra* note 76, at §81.

99 *Supra* note 95.

state of his memory at the time was so impaired as to make any kind of judicial examination ineffectual.

Certain Member States excuse relatives of the accused from testifying in court on the rationale illustrated earlier in this work.[100] No intrusion into the Right to Confrontation is justified in such situations, because no fundamental right may be said to justify the said privilege. Instead, the Court has twice approved the use in evidence of incriminatory out-of-court prior depositions of family members who later invoked their privilege to avoid cross-examination. In the Court's view, these rules make 'allowance for the special problems that may be entailed in a confrontation between "someone charged with a criminal offence" and a witness from his own family and is calculated to protect such a witness by avoiding his being put in a moral dilemma'[101]. Only sparse authority may be found on the admissibility in evidence of the adverse statements given during the preliminary investigation by a co-accused who later remained silent at trial.[102] Arguably, such evidence is admissible against other co-defendants, the reason being that the right to silence is sufficiently established[103] to justify an intrusion into the Right to Confrontation. However, the overall fairness of the proceedings under Article 6(1) may be in question when such evidence was obtained by granting the accomplice immunity from prosecution.[104]

More complicated matters arise with regard to prior declarants who simply fail to come to court. In Chapter 2, it was argued that their prior evidence ought to be admissible only when it is proved that the prior declarant was kept away against his or her will, or that the absence was due to some other specified and compelling reason. Evidence should not be admitted simply because efforts made by the prosecution to trace the witness were unsuccessful. In a few cases brought before the Court it was clear that no serious attempt to locate the person had been made,[105] but the evidence was still admitted on the basis that it was largely corroborated. Such an argument misses the point insofar as it employs the parameter for the evaluation of the evidence as a justification for its admissibility.

---

[100] See Chapter 2.

[101] *Unterpertinger, supra* note 91, at §30. The Commission endorsed such position in *G. v. Austria*, App. No. 15853/89 (19 February 1992).

[102] Cf. *Lucà, supra* note 74; *Craxi v. Italy*, App. No. 34896/97 (5 December 2002). For a commission decision on this respect cf. *Dorigo v. Italy*, App. No. 33286/96 (20 May 1998).

[103] The right to silence 'lies at the heart of the notion of fair procedure under Art. 6 of the Convention' cf. *Saunders v. U.K.*, [1996-VI] RJD 2044, (1997) 23 EHRR 313, at §68; *Funke v. France*, Series A No. 256-a, (1993) 16 EHRR 297, at §44; *Condron v. U.K.*, [2000-V] RJD 1, (2001) 31 EHRR 1, at §56. Also, see the Commission cases *Abas v. the Netherlands*, (1997) 88a DR 120; *Touvier v. France*, (1997) 88a DR 148; *Nikolova v. Bulgaria*, (1997) 88a D.R. 169.

[104] *X. v. U.K.*, (1977) 7 D.R. 115, at 118.

[105] *Barbera, Messegue and Jabardo v. Spain, supra* note 89; *Delta v. France*, Series A No. 191-a, (1993) 16 EHRR 574.

In a few cases brought before the Strasbourg organs, witnesses were absent because they were living abroad at the time of the trial. Since in such cases an examination had been held on commission, one would expect the Court to challenge the manner in which testimony was in fact taken.[106] In 1987, the Commission displayed some reluctance in this respect. In a German proceeding, a deposition had to be collected in Turkey by the Turkish authorities. Since no notice was given of the date of the examination, neither the applicant nor his counsel could question the witness. The use of such evidence was indeed justified, because 'the German authorities could not be held responsible for non-observance of Turkish law by the Turkish judiciary'.[107] Instead, in 1999, the Court challenged a request for evidence on commission sent by the Italian courts to the United States authorities. The latter were requested to forbid the presence of any representative of the parties at the examination of three decisive witnesses.[108] This very argument should have led the Court directly to declare a violation of the Confrontation clause. However, once again, the Court's reasoning was influenced to a decisive extent by considerations concerning the alleged lack of corroboration.

In any case, the distance between the seat of the trial and the foreign country should not become a tool for manipulation. The mere inconvenience of a journey abroad for the defendant's counsel is not acceptable as a ground for preventing reliance on this evidence. This is particularly true if, at the relevant time, the applicant had sufficient financial means to cover the travel expenses or, alternatively, had failed to appoint counsel in the foreign jurisdiction. Under these circumstances, later complaints concerning the alleged lack of an 'adequate opportunity' to challenge the witness' statements have been appropriately dismissed.[109]

Finally, it is also a rule of ECHR law that domestic courts may rely upon absent witnesses' prior depositions when the defendant had failed to request their summoning. In a recent case, the Court held that the request to examine two prosecution witnesses had been legitimately rejected, the defendants having failed to explain what they 'intended to prove by the witness evidence proposed and how this evidence could be relevant to the outcome of the case'.[110] This reasoning can be easily challenged: why should the accused be required to seek the appearance in court of those who are likely to give evidence against him or

[106] An early authority is *X., Y. and Z. v. Austria*, (1973) 43 CD 38.

[107] *P.V. v. F.R.G.*, (1987) 53 DR 182, (1988) 10 EHRR 503.

[108] *A.M. v. Italy*, [1999-IX] RJD 45, at §8. In fact, the absence of confrontation could be justified only with reference to the vulnerable witness G., minor, alleged victim of a sexual abuse. In comparison, there was no reason to exclude the defence from taking part in the interviews of Mr. D. (G.'s father) and Miss F. (the doctor in whom G. had first confided the alleged abuse).

[109] *Solakov v. The Former Yugoslav Republic of Macedonia*, App. No. 47023/99 (30 October 2001), at §60.

[110] *Laukkanen and Manninen v. Finland*, App. No. 50230/99 (3 February 2004), at §36.

her? One thing is explicitly to waive the Right to Confrontation, another thing is to bear an obligation to insist upon the examination of unfavourable witnesses. Further, this state of affairs contrasts with the underlying principle that a defendant should not be made to assume responsibility for the national authorities' failure to ensure respect for his or her rights.[111]

6.2 Evaluation

Under ECHR law it is then crucial to determine when the statement of an absent witness constituted the *only* or *main* piece of evidence. One would expect the Strasbourg judiciary to elaborate an independent and solid conception of corroboration and to place little reliance upon the wording of domestic rulings. Instead, the Court has failed to take a firm theoretical stand and reiterates that each case turns on its own specific facts. This approach has resulted in significant inconsistencies over the years.

Points of certainty are few and quite limited in their effects. Proceedings in which no other evidence but the absent witnesses' statements had been relied upon by the prosecution are rare, and certainly unfair if they resulted in the conviction of the defendant. 'Suicidal' reasoning by national courts cannot be expected that often. In *Lucà*, nevertheless, the Italian courts admitted that the 'main evidence against the accused was the statements which N. [a co-accused, absent witness] had made to the public prosecutor':[112] the Court obviously found a breach of the Confrontation clause.

It is also settled that the evidence of multiple absent witnesses does not meet the test of corroboration.[113]

When judgments are in the form of unreasoned verdicts, attention must focus on the directions given by the presiding judge to the jury. On one occasion, the Commission approved a direction according to which jurors should have attached 'less weight'[114] to the deposition of an absent witness than to live testimonies.

As one would imagine, more difficult problems emerge whenever national courts claim to have grounded a criminal conviction on absent testimonial statements *as well as* other evidence. It is precisely in these circumstances that a firm

---

111 S. Stavros, *The Guarantees for Accused Persons under Article 6 of the European Convention on Human Rights: an Analysis of the Application of the Convention and a Comparison with Other Instruments*, Martinus Nijhoff, London, 1993, 235.

112 *Lucà v. Italy, supra* note 74, at §17.

113 In *Craxi, supra* note 102, the prosecution case relied on pre-trial deposition of a deceased person and several co-defendants who remained silent at trial. In *Rachdad v. France*, App. No. 71846/01 (13 November 2003) the domestic conviction of the applicant was grounded on the prior depositions of six absent witnesses but, notwithstanding their accuracy and consistency, the Court found a violation of Article 6.

114 *Trivedi, supra* note 95.

and selective concept of corroboration should come into play. In comparison, ECHR practice shows an assortment of variable responses, based upon rather blurred arguments.

In *Unterpertinger*, the strictest conclusion ever reached by the Court on the issue of corroboration can be found. Although the statements of two absent witnesses were supported by a police report, a medical report and a further live testimony,[115] the Court took the view that the applicant's conviction was based *mainly* on the former source of evidence and, therefore, it failed to ensure confrontation. The Court was not satisfied with the presence of certain autonomous items of proof, but it verified the specific evidentiary *weight* attached to the out-of-court statements. This straightforward line of interpretation was revised shortly afterwards. In *Asch*, no unfairness was found because the absent witness's depositions were allegedly corroborated not only by medical certificates and police reports but also by 'the personal assessment' made by a police officer who had personally interviewed the declarant before the trial. The argument is particularly weak, since such derivative evidence clearly cannot serve the purpose of corroboration.[116] Furthermore, in *Artner* the Court ruled that certain documents produced in corroboration, even if not 'providing a precise indication as to the interests paid by the applicant' in a case of usury, nevertheless 'helped the judges to form their opinion'.[117] Following this approach, even inconclusive circumstantial evidence could counterbalance the departure from the confrontational paradigm.

It must also be noted that material evidence almost always satisfies the Strasbourg bodies that the test of corroboration had in fact been met.[118]

7 The Evidence of the Anonymous Witness

The Strasbourg organs have shown remarkable concern over the 'almost insurmountable handicap'[119] with which the defence is confronted in the case of anonymity. For a start, the employment of anonymous[120] evidence

---

115 *Unterpertinger, supra* note 91, at §33.

116 For a critical assessment of the Court's reasons in *Asch*, see C. Osborne, *Hearsay and the European Court of Human Rights*, [1993] Crim. L.R. 255-267. The author argues that there was 'no logical and consistent basis for a distinction' between *Asch* and *Unterpertinger*.

117 *Artner, supra* note 94, at §23.

118 *Kennedy v. U.K.*, App. No. 36428/97 (21 October 1998), (1999) 27 EHRR CD 266 (footprint and blood stains); *Raniolo, supra* note 89 (traces of gunpowder on the clothes of the accused).

119 *Windisch v. Austria, supra* note 81, at §28.

120 The very concept of anonymity has once caused some confusion. In *Baegen v. The Netherlands*, Series A No. 327-b, Ms. X. reported to the police to the effect that she had been raped by two men. She had met them in a night club and had accepted their offer to drive her home. The violence purportedly took

forces the defence to face 'difficulties which criminal proceedings should not normally involve'.[121] Further, the Court has held that:

> If the defence is unaware of the identity of the person it seeks to question, it may be deprived of the very particulars enabling it to demonstrate that he or she is prejudiced, hostile or unreliable. Testimony or other declarations inculpating an accused may well be designedly untruthful or simply erroneous and the defence will scarcely be able to bring this to light if it lacks the information permitting it to test the author's reliability or cast doubt on his credibility.[122]

ECHR cases on anonymous witnesses refer to domestic proceedings for extremely serious offences: drug[123] and weapon[124] trafficking, terrorist murder,[125] attempted murder and robbery with the threat of violence,[126] armed robbery,[127] kidnapping and extortion[128], prison riot[129] and a serious incident of burglary.[130] Most national convictions imposed custodial sentences on the applicants.[131] Strasbourg cases concerning anonymous witnesses are fewer than those related to absent witnesses. This may be because the number of proceedings involving anonymous evidence is itself smaller at national level, since the legislation of some Member States lacks a specific policy on anonymous witnesses. The comparative analysis of Chapter 6, however, will disclose that the admissibility of the evidence of anonymous witnesses, even if not laid down in *ad hoc*

place in the car. Ms. X. opted to remain anonymous on the ground of fear and she was indeed referred to as an 'anonymous witness' in the national and Strasbourg rulings. However, her home address was mentioned in the police file disclosed to the counsel so that her identity could be easily traced. In accordance with the definitions provided in Chapter 2, Ms. X. should not be regarded here as an anonymous, but rather as a vulnerable witness.

121 *Van Mechelen v. The Netherlands*, [1997-III] RJD 691, (1998) 25 EHRR 647, at §54.

122 *Kostovski, supra* note 71, at §42.

123 *Saïdi v. France*, Series A No. 261-c, (1994) 17 EHRR 251; *Lüdi v Switzerland*, Series A No. 238, (1993) 15 EHRR 173; *Doorson, supra* note 24. See also *Hayward v. Sweden*, App. No. 14106/88 (6 December 1991); *Kurup v. Denmark*, (1985) 42 DR 287.

124 *Kok v. The Netherlands*, [2000-VI] RJD 597.

125 *A.M. v. U.K.*, App. No. 20657/92 (2 December 1992), (1993) 15 EHRR CD 113.

126 *Van Mechelen, supra* note 121.

127 *Kostovski, supra* note 71.

128 *Visser v. The Netherlands*, App. No. 26668/95 (14 February 2002) and *Taal v. Estonia*, App. No. 13249/02 (22 November 2005).

129 *Birutis and others v. Lithuania*, App. No. 47698/99 (28 March 2002).

130 *Windisch, supra* note 81.

131 The applicants were sentenced to one-year imprisonment in *Visser*, 15-month in *Doorson*, three years in *Lüdi* and *Windisch*, six years in *Kostovski*, six years and six months in *Kok*, eight years in *Saïdi* and 14 years in *Van Mechelen*. As for the non-admissibility decisions five years in *Hayward* and five years and six months in *Kurup*. No report is available on the penalty in *A. M. v. U.K.*

provisions, might also result from certain rules on identity change. Further, complaints concerning anonymous witnesses may arise when discretionary powers allow the courts of criminal justice to circumvent the ordinary process of adjudication.[132]

7.1 Admissibility

In the Court's view, 'the use of statements made by anonymous witnesses to found a conviction is not under all circumstances incompatible with the Convention'.[133] This principle stems from the appreciation of an array of competing interests and values. In *Doorson*, the Court affirmed that even if Article 6 does not require the rights of witnesses and victims called upon to testify to be taken into account,

> their life, liberty or security ... may be at stake, as may interests coming generally within the ambit of Article 8 of the Convention. Such interests ... are in principle protected by other, substantive provisions of the Convention, which imply that Contracting States should organise their criminal proceedings in such a way that those interests are not unjustifiably imperilled. Against this background, principles of fair trial also require that in appropriate cases the interests of the defence are balanced against those of witnesses or victims.[134]

In such circumstances the establishment of special measures of protection (including anonymity) for the witnesses and victims appears to be not only a 'possibility' but an 'obligation' of the Member State under Article 8.

Anonymous evidence may be used in the case of a serious risk of threats and intimidation against the witness in person, or his or her relatives. In the assessment of such a risk, national courts must base their decision on presumptions, drawn from the seriousness of the offence, the character of the supposed offender or other circumstances. These presumptions must necessarily be case specific, although some looser standard could be applied in the risk assessment in the case of organised crime (mafia, paramilitary groups), since it is established that ordinary means of social control are ineffectual.[135]

In *Doorson*, the Court dealt with an incident of drug trafficking. The Dutch prosecuting authorities had decided to take action against the nuisance

---

[132] European jurisprudence on anonymous witnesses is analysed by B. De Smet, *La Défense Face aux Témoin Anonymes et les Exigences d'un Procés Equitable dans la Jurisprudence de la Cour Européenne des Droits de l'Homme'* (1999) 70 R.I.D.P. 761-776, M. Vogliotti, *La Logica Floue della Corte Europea dei Diritti dell'Uomo tra Tutela del Testimone e Salvaguardia del Contraddittorio: il Caso delle Testimonianze Anonime'* [1998] Giur. Ital. 851-860.

[133] *Van Mechelen, supra* note 121, at §52.

[134] *Doorson, supra* note 90, at §70.

[135] As in the case of I.R.A., dealt with in *A.M. v. U.K., supra* note 125.

caused by the market of heroin in the streets of Amsterdam and compiled a set of photographs of persons suspected of being drug dealers. These were shown to a number of addicts (referred to by the police under code names) who recognised the applicant but expressed their wish, which was later granted, to remain anonymous. The Court held that: 'although there has been no suggestion that Y15 and Y16 were ever threatened by the applicant himself, the decision to maintain their anonymity is not unreasonable per se [considering how] drug dealers frequently resorted to threats or actual violence against persons who gave evidence against them'.[136] No evidence was given to prove that those informants were in fact in immediate danger, but nevertheless – and regrettably – the Court regarded the whole category of proceedings for drug offences as a legitimate excuse for curtailing the Right to Confrontation. In comparison, more convincing arguments have been followed in *Kok*. There, the applicant had been convicted for possessions of arms, ammunition and high explosive. At the time of his arrest in an Amsterdam coffee shop, he was found in possession of a loaded and illegal gun. This led the Court to accept the Dutch court's arguments according to which the applicant could reasonably expect to 'be perceived as a threat by persons aware of his dealings'.[137]

It was argued in Chapter 2 that fear of reprisal ought not to become an expedient to circumvent the duty to give evidence in judicial proceedings: the Strasbourg organs seem responsive to this concern. In *Visser*, the veracity and reasonability of the fear adduced by the witnesses came under scrutiny. Eventually, the Court dismissed the national decision to grant anonymity on the basis of the violent reputation of the applicant's co-defendant,[138] in the absence of any evidence as to the specific capability of the applicant to harm the life and well-being of the witnesses.

Police officers are to be treated differently to ordinary civilians. In the Court's view,

> The anonymity of witnesses raises special problems if the witnesses in questions are members of the police force of the State. Although their interests – and indeed those of their families – also deserve protection under the Convention, it must be recognised that their position is to some extent different from that of a disinterested witness or a victim. They owe a general duty of obedience to the State's executive authorities and usually have links with the prosecution: for these reasons alone their use as anonymous witnesses should be resorted to only in exceptional circumstances.[139]

---

136 *Doorson*, *supra* note 90, at §71.

137 *Kok*, *supra* note 124, at 623.

138 *Visser*, *supra* note 128, at §47.

139 *Van Mechelen*, *supra* note 121, at §56.

7.2 Anonymous Absent Witnesses

In some early judgments on anonymous witnesses, the Court praised their information as an invaluable means for the performance of successful investigations.[140] It also acknowledged that the use of anonymous statements as evidence 'to found a conviction is a completely different matter. This involves ... limitations on the rights of the defence that deserve careful scrutiny to ensure that the infringement of defence rights is kept to a reasonable extent'.[141] In spite of such clear vision of the competing interests involved, the Strasbourg bodies failed for a long time to draw a distinction between the legal rules relevant to the *absent witness*, on the one hand, and the *anonymous witness*, on the other. Particularly unconvincing lines of reasoning were followed in relation to anonymous pre-trial declarants who also failed to take the stand. The topic is particularly important, because when the witness is simultaneously absent and anonymous the 'departure' from the confrontational paradigm reaches a peak, as all the components listed in Chapter 1, section 3.2 are derogated from.

In the very first case on anonymous witnesses, the Court held that compliance with the Confrontation Clause does not require 'that in order to be used as evidence statements of witnesses should always be made at a public hearing in court: to use as evidence such statements obtained at the pre-trial stage is not in itself inconsistent with Article 6(3)(d) provided the rights of the defence have been respected'.[142] Since then, case law developed under the assumption that discourse relevant to the absent witness could also automatically apply to the anonymous witness. Instead, this study endorses the view that absence from the courtroom should only be justified upon some other independent reason (death, poor health, residence abroad), since anonymity can be fully ensured through the performance of protected court examinations.

It is true that in four cases concerning the *absent anonymous witnesses* (*Kostovski, Windisch, Saïdi* and *Lüdi*) the Court found a violation of the Confrontation Clause. In all these cases, however, the crucial argument was that such evidence had not been corroborated.[143] If supporting evidence had been presented to the national courts, the Strasbourg bodies would have probably found no unfairness. This is precisely what happened in *Hayward*. There, Swedish authorities refused to summon an anonymous police informant whose previous depositions were read out at trial. His evidence, the reasoning went, 'was far from being the only evidence in the case'.[144] No obstacles prevented the

---

140 *Kostovski, supra* note 71, at §44; *Windisch, supra* note 81, at §30.

141 *Kostovski, supra* note 71, at §44.

142 Ibid at §41.

143 *Windisch* (*supra* note 71), at §31; *Saïdi, supra* note 123, at §44; *Lüdi, supra* note 123, at §47; *Kostovski, supra* note 71, at §44.

144 *Hayward, supra* note 123.

Swedish courts from holding a protected examination at the public hearing, as the defendant had repeatedly requested. Yet, the Commission approved the use of such prior depositions in evidence. In doing so, it regrettably failed to declare the attendance in court of an anonymous witness to be an essential element of a fair proceeding. In other words, the protected examination of anonymous witnesses at trial was not considered an indispensable element of judicial fairness. Therefore, national systems are *not* expected to ensure the attendance of those witnesses whenever the conviction can be largely based on some other supporting evidence. In this way, the typical 'counterbalance' suitable to the absent witness serves as a refuge for the evidence of the anonymous witness.

This state of affairs has partially been revisited in 2002. In *Birutis*, the applicants had been convicted for organising a prison riot, on the basis of the evidence of several anonymous co-detainees and a few prison guards. The Court first acknowledged that the domestic conviction was 'not based solely, or to a decisive extent, on the anonymous evidence'[145]. That being said, the Court also argued that, in their pleadings, the applicants had put forward an alternative explanation of events. They had alleged inconsistency and fabrication with regard to the anonymous statements, due to collaboration between the authors of such statements and the prison administration in order to obtain a more lenient regime of detention. Under these circumstances, the Court was not satisfied that the domestic courts' failure to question anonymous witnesses was compatible with Article 6. If followed in future judgments, this line of reasoning may pave the way for a complete revision of the ECHR approach to the 'absent anonymous' witness.

7.3 Collection

On four occasions the Court and the Commission have specifically discussed the modalities of a protected examination of the anonymous witness. The line between breach and compliance with Article 6 has been drawn by closely challenging the procedure followed by domestic courts.

In *Kurup*[146] the Commission declared the applicant's complaints unfounded and approved the action taken by Danish courts: they had ordered the defendant to leave the courtroom when anonymous witnesses A. and D. were heard. Instead, counsel was allowed to remain in the room and had every opportunity to take part in the examination.[147] In *A.M. v. U.K.*[148], the anonymous witness

[145] *Birutis and others, supra* note 129.

[146] *Supra* note 123.

[147] No breach of the Confrontation clause has been found in *X. v. Denmark*, (1982) 27 DR 50 (applicant excluded from courtroom to avoid the alleged intimidation of a non-anonymous declarant who was then cross-examined by defence counsel).

[148] *Supra* note 125.

was screened from the public and the accused, thus preventing the latter from seeing his physical appearance and detecting his demeanour during examination-in-chief and cross-examination. Nevertheless, the judge and representatives of both parties were able to observe the witness. Counsel was also allowed to pose any admissible question, save for those that could have led to a disclosure of identity, and no unfairness was found. In *Doorson*, two anonymous witnesses named Y15 and Y16 were questioned on appeal by an investigating magistrate, outside the courtroom, in the presence of the counsel. The personal appearance of the witnesses was disclosed to counsel, exactly as in *A.M. v. U.K.* The method of examination allowed counsel to ask the witnesses, through the magistrate's mediation, whatever questions it considered to be in its interest, except those that might lead to the disclosure of the witnesses' identity. It is reported that all questions were answered and, moreover, that the identity of the two individuals was known to the examining magistrate. For this reason, the Court dismissed the complaints of the accused. By contrast, in *Van Mechelen*, the investigating judge, a registrar and the anonymous witnesses[149] were connected by a sound link to the applicants, their lawyers and the prosecutor in a separate room. Counsel were requested to file their question in writing in advance and were also prevented from observing the demeanour of the declarants. The Strasbourg Court considered such a practice contrary to Article 6(3)(d).

This being said, rather stringent requirements must be met in the collection of evidence from the anonymous informant. For a start, a judge is always expected to lead or at least to supervise the interview. Secondly, the judge should also be aware of the identity of the interviewee and in a position to observe his or her behaviour under questioning. Thirdly, counsel should be given the chance to monitor the witness's demeanour and to pose all admissible questions at the time of the examination, with the exception of those questions intended, or capable, of revealing his or her real identity.

7.4 Evaluation

A presumption of unreliability applies to all anonymous statements: convictions 'should not be based either solely or to a decisive extent on evidence from anonymous witnesses'.[150] Such a presumption suffers no exceptions:[151] it applies to both 'absent' and 'testifying' anonymous witnesses.

---

[149] In *Van Mechelen, supra* note 121, eleven anonymous witnesses identified by a series of letters and numbers (*i.e.* 001-003-BRZ03-46204 etc.) were questioned in such manner. All of them were police officers, either members of the arresting unit or of the intelligence team.

[150] Cf. *Kostovski, supra* note 71, at §44, *Doorson, supra* note 90, at §76, *Van Mechelen, supra* note 121, at §61 and *A.M. v. U.K., supra* note 125.

[151] P. Van Dijk and G.J.H. Van Hoof, *Theory and Practice of the European Convention on Human Rights*, 3rd edn., Kluwer, The Hague, 1998, 475.

Once again, the aim of the corroboration straitjacket is to guarantee a solid and properly challenged basis for a guilty verdict. Contrary to cases concerning absent witnesses, however, the Court appears extremely vigilant in this context. In some recent rulings, the traditional nebulous considerations concerning the evidentiary material 'as a whole' were replaced by detailed and specific accounts[152] of each and every item of proof that allegedly supported the anonymous evidence. It is also settled that depositions from multiple anonymous witnesses cannot corroborate each other[153].

At this stage, the question is whether the standard of corroboration required in relation to anonymous testimonial statements is identical to the standard established for the absent witness. *Doorson* and *Visser* are extremely interesting in this respect since the Court took the view that national courts should treat anonymous sources of evidence 'with extreme care'.[154] This phrase has never been employed in judgments concerning non-anonymous absent witnesses. Regrettably, only minimal guidance can be found in ECHR law when attempting to assess its true meaning. Commentators face two interpretative options. The first might be to relate the 'extreme care' to the method of evidence collection. This would result in the addition of a further procedural guarantee to those enumerated in the previous section. Another, and far more convincing option, is to refer the 'extreme care' to the *degree* of corroboration required: the corroboration requirement should be treated differently when the witness is absent, or anonymous. In the former case, corroboration would be secured by *any* element capable of endorsing the prosecution case. In other words, corroboration would be ensured even though the items of proof in question did not specifically relate to the content of the absent testimonial statements. In the case of anonymity, by contrast, compliance with the corroboration requirement would only be guaranteed if the supportive items of proof provided specific confirmation of the allegations made by the anonymous informant.

A further distinction must be outlined. In jurisdictions that require judicial reasons to be stated by the courts, the 'extreme care' requirement establishes an obligation to provide a particularly cautious and accurate ruling on that matter. In trials by jury, a national practice of 'extreme care' could be proved by the issuing of appropriate warnings (ie 'urging caution') in the summing up to the jurors.

---

[152] See *Kok, supra* note 123, at 624.

[153] Cf. *Kostovski, supra* note 71.

[154] *Doorson, supra* note 90, at §76; *Visser, supra* note 128, at §44.

8 The Evidence of the Vulnerable Witness

ECHR discourse on vulnerable witnesses is still in its infancy. This is due, on the one hand, to the relatively limited number of applications filed with the Strasbourg bodies and, on the other hand, to a tendency to transplant onto vulnerable witnesses the arguments developed in relation to absent and anonymous witnesses. This is not to deny, however, that the special features of criminal prosecutions and trials concerning rape and other sexual offences are well known to the Court in Strasbourg:

> Proceedings are often conceived of as an ordeal by the victim, in particular when the latter is unwillingly confronted with the defendant. These features are even more prominent in a case involving a minor. In the assessment of the question whether or not in such proceedings an accused received a fair trial, account must be taken of the right to respect for the private life of the perceived victim. Therefore, the Court accepts that in criminal proceedings concerning sexual abuse certain measures may be taken for the purpose of protecting the victim, provided that such measures can be reconciled with an adequate and effective exercise of the rights of the defence.[155]

Once again, beyond theoretical speculation, the problem is to set the priorities between the Right to Confrontation and the protection of the vulnerable declarant.

8.1 Admissibility

ECHR discourse on vulnerable witnesses is based on applications concerning national proceedings for a variety of sexual offences, diversely defined and punished by Member States. These applications refer to incidents of rape[156] as well as common[157] and aggravated[158] abuse. All vulnerable witnesses had also been the victims of the violence, which was allegedly perpetrated by strangers, doctors, teachers or family members. In the Court's view,

---

[155] *S.N. v. Sweden*, App. No. 34209/96 (2 July 2002), at §47. See also *Baegen, supra* note 120 (Commission Report – 20 October 1994), at §77; *Slobodan v. The Netherlands*, App. No. 29838/96 (15 January 1997); *Lindqvist v. Sweden*, App. No. 26304/95 (22 October 1997); *Finkensieper v. The Netherlands*, App. No. 19525/92 (Commission Report – 17 May 1995).

[156] *Mattoccia v. Italy*, App. No. 23969/94 (25 July 2000) and *Baegen, supra* note 120. Commission cases concerning domestic proceeding for rape are *M. K. v. Austria*, App. No. 28867/95 (2 July 1997), (1997) 24 EHRR CD 59 and *Kremers v. The Netherlands*, App. No. 25205/94 (19 October 1995).

[157] *P. S. v. Germany*, App. No. 33900/96 (6 June 2000), reported in [2002] Arch. Nuova Proc. Pen. 367-368, with a comment by S. Maffei.

[158] See the Commission's decisions in *Lindqvist, supra* note 155 and *Finkensieper, supra* note 155.

cases involving the very young or the mentally handicapped 'often confront the prosecuting authorities and the courts with serious evidential difficulties in the course of the proceedings'.[159] These elements justify, the ECHR reasoning goes, some relevant departures from the confrontational paradigm.

A vulnerable person may be treated in domestic proceedings as an absent witness. In such a case, his or her depositions to the police or prosecutors count as evidence at trial. This approach is based on the assumption that vulnerability itself justifies non-appearance in the witness box. As in the case of anonymous informants, however, such a conclusion should be rejected, unless there is some other reason to suggests that the declarant be treated under the law as an absent witness. Consider the *M. K. v. Austria*[160] case. The applicant was charged with rape against R.R and his sister A.R., respectively 13 and 10-year-old. At the time of the trial, R.R. was detained in hospital for psychiatric treatment, following the deterioration of his mental health. For the purpose of this study, the R.R. is a 'vulnerable' 'absent' witnesses and the use of his deposition may be legitimate because poor health is one of the reasons that justify absence from the courtroom. The Strasbourg bodies, nevertheless, have largely approved the use in evidence of vulnerable absent testimonial statements, under the customary and improper shield of the corroboration requirement.[161]

8.2 Collection

Vulnerable witnesses may be interviewed through protected examinations, either in or outside the courtroom. The Strasbourg bodies have dealt only twice with this situation. As a consequence, although judicial reasoning explicitly refers to the implementation of 'special measures' of evidence collection, the present state of ECHR law provides only feeble guidance as to their specific content.

In *Kremers*[162], the applicants were convicted of abusing three young members of their extended family. At the investigation stage, the examining magistrate interviewed the girls in the presence of counsel, who had the opportunity to pose written questions. The defendants and public prosecutor followed the examination on a television monitor from a separate room. None of the girls was summoned at trial. In appeal, however, the court examined one of the alleged

---

159 *Mattoccia v. Italy, supra* note 156, at §71.

160 *Supra* note 156.

161 See the conclusions reached by the Commission in *Finkensieper supra* note 155.

162 This case was dealt with in three almost identical Commission decisions, following the submission of separate applications by three co-defendants in a Dutch proceeding. Two applications were filed under the title *Kremers v. The Netherlands*. The reference mentioned above (note 156) was to the application that was submitted first. The second one was recorded as *Kremers v. The Netherlands*, App. No. 26596/95 (19 October 1995) while the third one as *Hols v. The Netherlands*, App. No. 25206/94 (19 October 1995).

victims in the presence of the applicant's counsel. At that stage, he was given the chance to question her directly. Once again, the defendants followed the examination via video-link. The interview was dramatic: the girl panicked and could not answer the more emotionally burdensome questions. After detailed scrutiny, the Commission considered the procedure fair to the applicants and their complaint inadmissible. It argued:

> Insofar as the applicant complains that B. was heard in his absence and that she was allowed not to answer emotionally burdensome questions, the Commission recalls that the rights secured by Article 6(1) and 6(3) of the Convention are those of the accused and the defence in general. In order to determine whether these rights were respected, it is not sufficient to consider the situation in which the accused himself is placed. Consideration must rather be given to the situation in which the defence as a whole is placed. In exceptional circumstances there may be reasons for hearing a witness in the absence of the accused on condition that his lawyer is present, or to allow a witness not to answer certain questions.[163]

Identical conclusions were reached in *Slobodan*. The applicant was convicted of sexually abusing a number of persons, including his former wife and daughter. Pending enquiries, the investigating judge had heard them in the presence of counsel, who nevertheless did not pose any questions. This procedure was accepted as being compatible with judicial fairness.[164]

As anticipated, no detailed requirements have been yet laid down with regard to the examination of the vulnerable. The contrast with the regulations applied in the case of anonymous witnesses is striking. Furthermore, nothing can be found in the Strasbourg rulings, on the role of intermediaries (such as psychologists, social workers, doctors, parents) in the performance of such protected interviews.

8.3 Evaluation

No corroboration is required when the vulnerable person has been interviewed in protected hearings, either in or outside the courtroom. After having approved the actions taken by Dutch courts in *Slobodan*, for instance, the Commission made no investigation as to the amount of evidence employed to pass a guilty verdict.

In comparison, a presumption of unreliability applies to 'vulnerable absent statements'. Given the sexual nature of the related offences, the ultimate corroborative value would reasonably be attached to forensic evidence, based on analysis of samples taken from the alleged offender and victim. Great weight is

---

163 Cf. *Hols*, *supra* note 162.

164 *Slobodan*, *supra* note 155.

also given to medical examinations. In *Lindqvist*, the applicant's complaint was deemed inadmissible precisely because the Swedish courts relied heavily upon corroborative medical evidence that strongly confirmed the involvement of the accused in the incident.

When no material evidence is available to the courts or the victim's consent to sexual intercourse is at issue, matters unavoidably become more complicated. Major examples of inconsistencies in the implementation of the corroboration test in these circumstances are easy to find under ECHR law. In *Finkensieper*,[165] the Commission enumerated four statements that, according to its view, endorsed the complaint of the victim, one Ms. C., a former patient in a psychiatric ward named D.L. The list included: (i) statements of V., a friend of C., whom she had met and had associated with when both of them were patients in D.L. and to whom C. had confided that she was repeatedly being abused by the applicant and who had advised C. to write about the matter to C.'s therapist; (ii) statements of K., a group leader at D.L., who had received a letter from C. about the applicant's abuse and who had taken the matter up with his superiors; (iii) statements of C.'s therapist H.C, to whom C. had complained that the applicant was abusing her; (iv) statements of therapist A.H., who had treated C.'s friend V. and to whom C., V. and H.C. went in order to discuss the applicant's abuse of C. It is apparent that all these depositions were directly or indirectly based on the victim's account of the related facts and thus inadequate as a lawful means of supporting the prosecution case.

In a recent judgment, however, the Court has moved to a more stringent standard for the corroboration test in cases concerning vulnerable witnesses. In *P.S. v. Germany*, the sexual violence was allegedly perpetrated by the piano teacher of an 8-year-old girl. German courts based the conviction on the out-of-court depositions of the victim, her mother's account of her demeanour at the relevant time and a psychological expert's opinion on her credibility. Remarkably, the Court pointed out that 'the information given by the girl was the only direct evidence of the offence'[166] and, therefore, the proceedings violated the Confrontation Clause of the Convention.

9 Conclusion: Contribution of ECHR Law to a Theory of Confrontation

It is now time to summarise the contribution of ECHR law to a general theory of confrontation. It was expected that no well-rounded model for the administration of testimonial evidence in criminal proceedings could

[165] *Supra* note 155, at §68. The case was eventually struck out of the list for procedural reasons, cf. *Finkensieper v. The Netherlands* [1996-II] RJD 396.

[166] *P.S. v. Germany, supra* note 157, at §30.

result from the to-do and not-to-do instructions of the Strasbourg organs. Also, it is acknowledged that it is not the task of the Court to outline detailed rules of procedure and evidence. Nevertheless, some lessons may still be learned, while a number of topics deserve further clarification.

Research has shown that Article 6(3)(d) applies not only to court declarants, but also to the authors of other types of 'testimonial statements' that a court of justice may employ as evidence of the matter stated. The Court in Strasbourg is aware that the values protected by the Right to Confrontation may be impaired by such statements, regardless of the manner in which they are presented to the court (readings of previous depositions, first-hand hearsay, documents). This is quite a remarkable difference from U.S. constitutional law, where the use of the evidence of 'absent witnesses' is entirely abandoned to the technicalities of the law of hearsay, and no constitutional challenge based on the Sixth Amendment is possible.[167] Further, ECHR law sets out some interesting guidelines for the performance of 'protected examination' of anonymous witnesses.

Regrettably, research has also shown that the case law on the Confrontation Clause sets only a few parameters to which national laws are strictly required to comply. The evidence of an absent witness, for example, is almost always admissible under ECHR law, and the question of fairness rests almost entirely on the issue of corroboration.

Indeed, corroboration is a key that opens far too many doors to the access of unchallenged testimonies. Domestic courts are excused from making any reasonable effort to trace a prosecution witness, when his or her previous depositions are allegedly supported by other evidence. Also, anonymous witnesses may not necessarily be called to testify in a protected examination, when their prior evidence is corroborated. Very similar conclusions apply to the vulnerable witness. A further problem is that the corroboration test has been applied rather inconsistently over the last fifteen years. While lacking a solid theoretical foundation, such a test is of little selective value and often appears to be purely accessorial to the Strasbourg decision making process.

These are unambiguous signs that confrontation is too easily surrendered against ostensibly competing interests and that ECHR law still does not take this fundamental right as seriously as it should. In the following Chapter, discussion turns to the protection afforded to the Right to Confrontation at national level. Conclusions will be twofold. On the one hand, I will show that not all the *minimal* standards set by ECHR law are as yet rigorously met by Member States. On the other hand, I will also disclose that some national jurisdictions exceed the requirements of ECHR law – especially with regard to certain topics, such as the evidence of the anonymous witness – and therefore afford a greater degree of protection for this fundamental right of the accused.

---

167 For an analysis of the ECHR version of the Right to Confrontation from a United States perspective see R.W. Kirst, *Hearsay and the Right to Confrontation in the European Court of Human Rights*, (2003) 21 Q.L.R. 777.

CHAPTER 4

Criminal Evidence and Confrontation: A Comparative Approach

1 Outline

The present chapter places this research effort in the context of comparative[1] criminal procedure and serves as an introduction to the subsequent cross-national study on matters of confrontation, carried out in Chapters 5 and 6. Discussion is in three main parts. Firstly, I will outline the problem under investigation and cast some light upon the peculiarities of macro and micro-comparisons in the field of criminal evidence. The dualism between adversarial and inquisitorial models will also be revisited. Secondly, I will justify the choice of France, England[2] and Italy as 'model' European countries and locate the sources of their criminal evidence law. Thirdly, I will discuss and compare certain basic features of their domestic law.

2 The Macro Comparative Framework

2.1 Preliminaries

The English, French and Italian legal orders are committed to the upholding of basic safeguards for defendants in criminal proceedings. They are also bound to comply with the provisions of the European Convention on Human Rights, including the Confrontation clause of Article 6(3)(d). Chapter 5 and 6 will later discuss the extent to which the law of these countries affords protection to the Right to Confrontation. While fundamental rights are proclaimed, other highly respected values – such as the accuracy and efficiency of the adjudication process – are also invoked as central to criminal discourse. It is crucial to this work to try and explain how conflicts of values are resolved and how these goals are prioritised. The study of confrontational matters is a good test for this purpose, since it is now established that the incursions into this fundamental right are symptoms of the overestimation of arguments of public interest and social defence by national courts and legislators.

Scholars in comparative law argue that the systems of each and every society face essentially the same problems[3], and that identical goals are often pursued

---

1 No longer described as the 'Cinderella of the legal sciences' (H.C. Gutteridge, *Comparative Law*, 2nd edn., Cambridge Univ. Press, Cambridge, 1949, 23), comparative law is now acknowledged as an established academic discipline. Its methodology and scope are comprehensively exposed by L.J. Constantinesco, *Traité de Droit Comparé*, Paris, 1972, vol. II, 289-480. See also B. Grossfeld, *The Strength and Weakness of Comparative Law*, Clarendon, Oxford, 1990.

2 For these purposes, England includes Wales but not Scotland, which has its own system (below, n 85). For brevity's sake, in this work I will refer to 'England' and the 'English legal order'. References to the United Kingdom are sometimes made in relation to matters of international law.

3 K. Zweigert and H. Kötz, *Introduction to Comparative Law*, 3rd edn., Clarendon, Oxford, 1998, 34.

through quite dissimilar means.[4] This theory fully applies to the topic of this book: although domestic laws express a serious commitment to confrontation, they also allow penetrating intrusions into it. Although departures from the 'confrontational paradigm' may be found in rules of evidence that are construed in several different ways, such rules serve – in the minds of their supporters – the very same purpose, that is the alleged enhancement of the efficacy of the adjudication process.

The key methodological principle of comparative scholarship is *functionality*: sensible comparisons should refer to the legal tools employed by different jurisdictions to fulfil parallel functions ('functional equivalents'). For this reason, discussion ought to disregard national terminology and proceed on the basis of the neutral concepts coined in Chapter 1: 'testimonial evidence', 'confrontational paradigm', 'departures' from the paradigm and 'counterbalances'.

2.2 Macro and Micro Comparisons

Before a micro comparative study of testimonial evidence law is presented in Chapter 5 and 6, something must be said about the macro comparative framework that surrounds this field of the law. Macro comparisons are studies of two or more legal systems (e.g. common law, civil law) or branches of law (e.g. criminal law, criminal procedure) while micro comparisons are the investigations of specific topics (e.g. the criminal responsibility of corporations, the law of homicide, the probative value of public records). These two variants diverge on both methodology and scope. Macro comparisons are intended to make the features of a jurisdiction or branch of the law accessible to foreign jurists. They group systems of law into legal families[5] and widely employ theoretical generalisations. Unsurprisingly, they also tend to place their findings within a broad context of historical, economical and social considerations. Their focus is on the fundamental institutions, sources of law and underlying principles and values. Inevitably, the need for widely acceptable generalisations forces macro-comparison studies to focus their attention to mainstream doctrine and case law. In comparison, the narrow focus of micro comparisons requires a certain degree of familiarity with the features of the concerned jurisdiction. It is precisely for this reason that the present chapter later provides an insight into the foundations of English, French and Italian law. Micro comparisons also draw upon a high degree of technicality and they not only have the opportunity but also the obligation to focus on details, as well as domestic minority opinions.

Micro comparisons are mostly effective when provisions of different jurisdictions apply simultaneously to a legal case: multinational companies' agreements are precious tests for micro-comparative research in the area of contract law, as

---

4 J.C. Reitz, *How to Do Comparative Law*, (1998) 46 Am. J. Comp. Law 621-622.

5 K. Zweigert and H. Kötz, *Introduction...*, *supra* note 3, 63-74.

well as international arbitrations in the area of civil procedure. Criminal procedure is short of such opportunities, as the principle of territorial jurisdiction isolate the States from each other. Resistance against international co-operation also remains a universal feature of domestic criminal law. Even among European Union countries, this subject is immune to the wide-ranging pattern of integration that affects most other fields of the law.[6] Because rules of evidence are also strictly 'national', it is hardly surprising that comparative endeavours in this area mostly amount to macro, not micro, comparisons.[7] Micro comparative research, however, has never been entirely abandoned[8] and, in the last decade, nourishment for it has been provided by the study of the evidence and procedural rules of the International Criminal Tribunals,[9] and , more recently, the European arrest warrant.

A good understanding of the macro-comparative framework requires a brief analysis of the dualism between the adversarial and inquisitorial models

6 The macro comparative approach was inaugurated by the founder of modern comparative criminal procedure: K.J.A. Mittermaier, *Das Englische, Schottische und Nordamerikanische Strafverfahren*, Enke, Erlangen, 1851 and *Erfahrungen über die Wirksamkeit der Schwurgerichte in Europa und Amerika über ihre Vorzüge, Mängel und Abhülfe*, Enke, Erlangen, 1865. In contemporary literature, comparative studies of criminal procedure may be found as part of broad projects exploring criminal legal families across the world: cf. G.F. Cole, S. Frankowsky and M.G. Gertz, *Major Criminal Justice Systems: a Comparative Survey*, 2nd edn., Sage, Newbury Park, 1987; E. Fairchild and H.R. Dammer, *Comparative Criminal Justice Systems*, 2nd edn., Wadsworth, Belmont, 2001; P.L. Reichel, *Comparative Criminal Justice Systems – A Topical Approach*, 2nd edn., Prentice Hall, Upper Saddle River, 1999. In Europe, several studies apply a common format in the description of national laws of procedure and evidence: see J. Hatchard, B. Huber and R.A. Vogler, *Comparative Criminal Procedure*, British Institute of Intl. & Comp. Law, London, 1996; M. Delmas-Marty and J.R. Spencer (eds), *European Criminal Procedures*, Cambrige Univ. Press, Cambridge, 2002; C. Van den Wyngaert (ed.), *Criminal Procedure Systems in the European Community*, Butterworths, London, 1993. See also A. Braunschweig, *La Procédure Pénale en Droit Français*, 64 (1993) R.I.D.P. 1089-1113; P. Alldridge, *Reform Movements in Criminal Procedure and the Protection of Human Rights in England*, 64 (1993) R.I.D.P. 1115-1125; M. Chiavario, *Les Mouvements de Réforme du Procès Pénal et la Protection des Droits de l'Homme en Italie*, 64 (1993) R.I.D.P. 1193-1211.

7 For a comparative study of criminal evidence see the symposium *La Preuve en Procédure Pénale Comparée – Evidence in Comparative Criminal Procedure*, published in (1992) 63 R.I.D.P. The symposium included the following papers: J. Pradel, *Rapport Général*, 13-31; J.R. Spencer, *Le Droit Anglais*, 83-103; F. Casorla, *Le Droit Français*, 183-204; P. Corso, *Le Droit Italien*, 205-236. See also J.R. Spencer, *Evidence*, in M. Delmas-Marty and J.R. Spencer (eds.), *European Criminal Procedures*, *supra* note 6, 594-640.

8 For a cross-national study on testimonial evidence see R Screvens, *Le Statut du Témoin et sa Protection Avant, Pendant et Après le Procès Pénal*, [1989] R.D.P.C. 3-15. Specific focus on the testimonial evidence of the defendant is provided by G. van Kessel, *European Perspectives on the Accused as a Source of Testimonial Evidence*, (1998) 100 W. Virginia L.R. 799-845.

9 M. Findlay, *Synthesis in Trial Procedures? The Experience of International Criminal Tribunals*, (2001) 50 I.C.L.Q. 26-53. The Rules of Procedure and Evidence for the International Criminal Court were approved by the Preparatory Commission on 30 June 2000.

of procedure. Such models can be understood not only as conflicting cultural paradigms in allocating powers and responsibilities between the actors of the criminal process, but also as opposing "proof-taking" styles.

2.2.1 Adversarial and Inquisitorial Styles

It is a long-standing habit among commentators to introduce comparative efforts in criminal procedure by outlining the distinctions and relative merits of the adversarial and the inquisitorial model.[10] Historically, the former is the quintessence of the common law tradition in Great Britain and its former colonies, including Australia, Canada and the United States, while the latter is the product of civil law in the European continent. The term *inquisitorial* bears no pejorative nuance here: the subsequent discussion of the inquisitorial model does not refer to the sinister practice of the Inquisition, whose principles of law were codified by the 1670 *Ordonnance Criminelle de Saint-Germain-en-Laye* of Louis XIV,[11] but to the modern French tradition, stemming from the 1808 *Code d'instruction criminelle.*

Although the opposition between the adversarial and inquisitorial paradigms is too deeply engrained to be abandoned, it should be tailor-made to the purposes of this work. Several fruitful perspectives have been adopted to contrast the paradigms, since their features are not only relevant to the course of evidence but also the overall ideology of the adjudicating process and the respective roles of judiciary and counsel. This being said, the most captivating question to be answered has traditionally been which of the two models is better equipped to discover the truth of factual propositions.[12] Although both forms of trials have the establishment of past occurrences as a central aim,[13] they strongly disagree on the process of adjudication that best suits such an aim. It is precisely in the law of evidence that diversity most clearly materialises.

The essence of the adversarial style resides in 'a system of adjudication in which procedural action is controlled by the parties and the adjudicator remains essentially passive'.[14] Literature describes the adversarial trial as a one-day-in-

---

10 J.D. Jackson, *Two Models of Proof in Criminal Procedure,* (1988) 51 Modern L.R. 549-568; J. Pradel, *Inquisitoire-Accusatoire: une Redoutable Complexité,* (1997) 68 R.I.D.P. 213-229; B. Deleuze and J.R. Spencer and D. Vorms, *La Preuve: Une Question Inclassable,* (1993) 15 Arch. Pol. Crim. 37-53.

11 See Chapter 1.

12 See the empirical study of E.A. Lind J. Thibaut and L. Walker, *Discovery and Presentation of Evidence in Adversary and Non Adversary Proceedings,* (1973) 71 Mich. L.R. 1129. These findings have been reviewed by M.R. Damaška, *Evidentiary Barriers to Conviction and Two Models of Criminal Procedure: a Comparative Study,* (1973) 121 U. Penn. L.R. 506-589.

13 C. Brants, N. Jörg and S. Field, *Are Inquisitorial and Adversarial Systems Converging?,* in P. Fennell and others (eds.), *Criminal Justice in Europe: A Comparative Study,* Clarendon, Oxford, 1995, 41, at 42.

14 M.R. Damaška, *Evidence Law Adrift,* Yale Univ. Press, New Haven, 1997, 74.

court contest between two equal parties, seeking to resolve a dispute before an impartial judge who acts as an umpire. In principle, peers of the accused – empanelled in a jury – play the decision-making role. Their assignment is to affirm whether the charges brought against the accused are worthy of belief. As neither the umpire nor the decision-maker have prior knowledge of the case, parties conduct the process with each side attempting to convince the jury of the rectitude of their conflicting positions. Information reaches the fact finder in the form of two *one-sided* accounts. In the theatrical scene of the adversarial trial, equality of parties and the oral process of evidence collection are essential ingredients. As a party exposes the weakness in the opponent's case, the decision-maker is in the best position to assess where the truth rests beyond reasonable doubt. The very concept of *truth* is rather relative and consensual: if the parties agree that certain facts have happened in a certain way, that matter is usually settled with no further investigation. Under this variant, it is also left to the parties to decide what evidence to collect, present, agree or dispute.

Rather than a competition between opposing sides, a trial under the modern inquisitorial paradigm resembles more closely a continuing investigation and consists of a public verification of the findings made at the investigation stage. As the assumption is that the truth can – and should – be discovered through a systematic and scientific procedure, inquisitorial judges are expected to move towards it by their own exertions.[15] Since it may be in the parties' interest to conceal what happened, the State is the best-equipped authority to lead the course of criminal adjudication. As a result, public authorities act as the benevolent promoters and guarantors of the public interest. While counsel are assigned a relatively limited role, State functions are embodied in the influential examining judge,[16] a theoretically neutral officer in charge of performing the investigation. The *instruction* is indeed the crucial stage of the process, since most evidence is collected there. Instead, the trial is a relatively brief and informal affair primarily meant to test the veracity of the investigation findings. The trial is presided over and conducted by a professional judge – or a panel of judges – who not only has full access to the investigation file, but also will have read it very scrupulously.

In another perspective, adversarial trials bear a negative perception of the authority of the State and a minimalist view of its functions.[17] It has also been suggested that the two models assume opposing underlying visions of the purposes of criminal justice systems: conflict-solving as opposed to policy

---

[15] G. Williams, *The Proof of Guilt*, 3rd edn., Stevens, London, 1969, 28.

[16] In the 19th century, the *juge d'instruction* was said to be 'the most powerful man of France': H. de Balzac, *La Comedie Humaine – Splendeurs et Misères de Courtisanes – III*, Paris, 1840.

[17] History shows that there is a link between inquisitorial proceedings and centralised structure of government. This tendency dates back to the Roman criminal trial, which was adversarial during the Republic (509 B.C. – 27 B.C.) and inquisitorial at the time of the Empire (from 27 B.C. onwards).

implementing.[18] It is therefore expected that adversarial trials will be in principle reluctant to serve the purposes of protecting society for the sake of the public interest, while inquisitorial proceedings would more promptly fall into the temptation to place restrains on the fundamental rights of the accused. These theoretical assumptions are tested later in this work, when the intrusions against the Right to Confrontation in English, French and Italian law are illustrated and compared.

2.2.2 Multi-directional Changes in Contemporary Criminal Procedure

No contemporary jurisdiction exactly conforms to the theoretical paradigms described above. National systems operate procedural hybrids aimed at reducing the inherent weakness and flaws of both models. On the one hand, trials of an inquisitorial nature can often be perceived as unfair to the defendant. In the light of the unilateral process of evidence collection, an innocent defendant might be convicted simply because he appears to be the likeliest suspect to the court.[19] On the other hand, the adversarial system is commonly believed to skew the truth-finding process. Commentators suggest that the destiny of defendants relies greatly on the skills of counsel in arguing to the jury and cross-examining the witnesses, regardless of actual guilt or innocence.[20] Besides, due to the high costs of jury trials, the majority of cases are resolved out of court anyway. Hence, a typical feature of adversarial systems is the mass production of guilty pleas,[21] often achieved by offering convictions for less serious offences and sentence discounts.

It also interesting to consider how scholars perceive and describe their own domestic realms. French commentators firmly refuse to label their procedure as 'inquisitorial'. Instead, whilst contrasting the alleged adversarial nature of

---

18 M.R. Damaška, *The Faces of Justice and State Authority: a Comparative Approach to the Legal Process*, Yale Univ. Press, New Haven, 1986, 97-180.

19 C.M. Bradley, *The Convergence of the Continental and the Common Law Model of Criminal Procedure*, (1996) 7 Crim. Law Forum 472.

20 For an attack against the truth-finding deficiencies of the adversarial model from a U.S. perspective, see W.T. Pizzi, *Trials Without Truth: Why our System of Criminal Trials Has Become an Expensive Failure and What We Need to Do to Rebuild It*, N.Y. Univ. Press, New York, 1999, 25-45.

21 According to the figures of Home Office, *Criminal Statistics England and Wales 1998 (Cm 4649)*, London, Stationery Office, 1998, 60.6% of cases in the Crown Court were terminated by a guilty plea in 1998. This figure is even higher (82%) at the magistrates' courts. In the U.S. federal justice system, the proportion of convictions obtained through pleas of guilty or *nolo contendere* reaches 95%, and has been climbing steadily for over 30 years. In the state systems, guilty pleas accounted for 94% of felony convictions in 1998, according to The Bureau of Justice Statistics – U.S. Department of Justice, *Felony Sentences in State Courts – 1998*, (2001) 8-9.

the trial with the inquisitorial investigation that precedes it, they describe it as a *system procédural mixte.*[22] Conversely, despite the implementation of an adversarial Code of criminal procedure in 1989, the Italian doctrine is proud to affirm that the law looked at the Anglo-American model through pragmatic lenses, in full awareness of both its advantages and drawbacks, and 'the new Italian criminal procedure has by no means resulted in a mere transplantation of Anglo-American patterns. The procedural institutions that the Italian drafters borrowed from British or American models were in fact modified and adjusted to the continental tradition'.[23]

Owing to the influence of shared Human Rights institutions, the present tendency of European jurisdictions is to slide towards a *rights-oriented approach* in interpreting and applying rules of procedure and evidence. It is now settled that the truth, in so far as it can be established, should be established in a manner that is fair to the defendant. Nonetheless, these considerations should not lead one to conclude that inquisitorial and adversarial systems are in a slow, yet continuous, process of mutual convergence.[24] By definition, the adversarial and the inquisitorial are contrasting theoretical paradigms. They cannot converge for the obvious reason that their features are shaped in mutual opposition. Instead, it is true that a blend of inquisitorial and adversarial features can be found in existing criminal jurisdictions since national orders find it harder and harder to function in accordance with their own long-standing principles. Even a cursory look at the administration of present criminal justice reveals that multidirectional changes are in progress.

Dramatic reforms have recently been implemented within most European criminal procedures[25] and, as a consequence, domestic systems resemble less and less the stark theoretical models outlined above. This process also eludes conventional points of reference. Consider, for example, the exclusionary rules for hearsay evidence, which have been abolished in England by *C.J.A. 2003*, s. 114 and, instead, have been amidst difficulties transplanted in Italy.[26] Attracted by alien shapes, designers of newly mixed procedural forms may have created a terrain in which one can easily encounter odd angles of disparate procedural traditions and lack of orientation is a rather common feeling of researchers in the field.

---

22 M.L. Rassat, *Traité de Procédure Pénale*, PUF, Paris, 2001, §17; P. Conte and P Maistre Du Chambon, *Procédure Pénale*, 3rd edn., Dalloz, Paris, 2001, §325.

23 E. Amodio and E. Selvaggi, *An Accusatorial System in a Civil Law Country: the 1988 Italian Code of Criminal Procedure*, (1989) 62 Temple L.R. 1211, 1212.

24 C. Brants and others, *Are Inquisitorial and Adversarial Systems Converging?*, *supra* note 13, 42-48; C.M. Bradley, *The Convergence...*, *supra* note 19, 472-75.

25 Cf. discussion below, s C.3.

26 Cf. Art. 195 I-CPP.

This being said, the question is whether the contrast between adversarial and inquisitorial models can still be of some assistance in explaining the peculiarities of national laws of evidence. Although the core assumptions of national evidence law may not have been given away by recent reforms, more and more exceptions, deviations, departures from the mainstream principles are implemented, with a view to accommodate values and interests that may theoretically be conflicting with such principles. It should not surprise the reader, therefore, to discover that in England the need to protect vulnerable or intimidated witnesses has resulted in the elimination of the legendary right of the accused to cross-examine the accusers in person,[27] while in France parties may now directly question the witnesses, at odds with the inquisitorial tradition that attributed such a power to the president alone. This being said, however, a perception remains that criminal proof-taking styles represent the core of the social and political values of the society in which they exist, and they express the beauty of diversity of European cultures. Chapter 3 showed that the European Court of Human Rights is reluctant to elaborate comprehensive theories in the field of criminal evidence. Chapter 5 will later show that the major differences between domestic rules for the collection of the evidence of court witnesses are still the outcome of the adversarial or inquisitorial inspiration of the concerned systems.

As Prof. Pradel suggests, contemporary continental and common law criminal trials are reminiscent of 'two brothers who anxiously compare experiences, but for all that, each remains privately convinced of the superiority of his own'.[28] In comparison, Chapter 6 will then demonstrate that incursions into the fundamental Right to Confrontation are surprisingly common to all the European Countries chosen as models.

2.2.3 'Substantive' v 'Procedural' Exclusionary Rules of Evidence

Since the protection of the fundamental Right to Confrontation requires that some unchallenged testimonial evidence is excluded from the adjudication process, discussion will now turn to the topic of the exclusionary rules of evidence. It is often suggested that 'adversarial' evidence law consists precisely of a compilation of exclusionary rules that prevent courts of justice from using items of potentially relevant evidence. Evidence provisions of the U.S. and English legal orders are traditionally phrased so as to state what, as the expression runs, is not to be deemed as evidence. Matters have changed in England after the coming into force of *C.J.A. 2003*, which pursues an inclusive approach towards hearsay and character evidence.

---

27 Cf. Chapter 5, section 3.3.1.

28 J. Pradel, *Rapport Général, supra* note 7, 31.

It would be inaccurate to deduce that no exclusionary rules of evidence apply to proceedings of an inquisitorial nature. Confusion in this regard may result from a superficial reading of certain statutory provisions. Article 310 of the French Criminal Procedure Code, for example, accords 'full discretion to the presiding judge in the pursuance of any measure useful in the pursuance of truth'. Further, Article 427 states that a criminal offence can be proved by any means of proof. Does the principle of the *liberté de la preuve* mean that all evidence that might be relevant to the determination of a fact in issue is admissible pursuant to French law? Certainly not. Any adjudication process that claims to be fair establishes some limitations against the presentation of potentially relevant evidence to the criminal courts. Examples common to both adversarial and inquisitorial jurisdictions are easy to find. Evidence of confidential correspondence between the defendant and counsel may be relevant to the determination of the alleged culpability of the latter for obstruction to justice. Yet, such documents are covered by the legal profession privilege. The confession of the defendant may well be relevant to the determination of his or her liability. Yet, if obtained by torture or subterfuge, it is not admissible. Needless presentation of cumulative evidence and risk of undue delay are also recurrent grounds for exclusion of evidence in both adversarial and inquisitorial models.

If exclusionary rules are common to proceedings of both adversarial and inquisitorial inspiration, the problem is then to establish where their respective uniqueness lie. The search for a convincing answer requires investigation of the manner in which exclusionary rules operate. Some exclusionary rules are *substantive* in nature, while others are merely *procedural*.

Under the inquisitorial variant, evidence is part of procedural law and evidentiary problems are tackled as 'procedural nullities' of the judicial acts that technically bring such evidence before the court. Consider French law as an example. There, statutory provisions provide meticulous regulations for the administration of each and every means of proof (documents, testimonies, confessions, etc...). The principle de *la legalité de la preuve* states that any departure from the legal requirements may be subject to the sanction of nullity and result in the exclusion of evidence.[29] As far as testimonial evidence is concerned, provisions dictate which witnesses can be summoned, how summons shall be served and under what formalities out-of-court depositions should be recorded. Compliance with these *procedural* guarantees is the one and only test to which evidence is submitted. If such a test is satisfied, testimony counts as evidence and the law is indifferent to its specific content. The appreciation of the content of a testimony is entirely left to the *intime conviction* of the court while any exclusionary rule of evidence referring to 'parts' of the depositions would be perceived in those systems as a barrier to the quest for truth.

[29] P. Conte and P. Maistre Du Chambon, *Procédure Pénale, supra* note 22, §67.

Under the adversarial variant, the heart of the law of evidence lies precisely where discussion of evidentiary matters in inquisitorial proceedings ends. Procedural exclusionary rules exist, but play a relatively limited part. Testimonial matters provide a paradigmatic example for my discussion, since the problem of admissibility raises completely different questions. Also in adversarial systems, police and prosecutors must follow certain formalities in the collection of out-of-court depositions. Even if such formalities are complied with, however, pre-trial depositions may be inadmissible as evidence of the facts stated and may only impeach the credibility of their author. In addition, admissibility provisions typically refer to statements given at trial and are mainly concerned with their substance (i.e. the content of the statement). This is why evidence rules primarily dictate which questions may be asked to elicit a deposition and which answers the witness is allowed to give in the presence of the jury. Major grounds for refusing admissibility are 'opinion', 'character' and, to a more limited extent, 'hearsay'. At this stage, what matters most is to understand that adversarial evidence law attaches great importance to the scrutiny of the actual *content* of a testimonial deposition and the reason for which such deposition is tendered in evidence. Concerns of this kind are instead foreign to the inquisitorial discourse.

To the majority of continental jurists, the typical adversarial evidentiary rules appear puzzling and obscure. Consider the example of hearsay logic. The difference between evidence offered to prove the matter asserted and evidence offered to prove that a statement was made is simply ignored in inquisitorial jurisprudence.[30] Considerations over the reliability of the unchallenged statements of a third person that does not come to court would certainly cross the mind of an inquisitorial judge, but inquisitorial law expresses no interest in governing the exercise of his or her discretion. From an historical perspective, it is fair to say that the absence of substantive exclusionary rules contributed greatly to the perception of the immense distance between the adversarial and inquisitorial discourse. French law has never experienced a hard system of rules regarding what is relevant or admissible evidence and what is not, or what may or may not be proved by a specific statement of a witness, such as exists in England and America, and still consumes so much time in the courts of those countries.

In England and the U.S. much academic ink has been spilt over the classification of exclusionary rules and their inherence in adversarial proof style.[31] Common law judges acknowledge that '[adversarial-based] law excludes evidence

[30] It must be acknowledged that the theoretical opposition between 'evidence that a statement is made' and 'evidence that the matter therein stated is true' still permeates *C.J.A. 2003*, despite the fact that the Act renders the majority of hearsay evidence admissible in criminal proceedings.

[31] M.R. Damaška, *Evidence Law Adrift*, *supra* note 14, 12-14 accepts that virtually all observers consider the intense preliminary screening of evidence a salient trait of the Anglo-American fact-finding style, but later argues that only a small subset of exclusionary rules is truly idiomatic to the common law.

of many matters which in life outside the courts sensible people take into consideration when making decisions'.[32] In the 19th century, Charles Dickens engaged in acute criticism of the complexity of this branch of the law and the alienation of the English middleman from the technicalities of the adjudication process.[33] Two theories present themselves as explanations for the peculiarities of the Anglo-American fact-finding process. According to the most commonly referenced one, the reason lies entirely in the deployment of lay people as judges of fact.[34] Jurors are not professionally trained to assess evidentiary matters and, the reasoning goes, the screening of a great deal of evidence is essential to provide guidance to their assessment of the case. More recently, this position has been partially reviewed by those who suggest that the evidentiary arrangements of the Anglo-American trial result from the strongly partisan role that counsel play, in the selection and presentation of evidence before the courts. According to this view, exclusionary rules should be regarded as a means for 'the control of lawyers, rather than juries'.[35]

The staged opposition between *procedural* and *substantive* exclusionary rules of evidence will be referenced in subsequent parts of this book, since it may assist in clarifying the domestic approaches to matters of confrontation.

3 Model Countries and Boundaries of the Comparison

3.1 Three Countries as European Models

In broad terms, all Western European countries would be suitable for comparison because they are at parallel stages of social and economic development, share the cultural values entrenched within the body of the ECHR law and experience very similar conflicts of values and interests. Recent studies[36] also suggest that EU countries face almost identical criminal environments: a general increase of the crime rate, especially in the field of organised

---

[32] *R. v. Turner*, [1975] Q.B. 834 (C.A.).

[33] See the fictional case *Berdell v. Pickwick* in C. Dickens, *The Pickwick Papers*, London, 1836-37, 537.

[34] The common law's fact-finding arrangements are the 'child of the jury system' according to J.B. Thayer, *A Preliminary Treatise on Evidence at the Common Law*, Sweet & Maxwell, London, 1898, 266. They are based upon the idea of 'the fallacy, that, whatever is morally convincing, and whatever reasonable beings would form their judgements and act upon, may be submitted to the jury', *Wright v. Tatham* (1838) 5 Cl. & Fin. 670, 7 E.R. 559 (H.L.) (L.J.Coleridge).

[35] D.A. Nance, *The Best Evidence Principle*, (1988) 73 Iowa L.R. 229. An early promoter of this approach was E.M. Morgan, *The Jury and the Exclusionary Rules of Evidence*, (1937) 4 Univ. Chicago L.R. 247-258.

[36] The findings of a recent survey founded by the Council of Europe are reviewed in K. Auromaa, *Trends in Criminality*, in *Crime and Criminal Justice in Europe*, Council of Europe Publishing, Strasbourg, 2001, 13-34.

crime, economic fraud and sexually-related offences, a chronic insufficiency of financial means for the enforcement agencies (police, prosecutors, courts, prisons), an increasing demand for a high-quality administration of justice and a prompt reparation of its miscarriages.

Comparisons are mostly valuable when they focus on jurisdictions that constitute prime examples of the legal family to which they belong. Since criminal evidence discourse is still partly influenced by the dualism between the adversarial and the inquisitorial paradigms, the choice of Italy, France and England[37] as model countries is by no means accidental. Despite the national commentators' effort to draw a clear-cut line between the inquisitorial preliminary investigation and a supposedly adversarial trial, France remains the prime example of the continental tradition.[38] Similarly, England is the bastion of the adversarial proof-taking style on European soil.[39] Instead, Italy is represented as a true hybrid since 1989, when a adversarial Code of criminal procedure was transplanted into a French-influenced legal culture.[40]

3.2 Sources of Law: Definition and Typology

The aim of this section is to familiarise the reader with the sources of English, French and Italian evidence law. A very broad definition of source of law is adopted here: it includes whatever 'moulds or affects the living law [of] the chosen systems and whatever the lawyers there would treat as a source of law'.[41]

---

37 For a comparative approach see generally M. Delmas-Marty and J.R. Spencer (eds.) *European Criminal Procedures, supra* note 7, and, specifically, the following national reports: J.R. Spencer, *The English System*, 142-217, V. Dervieux, *The French System*, 218-291 and A. Perrodet, *The Italian System*, 348-412.

38 J.Y. Chevallier, *La Preuve en Procédure Pénale Comparée – Rapport de Synthèse pour les Pays d'Europe Continentale*, (1992) 63 R.I.D.P. 43-55.

39 S.J. Schulhofer, F Greenberg and B.J. Greenberg, *La Preuve en Procédure Pénale Comparée – Rapport de Synthèse pour les Pays de Common Law*, (1992) 63 R.I.D.P. 33-42.

40 A. Amodio and E. Selvaggi, *An Accusatorial System..., supra* note 23, 1211-1124; L.J. Fassler, *The Italian Penal Procedure Code: An Adversarial System of Criminal Procedure in Continental Europe*, (1991) 29 Colum. J.T.L. 245-278; E. Zappalà, *Le Procès Pénal Italien entre Système Inquisitoire et Système Accusatoire*, (1997) 68 R.I.D.P. 111-124; W.T. Pizzi and L. Marafioti, *The New Italian Code of Criminal Procedure: The Difficulties of Binding an Adversarial Trial System on a Civil Law Foundation*, (1992) 17 Yale J. Intl. Law, 1-40; E. Grande, *Italian Criminal Justice: Borrowing and Resistance*, (2000) 48 Am. J. Comp. Law 227-259.

41 K. Zweigert and H. Kötz, *Introduction to Comparative Law, supra* note 3, 35-36.

3.2.1 Constitutional Law

The supreme source of French and Italian law is the national Constitution.[42] In France, constitutional value is also borne by the so-called *bloc de constitutionalité*, which includes the 1789 Declaration of the Rights of Man and the Citizen,[43] the preamble of the former 1946 Constitution, as well as the fundamental principles of the legislation and rulings of the Constitutional Council. Italian legislation is subject to the permanent judicial review of the Constitutional Court: any domestic court of justice may submit to the Court a 'not manifestly unfounded' claim of unconstitutionality.[44] In France, the process of judicial review is more limited: the Constitutional Council may only challenge the constitutionality of the Acts passed by the French Parliament *before* they are formally enacted (cf. Article 61 F-CONST).

While both the Italian and the French Constitution acknowledge basic principles of criminal procedure (e.g. the presumption of innocence, the right to counsel, *nulla poena sine lege*), only the Italian Constitution specifically addresses evidentiary matters. After the 1999 'fair trial' amendment,[45] Article 111 I-CONST almost literally reproduces Article 6 of the European Convention of Human Rights, including the Confrontation Clause. It also includes the principle of adversarial adjudication (*principio del contraddittorio*) in criminal proceedings and a significant exclusionary rule against the use in evidence of the depositions given by those 'who have always voluntarily avoided confrontation with the accused or counsel'.[46] These provisions were inserted into the Constitution to contrast the anti-adversarial role played by the Italian Constitutional Court in the last decade. On three occasions during the year 1992, the Constitutional Court affirmed that some of the adversarial exclusionary rules of evidence embedded in the 1989 Code offended allegedly superior constitutional principles. To be more accurate, the Court deemed the exclusion of hearsay evidence of police officers,[47] previous inconsistent statements of witnesses[48] and prior statements of silent or absent co-defendants[49] as causes of an 'unreason-

---

[42] The Italian Constitution was passed by the Constitutional Assembly on December 22, 1947 and entered into force on January 1, 1948. The Constitution of the 5th French Republic was passed on October, 4, 1958 and approved by public referendum on September 28, 1958.

[43] *Dèclaration des Droits de l'Homme et du Citoyen*, approved on August 26, 1789.

[44] Cf. Art. 137 I-CONST; Law No. 87, 11 March 1953.

[45] The amendment was made by Law Const No. 2, 23 November 1999 emphatically entitled 'Incorporation of fair trial principles into Art. 111 of the Constitution'.

[46] Art. 111(4) I-CONST.

[47] (I) Corte cost., judgment No. 24/1992, [1992] Giur. Cost.114, concerning Art. 195 I-CPP.

[48] (I) Corte cost., judgment No. 255/1992, [1992] Giur. Cost. 1961, concerning Art. 500 I-CPP.

[49] (I) Corte cost., judgment No. 254/1992, [1992] Giur. Cost. 1932, concerning Art. 513 I-CPP.

able loss' of reliable evidence.[50] When amendments to the procedural code were passed to comply with the aforementioned judgments,[51] its overall structure was affected and the shadow of the inquisitorial practice was cast again on the Italian criminal trial.[52] It must also be acknowledged that, at the time, Italy was shaken by the assassination of two famous crusading mafia prosecutors.[53] Large sectors of the public opinion and doctrine perceived exclusionary rules as dangerous obstacles in the fight against organised crime. In 1998, a further ruling of non-constitutionality of Article 513 of the code stated that a criminal conviction could be based on the pre-trial depositions of a co-defendant who had refused to give evidence in the courtroom.[54] Faced with the persistent anti-adversarial attitude of the Constitutional Court, the Parliament then took the matter in its own hands and amended the Constitution as reported above. This was clearly intended to prevent any further interference by the Constitutional Court in this field of the law. The related provisions of the Code were amended accordingly in 2001 and adversarial principles were, after 12 years, fully restored.[55]

In comparison, no formal Constitution exists in English law, where all Acts of Parliament have in principle the same legal value. The concept of Parliamentary sovereignty implies that Parliament has the power to enact, revoke or alter such, and any, law it sees fit to deal with while no one Parliament can bind its successors.[56] However, there have always been social and political influences, which have imposed restraints of the abrogation or passing of certain pieces of legislation. As a consequence of this, a few Acts of pivotal importance in the history of English law have never been abrogated and are widely acknowledged as foundations of the legal culture. Among them, relevant to criminal procedure, are the *Magna Carta 1297*,[57] the *Petition of Right 1627*,[58] the *Habeas Corpus*

---

50 Sharp criticism of the Constitutional Court's rulings was voiced by cf. O. Dominioni, *Un Nuovo Idolum Theatri: il Principio di non Dispersione Probatoria*, [1997] R.I.D.P.P. 736.

51 Cf. Law No. 356, 7 August 1992.

52 G Di Chiara, *L'Inquisizione come "Eterno Rimedio": Tecnica delle Contestazioni ed Usi Dibattimentali delle Indagini a Seguito della Sentenza 255/92 della Corte Costituzionale*, [1992-I] Foro Ital. 2013-2023.

53 On May 23, 1992, Giovanni Falcone, his wife and several bodyguards were driving from Palermo airport into the city center when dynamite a bomb, triggered with a long-distance device, made a 30-foot wide crater in the motorway and took their lives. A few weeks later, on July 19, 1992, Paolo Borsellino was killed by a car-bomb in Palermo.

54 (I) Corte cost, judgment No. 361/1998, [1998] Giur. Cost 2083.

55 Cf. *Law No. 63, 1 March 2001. For a comment cf* P Tonini (ed.), *Giusto Processo: Nuove Norme sulla Formazione e Valutazione della Prova*, Cedam, Padova, 2001; R.E. Kostoris (ed.), *Il Giusto Processo tra Contraddittorio e Diritto al Silenzio*, Giappichelli, Torino, 2002.

56 W. Wade, *Constitutional Fundamentals*, Stevens, London, 1989, 27-50.

57 25 Edw. I ch. I.

58 3 Cha. I ch. I.

Act 1679,[59] and the *Bill of Rights 1688*.[60] The *Human Rights Act 1998* may also well join this group.

3.2.2 ECHR law

The European Convention system does not impose upon Contracting States the obligation to make the Convention[61] part of domestic laws or otherwise to guarantee its prevalence over national law. International law gives the States a discretion to decide how to comply with international obligations and implement the concerned provisions. The consequence is that in some Contracting States no internal effect is assigned to the Convention, while in others it is. Italy, France and the United Kingdom fall in the latter category, as the Convention is directly enforceable in their domestic domain. Therefore, not only does it bind national governments as a matter of international law, but also domestic courts and authorities in the daily administration of legal affairs. Criminal suspects are thus entitled to invoke and rely upon the provisions of the Convention before national courts of justice.

The determination of the specific place of ECHR law in the sources of law of the jurisdictions covered by this study deserves further discussion. Relationships between international and municipal law may be governed according to two contrasting approaches, the dualistic and the monistic. Under the dualistic variant, international and national systems form two independent spheres, and international law has internal effect only after it has been duly transformed into national law. The latter model describes the situation in the United Kingdom. Despite its early ratification of the Convention in 1951 (first among all European countries), it was only with the coming into force of *H.R.A. 1998* that the Convention provisions were incorporated into U.K. law. The enactment of this statute is largely due to the manifesto commitment of the English Labour Government elected in 1997 to 'bring rights home'.[62] It is far beyond the scope of this study to discuss why it took almost half a century to reach this result, which was emphatically welcomed by commentators as bringing English criminal practice into an entirely new dimension.[63] Since 2 October 2000, Conven-

---

59 31 Cha. 2 ch. 2

60 1 Will. & Mary (sess 2) ch. 2

61 The Convention was ratified by the United Kingdom on March 8, 1951, by Italy on October 26, 1955 and by France on May 3, 1974.

62 Cf. Home Office, *Rights Brought Home: The Human Rights Bill (Cm 3782)*, London Stationery Office, 1997; Lord Irvine, *The Development of Human Rights in Britain under an Incorporated Convention on Human Rights*, [1998] P.L. 221-36.

63 The impact of *H.R.A. 1998* into English criminal law, litigation and sentencing is exposed by B. Emmerson and A. Ashworth, *Human Rights and Criminal Justice*, Sweet and Maxwell, London, 2001. For critical views, see also T. Campbell, K.D. Ewing and A. Tomkins, *Sceptical Essays on Human Rights*, Oxford Univ. Press, Oxford, 2001.

tion rights take precedence over any rule of common law and most delegated legislation. Existing statutes must now be given effect in a manner that is 'compatible'[64] with the Convention rights, in so far as it is possible. For the case in which such an interpretation is impossible, a complex procedure has been established to formally preserve Parliament's sovereignty and promote prompt amendments of the law.[65] None of the central features of English law of criminal procedure and evidence have been left untouched by this reform[66] and a number of topics are still undergoing judicial and statutory review. Among them, a mention is due to the statutory restrictions to cross-examination on certain witnesses' prior sexual history, which the House of Lords has deemed contrary to the defendant's right to a fair trial.[67] It is also agreed that conflict with ECHR may sometimes be prevented by a tailor-made use of some of the typical English court's discretionary powers to stay proceedings, to exclude relevant evidence or to allow a submission of 'no case to answer'. The Court of Appeal has also recently held that any breach of Article 6 of the Convention in the proceedings before courts of first instance would 'almost inevitably'[68] result in the quashing of criminal convictions on appeal. Indeed, since the coming into force of the Human Rights Act several convictions have been quashed – pursuant to *C.A.A. 1968*, s. 2(1)[69] – as the proceedings which secured them were deemed unsafe due to violations of the appellant's Article 6 rights.

In comparison, France and Italy apply the monistic view, according to which national authorities are bound by international law in their relations with individuals, regardless of whether the rules of international law have been transformed into municipal law. Precedence of the Convention provisions over national laws – yet not the Constitution – is ensured by the related constitutional provisions.[70]

---

64 *H.R.A. 1998*, s. 3. This obligation is to be interpreted extensively, as suggested by the House of Lords in *R. v. A. (No 2)*, [2002] 1 A.C. 45 (H.L.) (Lord Steyn).

65 This procedure allows the High Court, Court of Appeal and House of Lords to declare a provision of primary legislation incompatible with the Convention (*H.R.A. 1988*, s. 4). This declaration, however, does correspond to a formal abrogation of the legislation in question, but only confers a power to the relevant Minister to amend the law by remedial order. Such amendments may operate retrospectively, in order to be applied to the trial in which the issue had been raised (Sched. 2 para 1(1)(a)).

66 For discussion cf. B. Emmerson and A. Ashworth, *Human Rights…, supra* note 63, 255-531.

67 See Chapter 6, section 4.

68 *R. v. Togher*, [2001] 3 All. E.R. 463 (C.A.).

69 *R. v. Forbes*, [2001] 1 A.C. 473 (H.L.), *R. v. Francom*, [2001] 1 Cr. App. R. 237 (C.A.).

70 Cf. Art. 55 F-CONST; Art. 11 I-CONST.

3.2.3 Statutory Law

On the continent of Europe, criminal law and procedure are codified since the early 19th century. At that time, the Napoleon's Codes were the symbols of his determination to reorganise the rules of society, following the political upheaval of the *Révolution*. Although later judged to be the most unsuccessful among Napoleon's legal products,[71] the 1808 *Code d'instruction criminelle* was transplanted in several European countries and is still today the source of Belgian criminal procedure. In France, however, it has been replaced in 1959 with the present *Code de procédure pénale*.[72]

In Italy, the French model was closely followed by the first procedural Code of the Reign in 1865, while an enlightened liberal, yet still inquisitorial, approach is said to have inspired its successor, in 1913.[73] The following 1930 Code, an early product of the Fascist regime, was still a French-influenced document that emphasised crime control to the detriment of the rights of the accused. It remarkably survived for some forty years after the birth of the Republic, while Italy was facing the ideological conflict between 'hierarchical' and 'coordinated' models of justice.[74] After almost two decades of vibrant academic and political debate and some unsuccessful attempts to enact a new Code, February 16, 1987 marked the departure from tradition. On that day, the Parliament delegated the Government to draft a new code of Criminal procedure. The delegating statute[75] listed 105 criteria based mainly upon adversarial principles to which the Code was to conform. The present Code came into force on October 24, 1989, a date that stands out as a turning point in the history of Italian law.[76]

Although in Italy and France provisions of some importance (*e.g.* juveniles' trials, proceedings before the justice of the peace) may be found in separate statutes, rules of evidence law are built in the Codes. In Italy, the subject is governed by a tailor-made book of the Code which is specifically entitled 'evidence'. Its first section enumerates principles of universal application concerning admissibility, evaluation, corroboration and sanctions for illegally obtained evidence.[77]

---

[71] J. Pradel, *Presentation du Code Français de Procedure Penale*, in S. Maffei (tr), *Il Codice di Procedura Penale Francese*, CELT, Piacenza, 2002, 7, quoting R. Garraud, *Traité Théorique et Pratique d'Instruction Criminelle et de Procédure Pénale*, Larose & Tenin, Paris, 1907, 90.

[72] The socio-political context in which the French Code was approved is described as 'unfortunate' by R. Vouin, *L'Application du Code de Procédure Pénale et le Malheur des Temps*, [1962] R.S.C. 65-66.

[73] M. Chiavario, *Procedura Penale – Un Codice tra Storia e Cronaca*, Giappichelli, Torino, 1994, 20.

[74] M.R. Damaška, *Structures of Authority and Comparative Criminal Procedure*, (1975) 84 Yale L.J. 480-543.

[75] Cf. Law No. 81, 16 February 1987.

[76] It has been suggested that, to a comparative law scholar 'looking at different systems of criminal justice, the new Italian Code appears as the most outstanding event in the 20th Century'; A. Amodio and E. Selvaggi, *An Accusatorial System...*, *supra* note 23, 1211.

[77] Arts. 187-193 I-CPP. This section is the very defining and most ambitious feature of the Italian Code, since it concentrates in relatively few provisions all the major assumptions of the law of criminal

Rules governing testimonies of witnesses, documents, expertise and other means of proof are also included.[78] By contrast, no section on evidence law exists in the French Code: there, the related provisions are to be found scattered in its five books. Occasionally, some references will also be made to the codified sources of French and Italian substantive criminal law (i.e. the 1996 French *Code pénal* and the 1930 Italian *Codice penale*).

In comparison, the English statutory sources relevant to criminal procedure are dispersed in conditions of 'shocking mess',[79] among more than 150 different Acts. Some of them, such as the *Justice of the Peace Act 1361*, are ancient and drafted in an archaic and obscure language. Even contemporary Acts tend to be mostly unsystematic, a feature that leads to striking incidents of inconsistency. Further, amendments and re-amendments of a single Act follow over the years without any official publication of a final consolidating text. In spite of the unintelligibility of legislative sources, the case for either a mere consolidation[80] or a proper re-constructive codification of English criminal procedure struggled for years to achieve widespread consensus among commentators and law makers.[81] The case for codification gained some momentum after the publication of an official review of the criminal justice system: Lord Justice Auld recommended the production and maintenance of a Code of Criminal Law that, in his view, should consist of four sections, two of which would be devoted to rules of criminal procedure and evidence.[82] The recommendations of Lord Auld were partly implemented in March 2005, when, for the first time in English history, the *Criminal Procedure Rules 2005* were published and laid in Parliament. The *Crimi-*

evidence; cf. F. Cordero, *Procedura Penale*, 7th edn., Giuffrè, Milano, 2000, 603-659. At the time of the coming into force of the new Code, all the leading commentators illustrated the new principles of evidence law: compare M. Nobili, *Il Nuovo "Diritto delle Prove" ed un Rinnovato Concetto di Prova*, [1989] Leg. Pen. 395-400, G. Illuminati, *Il Nuovo Dibattimento: l'Assunzione Diretta delle Prove*, [1988-V] Foro Ital. 355-366; G. Lattanzi, *La Formazione della Prova nel Dibattimento*, [1989] Cass. Pen. 2298-2305.

78 These means are testimonies (Arts. 194 to 207 I-CPP), parties' examinations (Arts. 208 to 210), identification parades (Arts. 213 to 217), judicial experiments (Arts. 218 to 219), expert opinions (Arts. 220 to 233), documents (Arts. 234 to 243) and live confrontation between the suspect and witnesses, or witnesses who submitted conflicting evidence (Arts. 210 to 217).

79 J.R. Spencer, *The Case for a Code of Criminal Procedure*, [2000] Crim. L.R. 519, 520.

80 Scotland provides two examples of consolidation-without-reformation. The success of the *Criminal Procedure (Scotland) Act 1975*, which gave rational form to more than 60 pieces of legislation passed between 1587 and 1973, was duplicated by the *Criminal Justice (Scotland) Act 1995* which consolidated the previous statute and the additions and amendments made over the succeeding years: cf. R.W. Renton and H.H. Brown, *Criminal Procedure According to the Law of Scotland*, 6th edn., Green-Sweet & Maxwell, Edinburgh, 1996.

81 J.R. Spencer, *The Case for a Code...*, *supra* note 79, 520. See also, with reference to issues of both substantive and procedural law, Lord Bingham, *A Criminal Code: Must We Wait Forever?*, [1998] Crim. L.R. 694.

82 Auld L.J., *Review of the Criminal Courts of England and Wales, Report*, London Stationery Office, London, 2001, 20-22.

nal Procedure Rules 2005 consolidated rules governing the practice and procedure of the criminal courts – the criminal division of the Court of Appeal, the Crown Court and magistrates' courts. Yet, statutory reforms of criminal evidence are still being carried out by single Acts: among them, the *Criminal Justice Act 2003* will deserve special attention in the following chapters.

3.2.4 Case Law

The value of precedents as a source of law truly distinguishes common and civil law families. For the purposes of the present research, this well established assertion deserves only brief discussion.

The doctrine of binding precedent, or *stare decisis*, lies at the heart of English law. Within the hierarchical structure of English judiciary, the *ratio decidendi* of previous judgments is binding on lower courts. Only the House of Lords, since 1966, considers it possible to depart from its own previous judgement when it appears right to do so.[83] Nevertheless, this potentially revolutionary opportunity has been used in very limited circumstances. By contrast, continental case law has no formal binding force for either the court that established it or lower courts. Furthermore, as a general principle, judicial decisions become relevant to jurists exclusively when a practice has been formed, creating what would there be described as an *usus fori*. It must be said, however, that in the vast majority of cases Italian and French criminal courts of first and second instance tend to conform to the authorities of their respective supreme Courts.

Despite such a deference to the supreme Courts, a clear-cut line can still be drawn between the value and implications of courts' dicta in common law and continental systems. In Italy and France, general principles of law are often established in the articles of the codes. Courts are required to apply principles to specific legal problems and, broadly speaking, enjoy discretion only when the legal provisions do not set forth a detailed regulation of the topic. Conversely, in England it is for the courts to announce and elaborate the principles of the common law, while statutory provisions often lay down regulations of details, as well exceptions and deviations to those principles.[84]

3.2.5 Jurisprudence

Although, strictly speaking, the opinions of academics and commentators are not a source of law in the countries under scrutiny, jurisprudence nevertheless plays a significant part in the enhancement of understanding of the law as well as in the education of lawyers. The matter deserves some

---

83 *Practice Note (Judicial Precedent)*, [1966] 1 W.L.R. 1234 (H.L.).

84 J.R. Spencer, *Le Droit Anglais*, *supra* note 7, 83.

attention here, since the attitude of commentators contributes to keep English and continental law on criminal procedure and evidence apart.

In accordance with the common law tradition, the features of the English criminal justice system are presented under three separate treatises: substantive law, procedural law and evidence.[85] Whilst evidence law has a long-established academic standing, criminal procedure is not always included in the university curricula, as it is mainly regarded as of interest to practitioners alone. In comparison, an in-depth understanding of the sophisticated and technical features of the law of evidence is considered a most challenging intellectual endeavour for the English lawyer.

On the other side of the Channel, evidence law is exposed as a relatively small chapter of civil and criminal procedures, which are two of the most distinguished academic subjects in the syllabus of the French Faculties of Law. Both historical and technical reasons lie behind this state of affairs. As the Napoleonic Codes were silent on matters of evidence, the exegetical method of French jurisprudence led commentators to neglect a comprehensive analysis of the subject. Moreover, the principle of *liberté de la preuve* and its corollaries brought about an extensive deregulation. As a result, evidence is regarded there as a purely procedural topic. In recent years, an eminent French scholar described as 'incredible and shocking'[86] the scarce attention devoted to criminal evidence by domestic jurisprudence, while calling for the development of a general theory of the subject.

The Italian situation is peculiar. For almost two centuries, jurisprudence and academic curricula have followed the French tradition. As noted earlier in this chapter,[87] the new procedural Code now follows adversarial assumptions and includes a specific book on the law of evidence. Although the subject is not yet independently taught in the Italian Faculties of Law, all textbooks of criminal procedure are being restructured in order to address the increased relevance of the topic.[88]

---

85 Traditionally, English textbooks on evidence exposed the rules of both civil and criminal proceedings: see J.P. Taylor, *A Treatise on the Law of Evidence as Administered in England and Ireland: with Illustrations from the American and Other Foreign Laws*, Maxwell & son, London, 1848 and C. Tapper, *Cross and Tapper on Evidence*, 9th edn., Butterworths, London, 1999. More recently, criminal evidence has also been treated autonomously by A.A.S. Zuckerman, *The Principles of Criminal Evidence*, Clarendon, Oxford, 1989 and R. May, *Criminal Evidence*, 4th edn., Sweet & Maxwell, London, 1999.

86 According to M.L. Rassat, *Traité de Procédure Pénale*, *supra* note 22, §192 only an average 3% of the pages of French criminal procedure textbooks discuss matters of evidence law.

87 See above, section 3.2.3.

88 Cf. F. Cordero, *Procedura Penale*, *supra* note 77, 603-661, A. Nappi, *Guida al Codice di Procedura Penale*, 7th edn., Giuffrè, Milano, 2000. For a noteworthy contribution to the establishment of a general theory of criminal evidence see P. Tonini, *La Prova Penale*, 4th edn., Cedam, Padova, 2000.

3.3 Temporal Boundaries

It is now time to illustrate and justify the temporal and structural boundaries of this comparative study. Whilst it would be valuable to describe the features of French, English and Italian evidence laws in their historical development, this work exclusively deals with the present state of the law. References to past rules is provided only when it is essential to clarify the scope of the current provisions, or to elucidate the reasons for their latest amendments.

In the last few years, criminal evidence laws have undergone major changes in all the model countries, under the increased pressure of active legislators. This unifying phenomenon has several reasons. Firstly, there is the need to address the rising concern of the public opinion over the quality of the national administration of criminal justice. Secondly, compliance with the fair trial standards established under ECHR law must be strictly enforced. It is hardly surprising, therefore, that the newly amended version of Article 111 Italian Constitution includes an almost plain reproduction of Article 6 of the European Convention. On the other side of the Alps, in 2000 a statutory reform[89] repealed and amended more than 170 articles of the *Code de procedure pénale* and inserted more than 80 new ones, thus leading commentators to announce the birth of a new French criminal procedure.[90] Its foundation and emblem is the new *article préliminaire* to the Code, under which literally all main features of ECHR jurisprudence are referenced: equality of arms, impartiality of the judiciary, reasonable time requirement and right to an effective remedy against unlawful convictions.[91]

In England, commentators described reform movements in the 1990s, culminating with the coming into force of the *H.R.A. 1998*, as the most significant in 350 years.[92] Amongst the statutory reforms relevant to criminal procedure and evidence a mention is due to the *C.J.P.O. 1994*, that introduced some limitations to the accused' s right to silence, and *Y.J.C.E.A. 1999*, which was an attempt to modify orthodox trial arrangements so as to reduce the personal stress and risks of vulnerable and intimidated witnesses. Finally, on November 20, 2003, *C.J.A. 2003* received the Royal assent. The provisions of *C.J.A. 2003* entered into force in different stages, the last of which on April 5, 2005, in conjunction with the commencement of the newly enacted *Criminal Procedure Rules 2005*. *C.J.A. 2003* promotes fundamental changes to pre-trial process,

89 Law No. 516, 15 June 2000, entitled 'loi renforçant la protection de la présomption d'innocence et les droits des victimes'.

90 M. Delmas Marty, *Une Nouvelle Procédure Pénale – Présentation*, [2001] R.S.C. 3.

91 The implementation of these principles was achieved through the insertion of new articles, chapters and titles into the French Code of criminal procedure.

92 Lord Bingham, *A Criminal Code...*, *supra* note 81, 694.

including reforms to bail, charging and disclosure. It also revolutionises the phase of the trial, with changes to evidence procedures, double jeopardy, juries and appeals, and sentencing. Further, in an attempt to establish an 'inclusionary approach to evidence', the Acts makes amendments to the most preserved sanctuaries of the common law, namely hearsay[93] (*C.J.A. 2003*, ss. 114 to 136) and character (*C.J.A. 2003*, ss. 98 to 113) evidence.

3.4 Structural Boundaries

3.4.1 Serious Offences

The present study focuses on criminal proceedings for the most serious offences. This should not be interpreted as an underestimation of the importance of simplified or abbreviated forms of proceedings in contemporary litigation. If the ordinary rules governing the course of trials were to be applied without any derogation for all offences, national justice systems would most likely collapse. At present, not only is this true for adversarial jurisdictions, whose trials are costly and constitute only a small fragment of litigation, but also for inquisitorial ones. Endemic lack of resources require all European jurisdictions to contain the workload of the courts, in order to comply with the reasonable time requirement set forth in the European Convention. Even in Italy and France, recent legislation promotes forms of negotiated criminal justice as alternatives to prosecution.[94]

Two reasons justify my decision to limit the analysis to proceedings for serious offences. Firstly, they are those in which the full panoply of evidentiary rules applies. Simplified or abbreviated forms of trial tend to be characterised by less vigilant standards of protection of the accused's rights. Secondly, those proceedings are most accessible to the assessment – and criticism – of public opinion. Standard rules of procedure and evidence should therefore closely reflect the national assumptions concerning the manner in which justice is to be served and past occurrences should be established.

---

93 The English law of hearsay is considered in Chapter 6, with specific reference to the evidence of the absent witness.

94 For insights into the various forms of negotiated criminal justice in Italy see S. Maffei, *Negotiations 'on Evidence' and Negotiations 'on Sentence': Adversarial Experiments in Italian Criminal Procedure*, [2004] Journal Intl. Crim. Just. 1050-1069. In France, at the early stages of the investigation of the minor offences listed in Art. 41-2 F-CPP, the prosecutor may recommend the implementation of a panoply of restrictive measures, to which the suspect may agree in writing. Such an agreement (*composition pénale*) comes into effect once it is validated by the president of the local tribunal.

3.4.2 The Course of Litigation

Focus is on the entire course of criminal litigation, from the early collection of the *notitia criminis* until the moment in which the judgment of the court becomes final.[95] Instead, no notice is taken of the evidentiary issues pertaining to the phase of sentencing in the English criminal process.

The stage of preliminary investigation is relevant to the discussion of confrontational matters for several reasons. Firstly, it is at this point that parties locate potential witnesses and collect information on the reliability of their account and their personal credibility. This information is essential to perform an effective adverse-questioning[96] at the time of the court testimony. Secondly, out-of-court depositions to prosecutors and police may be put in evidence when the witness is unavailable for a court examination.[97] Thirdly, dedicated hearings may be set up at the investigation stage for the collection of the evidence of the vulnerable or anonymous informant.

Once preliminary investigations are concluded, English French and Italian prosecuting authorities are required to satisfy a court of justice of the existence of a prima facie case against the suspect, in order to secure his or her committal for trial. In Italy, committal proceedings are held in a camera hearing termed *udienza preliminare* by a single professional judge.[98] In France, the *mise en accusation* is pronounced by the *juge d'instruction* (Article 181 F-CPP) and may be challenged before the *Chambre de l'instruction*.[99] In England, following the coming into force of *C.D.A. 1998*, s. 51 committal proceedings have been abolished in the case of indictable only offences.[100] As a consequence, magistrates' courts (composed of a single district judge or three lay justices) may send the case to the Crown Court immediately after a brief preliminary hearing held

---

95 For the purpose of this work, a criminal judgment is final when no 'ordinary' instrument of appeal or review is allowed under national law. Final judgments are usually subject to further judicial review, in the case of a miscarriage of justice: see the procedure for 'revision' in France (Arts. 622 to 626 F-CPP) and Italy (Arts. 629 to 647 I-CPP). In England the Criminal Cases Review Commission may at any time refer a conviction to the Court of Appeal, pursuant to *C.A.A. 1995*, s. 9(1) if there is a 'real possibility that the conviction would not be upheld'.

96 See Chapter 1, section 3.2.6.

97 The category of the absent witness in English, French and Italian law is illustrated in Chapter 6, section 2.

98 Cf. Arts. 416 to 433 I-CPP.

99 Cf. Arts. 212 and 214 F-CPP. The *Chambre de l'instruction* consists of a panel of three professional judges. It may discontinue proceedings for three reasons: lack of factual basis, perpetrator unknown or insufficient evidence. In such cases, a decision *de non-lieu* (short term for: *il n'y a lieu a suivre*) is pronounced.

100 Instead, for the offences triable either way, committal proceedings before examining justices come in two variants: with (so called 'full committals', *M.C.A. 1980*, s. 5A) or without (*M.C.A. 1980*, s. 6(2)) consideration of evidence.

before them. Committal proceedings are relevant to confrontational discourse whenever testimonial evidence may be collected at this stage and later tendered before the trial courts.[101]

Chapter 6 will later show that the procedure for the collection of testimonial evidence at trials at first instance mostly conform to the 'confrontational paradigm' described in Chapter 1. For the purposes of this work, the phrase 'trial at first instance' includes the English trial[102] on indictment with a jury[103] and the Italian and French proceedings before the Assize Courts.[104] Readers should also be aware that although Assize Court trials account only for a limited number of serious crimes, their rules of procedure and evidence closely resemble those applied by district courts (*tribunals correctionnels* or *tribunali di primo grado*), before which offences of an intermediate gravity are tried.

All the criminal courts of first instance considered in this work incorporate lay people. Nevertheless, the allocation of roles and responsibilities of lay and professional magistrates makes juries of English courts inherently different from their continental counterparts. A comprehensive analysis of this topic falls beyond the scope of the present research and only a few indications can be provided hereinafter.[105] In France and Italy lay and professional judges constitute a single panel[106], presided over by one of the professionals. The president of the Assize Court has overall control of the hearing and enjoys several discretionary powers that grant him or her a specific leading role. At the closure of the trial, lay and professional judges retire together and deliberate on questions of both fact and law, and also pass the sentence if the accused is found guilty. It is traditionally argued that the professional judges may easily exert their authority when closeted with the lay jurors, and that their presence plays a major role in

---

101 See Chapter 6, section 2.1.2.

102 In England no trial takes place when the defendant pleads guilty to the counts on the indictment. As a consequence, cases of guilty pleas could be relevant to this work only in the rare circumstances in which the Court of Appeal grants leave of appeal; cf. *R. v. Forde*, [1923] 2 K.B. 400 (C.A.) 403 (Avory J.) or when the accused is allowed to withdraw its plea, before the sentence is passed: cf. *R. v. Plummer*, [1902] 2 K.B. 339 (C.C.C.R.).

103 Pursuant to *C.J.A. 2003*, ss. 43-47, defendants in English criminal proceedings will soon be deprived of their traditional right to a trial by jury in the case of indictable offences. Under the terms of such provisions, the prosecution may apply to a judge of a Crown Court for the trial on indictment to be conducted without a jury in certain fraud cases and also where there appears to be a danger of jury tampering.

104 Governed respectively by Arts. 465 to 548 I-CPP and Arts. 231 to 380-15 F-CPP.

105 For comparative discussion of lay participation in criminal proceedings see R. Munday, *Réflexions Historiques et Comparatives sur le Procès par Jury*, in P. Legrand (ed.), *Common Law d'un Siecle à l'Autre*, Blais, Cowansville, 1992, 493-528 and S.C. Thaman, *The Lay Participation in the Criminal Trial in the XXIst Century*, (2001) 72 R.I.D.P. 19-23.

106 Assize Courts consist of a panel of 12 judges (9 lay, 3 professionals) in France, and 8 judges (6 lay, 2 pros) in Italy.

the deliberation.[107] As far as English law is concerned, the basic rule is that the judge resolves questions of law while the jury only addresses questions of fact. During trial, the jury plays an almost entirely passive role[108] while the judge acts as the umpire of the contest between the opposing parties and the guarantor of fairness to the defendant. In the summing up, it is the duty of the judge to instruct the jury in all matters of law. It is also settled that juries must accept these directions as correct. Conversely, juries remain sovereign as for the determination of any disputed fact.

Unreasoned verdicts are given by English Crown Courts[109] and French Assize Courts. The opposite applies in Italy because Article 111(6) of the Constitution requires all criminal courts to give reasoned judgments. In comparison, in England reasons are provided only by Appeal Courts and the House of Lords. Any attempt to obtain, disclose or solicit any particulars of statements made, opinion expressed, arguments advanced or votes cast by members of the jury sequestered for deliberation amounts to contempt of court.[110] As far as the French system is concerned, analysis of court reasoning is even more limited, given that also appellate judgements of the Assize Courts are delivered in the form of unreasoned verdicts. To ensure secrecy, all ballots cast for the decision of matters of fact, law or sentence are immediately burnt.[111] In France, thus, criminal judges' opinions with regard to the most serious offences[112] are only available in the judgements of the Supreme Court (*Cour de Cassation*).

Considerable differences among the model countries exist in relation to the procedure for appealing against a criminal judgment. Parties to the criminal trials before the Assize Courts in Italy and France[113] are always entitled to an appeal as long as they apply for it within certain time limits. As a consequence, appeal proceedings take place against most judgments as a matter of routine. In

---

107 F. Lombard, *Les Jurés: Justice Représentative et Représentation de la Justice*, L'Harmattan, Paris, 1993.

108 Members of English juries may also exceptionally question the witness: see Chapter 5, section 3.3.1.

109 Since the *H.R.A. 1998* came into force, English magistrate courts adjusted their practice to the official guidance of the Lord Chancellor and began to give oral reasons for their decisions. The Crown Court is also expected to state reasons when it dismisses a defendant's appeal from the magistrate courts: cf. *R. v. Harrow Crown Court, ex p. Dave*, [1994] 1 W.L.R. 98 (Q.B.D.). As explained above, however, this study only considers trials on indictment with a jury before the Crown Court, in which an unreasoned verdict is pronounced.

110 *Contempt of Court Act 1981*, s. 8.

111 Art. 358(3) F-CPP.

112 Reasons must also be provided in criminal judgements by Italian tribunals and Courts of appeal.

113 In France, appeal against Assize Courts verdicts was introduced only in 2000 (Arts. 380-1 to 380-15 F-CPP, as inserted by Art. 81, Law No. 516/2000), as a result of the increasing pressure of ECHR law. For discussion see F. Doroy, *Le Réexamen d'une Décision Pénale Consécutif au Pronuncé d'un Arrêt de Condamnation de la CEDH Mise en œuvre de la Réforme du 15 Juin 2000: Questions Juridiques et Problèmes Pratiques*, [2003-6] Droit Penal n°18.

England, the traditional rule was that only convictions, yet not acquittals, could be challenged in appeal. Those convicted before the English Crown Court must obtain leave to appeal by a single judge or, if he or she refuses it, the full Court. It has been calculated that the appeal rate of those convicted in the Crown Court after pleading not guilty is about 1 in 10.[114] Matters have been revolutionised by the entry into force, in April 2005, of *C.J.A. 2003*, ss. 75 to 97 according to which the prosecution may also apply to the Court of Appeal for an order quashing a person's acquittal, when new and compelling evidence emerges and a retrial appears to be in the interest of justice.

Furthermore, the very underlying features and nature of appellate proceedings differ sharply in the jurisdiction under scrutiny. Italian and French trials in appeal may involve a reconsideration of all factual matters, since courts in these jurisdictions may review questions of both law and fact. Some limitations to the admission of fresh evidence apply but the Court of Appeal is entitled to reverse judgments purely on the basis of a different evaluation of the very same evidence tendered before courts of first instance. Defendants may therefore be convicted by the Court of Appeal, although they had been acquitted at the trial at first instance. In comparison, the English Court of Appeal deals exclusively with matters of law and its main task (except for the aforementioned cases under *C.J.A. 2003*) is to quash 'unsafe' convictions[115] and order a retrial in the cases prescribed by the law.

As for the compositions of appeal courts, further differences emerge. While the English Court of Appeal is duly constituted by three professional judges,[116] Italy and France maintain the employment of a panel of lay and professional magistrates. To be more accurate, the Italian model based on the establishment of an autonomous judicial body named *Corte d'assise d'appello*[117] was not followed by the recent French statutory reform. The new amended version of Article 380-14 of the French Code, in fact, establishes a rotating system[118] whereby appellate proceedings are held before an ordinary Assize Court, different from the one

---

[114] A. Saunders and R. Young, *Criminal Justice*, 2nd edn., Butterworths, London, 2000, 634.

[115] *C.A.A. 1968*, s. 2(1), as amended by *C.A.A. 1995*. Matters which are capable of rendering a conviction unsafe typically include a wrong decision on the admissibility of evidence, irregularities during the course of the trial, errors in the summing up, misconduct of the trial judge, errors by defence counsel.

[116] Albeit very rare, it is possible that a Court of the Criminal Division of the Court of Appeal numbers more than three judges, when an extraordinary important case is dealt with (cf. *R. v. Turnbull*, [1977] Q.B. 224 (C.A.)) or there have been prior conflicting decisions on the matters raised on appeal (*R. v. Newsome*, [1970] 2 Q.B. 711 (C.A.)).

[117] Its composition is identical to the Assize Court of first instance (2 pros, 6 lay judges).

[118] Sharp criticism of the 'rotating' system has been expressed by those who subscribe to the view that appeals should always be held before a formally superior court of justice: cf. W. Roumier, *Pour en Finir avec un Réforme Inachevée: à Propos de l'Appel des Décisions en Matière Criminelle*, [2003-10] Droit Penal n°28.

that pronounced the verdict at first instance.[119] It is for the *Cour de Cassation* to designate which Assize Court is competent for the appeal on a case by case basis.[120]

Finally, an application for review on grounds of law may also be filed to the national Supreme courts (i.e. House of Lords, *Cour de Cassation, Corte di Cassazione*). All the judgments of such Courts are accompanied by written reasons.

4 English, French and Italian Criminal Evidence Law

After these introductory and methodological remarks on France, Italy and the United Kingdom, this book now turns its attention to a few general features of domestic evidence law. Readers should be aware that wide-ranging procedural analysis is far beyond the scope of the present work. Only a few topics that lie at the very heart of the law of evidence are considered, in the light of their influence on testimony and confrontation.

At the outset, it is worth noticing that it is extremely difficult to make any general statement regarding evidence law that is entirely correct. Under the three jurisdictions covered by this study, the subject is intermingled with derogations, exceptions and adjustments to all general principles. Sometimes, discussion of such principles could even be misleading, since certain ingrained formulas (such as orality, immediacy, directness) may serve multiple or even antagonistic purposes. Italy, France and England are also far from being monolithic societies: a variety of opposite views are subscribed to and promoted by commentators of different ideological and political background. Hence, in relation to key issues there are conflicting opinions about what the legal rules are and should be. In Italy, for instance, a rather simple matter such as the right of the defendant to cross-examine adverse witnesses in person is still unsettled, and it is far from clear whether the defendant is actually entitled to do so, or not.[121] As the analysis goes more and more in depth, the complexity of domestic legal discourse will gradually emerge.

4.1 What 'Evidence' Means

English, French and Italian discourses agree on a preliminary point of departure: evidence 'of a fact is that which tends to prove it – something which may satisfy an inquirer into the fact's existence'[122]; evidence is 'every ele-

---

[119] In appeal, nevertheless, French Assize Courts consist of an enlarged panel of 15 judges (3 pros., 12 lay).

[120] For critical views, see H. Temime, *L'Appel des Arrêt d'Assises*, [2001] R.S.C. 53-85, J. Pradel, *L'Appel contre les Arrêt d'Assises: un Apport Heureux de la Loi du 15 Juin 2000*, [2001] D. Chron. 1964, 1970.

[121] See Chapter 5, section 3.3.1.

[122] C. Tapper, *Cross and Tapper on Evidence, supra* note 85, 1.

ment on which a judge may ground the assessment as to the existence or non existence of a given fact, or the truth or falsity of a proposition';[123] evidence is 'any material or immaterial entity capable of establishing a demonstrative link with another entity'.[124] Inherent to these propositions is the assumption that evidence is a *means*[125] for the establishment of the truth of an assertion. Consequently, evidence law is seen as the subject that governs the judicial administration of any element from which some inference can be drawn upon a fact at issue.

It is then for *national* laws of evidence to select *which* elements (collected either at trial or out-of-court) may be employed as evidence of *which* specific facts. These matters are indeed the cause of profound divergences. In adversarial discourse, the term 'evidence' usually describes the statements of testifying witnesses. A perception exists that evidence is exclusively what is said in the courtroom, before the judge and jury. Information gathered at a pre-trial stage may well influence the determination and strategies of the parties, but is in principle no evidence for the jury. In the inquisitorial world, in comparison, the term evidence (*proof, prova*) refers both to the findings of the investigation and the trial depositions of witnesses. An opposing assumption stands that these elements may equally contribute to the pursuance of the truth. The implication of this difference in matters of testimonial evidence will become apparent as discussion unfolds in the following sections.

It must also be said that in England, France and Italy, as in most of the systems of the world, the burden of proof in criminal proceedings is on the prosecution. Indeed, before Article 6(2) of the Convention declared the presumption of innocence a cardinal principle of 'European' criminal law, most Member States' legal orders had already acknowledged it. While the presumption of innocence finds its authority in constitutional provisions in Italy and France,[126] in England it has been established by the House of Lords by means of the landmark metaphor of the 'golden thread throughout the web'[127] of the history of criminal law. Legal discourse on the corollaries of the presumption of innocence has autonomously developed and reached independent conclusions in the three jurisdictions under investigation. The presumption of innocence draws upon

[123] R. Merle and A. Vitu, *Traité de Droit Criminel – Procédure Pénale*, 5th edn., Cujas, Paris, 2001, 177.

[124] A Melchionda, *Prova (Diritto Processuale Penale)*, in *Enciclopedia del Diritto*, Giuffrè, Milano, 1988, vol. XXXVII, 650.

[125] *'Dans tous les cas la preuve est un moyen pour une fin'*; J. Bentham, *Traité des Preuves Judiciaires*, 2nd edn., Paris, 1830, vol. I, 17.

[126] Contrast the slightly different phrasing of Art. 27(2) I-CONST ('L'imputato non è considerato colpevole sino alla condanna definitiva') and Art. 9 Dècl. Droits Homme ('Tout homme étant présumé innocent jusqu'à ce qu'il ait été déclaré coupable').

[127] *Woolmington v. D.P.P.*, [1935] A.C. 462 (H.L.) 481.

various matters of criminal evidence and procedure. It has major consequences for the treatment of the accused pending proceedings against him: pre-trial detention, for instance, cannot have a punitive character and any detention on remand must comply with Article 5 of the Convention. For the purposes of this work, however, the presumption of innocence is central insofar as it suggests that any doubt concerning the prosecution case should benefit the accused. This explains why, when confrontational testimonial evidence is either not available or inadequate to support a case against the defendant, the non-confrontational depositions of absent, anonymous and vulnerable witnesses become so absolutely vital for the prosecution office.

4.2 Judicial Fairness

Article 6 of the Convention binds the European jurisdictions to ensure a fair criminal trial. As far as evidentiary matters are concerned, fairness calls for the respect of defence rights in the procedural collection of what may be used as a basis for an adverse judgment. In the first place, therefore, fairness is a criterion to be followed in the *establishment* of domestic evidence law by national law makers.

It is far more complex to assess whether fairness may also constitute a standard for the judicial *interpretation* of domestic evidence laws. The question to be answered here is whether domestic courts may legitimately refer to 'fairness' as an independent ground for excluding evidence adverse to the defendant.

It is a firmly established principle that at common law a judge has a discretion to exclude evidence if it is necessary in order to secure a fair criminal trial.[128] In England, the common law discretion has been buttressed by *P.A.C.E. 1984*, s. 78(1). Although at the time of its coming into force some case law suggested that the section did 'no more than restate'[129] the power which judges had at common law, it is now settled that its introduction has led to a significant broadening of the area of courts' discretion.[130] Under this provision, a court may

[128] *R. v. Christie*, [1914] A.C. 545 (H.L.). This discretion had two separate features. On the one hand, it provided for the exclusion of evidence that bears a prejudicial effect outweighing its probative value (*Noor Mohammed v. King*, [1949] A.C. 182 (P.C. British Guyana); *Harris v. D.P.P.*, [1952] A.C. 694 (H.L.); *Selvey v. D.P.P.*, [1970] A.C. 304 (H.L.)). On the other hand, it excluded improperly obtained evidence. This aspect was traditionally meant to put a limit on the English principle that the method by which the evidence was secured was generally irrelevant to its admissibility. This principle has been expressed in the oft-quoted words of Justice Crompton, in *R. v. Leatham*, (1861) 8 Cox C.C. 498, 501: 'It matters not how you get it; if you steal it even, it would be admissible in evidence'. The U.S. and other jurisdictions follow an opposite rule: for a comparative overview see S. Kines, *Why Suppress the Truth? U.S., Canadian and English Approaches to the Exclusion of Illegally Obtained Real Evidence in Criminal Cases*, [1996-2] R.P. 147-162.

[129] *R. v. Mason*, [1988] 1 W.L.R. 139 (C.A.) 144 (L.J. Watkins).

[130] *Matto v. D.P.P.*, [1987] R.T.R. 337 (D.C.) 346 (L.J. Woolf).

refuse to allow *any* evidence on which the prosecution proposes to rely if 'having regard to all circumstances of the case, including the circumstances in which the evidence was obtained, the admission of the evidence would have such an adverse effect on the fairness of the proceedings that the court ought not to admit it'. In practice, counsel raise numerous questions of unfairness before English courts and the provision in question is one of the most often referred to in criminal litigation. Discretion has been used in relation to a wide range of items of improperly obtained evidence, in the attempt to ensure the integrity of the criminal process.[131] By way of illustration, it may lead to the exclusion of confessions[132] as well as depositions of absent witnesses,[133] identification evidence,[134] co-defendant's pleas of guilty[135] and evidence obtained from an illegal search.[136] It must also be recalled that, in England, assessment of 'fairness' or the mere 'appearance of fairness' is often included among the criteria to be taken into account by the judge, when he is required to exercise judicial discretion in other evidentiary and procedural matters. Chapter 5 will later disclose that this also applies to the treatment of anonymous informants.

In France, findings of the preliminary investigation can only be excluded from the dossier when a nullity applies. A nullity is textual when the law explicitly establishes this sanction for the failure to comply with a specified formality. Conversely, a nullity is named 'virtual'[137] when it is left to the judge to appreciate the consequences of a procedural violation. In these comparatively few cases, the French judiciary has sometimes referred to the concept of *loyauté* (fairness) in order to exclude elements collected out-of-court, especially when the adjudication process of such elements originated from a criminal offence.[138] Nonetheless, the Supreme Court is generally 'reluctant to acquit convicted persons and disregard the truth in favour of unwritten principles whose exact definition is questionable'.[139] In practice, the majority of relevant cases refer to illegitimate

---

131 See generally P. Mirfield, *Silence, Confessions and Improperly Obtained Evidence*, Clarendon, Oxford, 1997.

132 It is approved practice to challenge confessions collected at the investigation stage under *P.A.C.E. 1984*, s. 76 and s. 78 in the alternative. Most of the section 78 cases involve allege breaches of the provisions of Code C (the Code of Practice for the Detention, Treatment and Questioning of Persons by Police Officers), according to which police should make contemporaneous and accurate recordings of the words spoken by a suspect in interview (the so called 'verballing' provisions); cf. *R. v. Keenan*, [1990] 2 Q.B. 54 (C.A.).

133 *R. v. O'Loughlin*, [1988] 3 All E.R. 431 (C.C.C.).

134 *R. v. Beveridge*, (1987) 85 Cr. App. R. 255 (C.A.); *R. v. Deenik*, [1992] Crim. L.R. 578 (C.A.).

135 *R. v. O'Connor*, (1987) 85 Cr. App. R. 298 (C.A.).

136 *R. v. Sultan Khan*, [1997] A.C. 558 (H.L.).

137 M.L. Rassat, *Traité de Procédure Pénale*, *supra* note 22, §433, cf. Art. 802 F-CPP.

138 (F) Paris Chambre acc., 26 April 1990, X., [1991-II] J.C.P. n°21704; (F) Cass. crim., 28 October 1991, *Bull. crim.* n°381, Tournier.

139 H. Leclerc, *Les Limites de la Liberté de la Preuve – Aspects Actuels en France*, [1992] R.S.C. 17; see also L. Raison Rebufat, *Le Principe de Loyauté en Droit de la Preuve*, [2002] Gaz. Pal. Doct. 1195.

searches and seizures, not testimonies. Besides, case law exclusively applies the standard of fairness to information gathered by public authorities, claiming that it is only they who carry a duty of *loyauté* towards the accused. Hence, evidence collected by witnesses and civil parties unfairly[140] or illegitimately[141] may well be employed in the final judgment, provided that it has been promptly disclosed to the defence counsel. This state of affairs raises serious concerns,[142] insofar as it could lead public authorities to circumvent strict procedural provisions by exploiting the actions of private citizens.

In Italy, there is hardly any place for the assessment of fairness as such on the part of criminal courts.[143] The law of evidence, in fact, is strictly governed by the rules of the Code of criminal procedure. Evidence adverse to the accused may thus be excluded only under statutory provisions that explicitly deem certain items of evidence 'non-usable', pursuant to Article 191 of the Code.[144]

4.3 Orality

A superior principle of orality (or directness) is said to inspire English, French and Italian criminal procedure.[145] In broad terms, such a principle reflects the preference for oral discussion between parties at the public hearing and the employment in evidence of oral statements rather than written depositions collected at earlier stages. Strange as it my sound, the concept of orality is of little use to this comparative research, since it is construed differently in the model countries so as to serve conflicting legal purposes.

In the adversarial variant, admissible evidence is limited to what witnesses report orally at the hearing, before the court and parties. Information on the case is adduced almost solely through the evidence of witnesses. The principle of

---

[140] In relation to secret recordings of private conversations, cf. (F) Cass. crim., 11 February 1992, *Bull. crim.* n°66, X.; (F) Cass. crim., 6 April 1993, J.-L. T., [1993-II] J.C.P. n°22144.

[141] (F) Cass. Crim., 30 March 1999, *Bull. crim.* n°59, X., (stolen documents); (F) Cass. crim., 15 June 1993, *Bull. crim.* n°210, X. (professional misconduct).

[142] M.L. Rassat, *Traité de Procédure Pénale, supra* note 22, §214.

[143] The small reservation concerns evidence for which no rule can be found in the procedural Code. Under Art. 189 I-CPP, the court may admit such evidence if (1) it is relevant and (2) it does not affect the 'moral freedom' of the individual concerned.

[144] Analysis of the major exclusionary rules in Italian criminal procedure is provided below, section 4.4.

[145] The 'most important feature of an English trial, civil or criminal, has been its orality', cf. C. Tapper, *Cross and Tapper on Evidence, supra* note 85, 263. In France, the Supreme Court held that 'the principle of an oral hearing bases and dominates the procedure before the Assize Courts, and prevails even over the discretionary powers of its president': cf. (F) Cass. crim., 8 November 1934, *D.* 1935, *Juris.* 7. Earlier authorities are (F) Cass. crim., 6 April 1894, *D.* 1898.1.284 and (F) Cass. crim., 19 March 1896, X., *Bull. crim.* n°107. In Italy, the 1987 delegating statute for the enactment of the new Code of criminal procedure mentioned the implementation of the 'oral method' as the underlying feature of the reform.

orality is thus the ultimate foundation of exclusionary rules concerning information that has been collected unilaterally by the parties before trial. In comparison, in the inquisitorial variant, orality merely calls for a 'live opportunity' for oral discussion between the parties on the evidence assembled in the court dossier. Information gathered by prosecuting authorities counts as evidence, insofar as the defence enjoys the opportunity to comment upon it before the court. It is essential to understand that this chance of an open discussion may be of little use to the defence, since the court can still rely either on oral evidence or on pre-trial information. In theory, prior depositions of witnesses are treated in opposite ways under the two variants. In adversarial discourse they are inadmissible as evidence of the facts they state and may only serve the purpose of impeachment. In the inquisitorial world they are fully admissible, provided that certain formalities had been respected at the time of collection and the defence enjoys the opportunity to comment upon them.

This theoretical framework, however, does not truly represent the current state of national laws. Even in England and Italy, in fact, prior statements of witnesses may count as evidence on many occasions, as evidence of the fact they state. In England, devotion to orality traditionally resulted in the limitation of the evidentiary value of pre-trial depositions. Such depositions fall within the ambit of the doctrine of hearsay, and they ought not to be relied upon as evidence of the fact they state, unless a statutory or common exception to the rule applies. The analogous 'rule against narrative' also excluded the previous statements of witnesses who take the stand, except for the purpose of impeachment. The traditional assumption was that oral presentation of evidence alone ensured a fair assessment of the case on the part of the jurors.[146] It remains to be seen whether these assumptions will still permeate the procedure after the entry force – occurred in April 2005 – of the relevant provisions of *C.J.A. 2003*. The Act, in fact, promotes an inclusive approach to hearsay evidence and makes prior inconsistent statements of witnesses routinely admissible in criminal proceedings.[147] In Italy, prior statements may be used in evidence if it is proved that the court declarant had been intimidated or bribed to give a false oral testimony (Article 500(4) I-CPP) or when unpredictable circumstances make it absolutely impossible to obtain a court testimony (Article 512 I-CPP).

More discussion on this topic is provided in Chapter 5, with reference to the use of prior inconsistent statements in evidence, and Chapter 6, with regard to the prior depositions of the 'absent witness'.

---

[146] *Butera v. D.P.P.*, (1987) 164 C.L.R. 180 (H.C.-Aus.) 189.

[147] *C.J.A. 2003*, s. 119. In civil proceedings, the exclusionary rule for hearsay evidence had already been repealed by C.E.A. 1995, s 1, following the recommendations of Law Commission, *The Hearsay Rule in Civil Proceedings* (Law Com. No. 216, 1993).

4.3.1 The Finding of the Investigation Before the Court

While English juries know nothing of the findings of the investigation, French courts are fully aware of them. In comparison, Italian courts have only a limited access to the information gathered by the parties before the trial.

In line with adversarial assumptions, English judges and jurors enter the courtroom innocent of what happened at the investigation stage. Previous knowledge of circumstances relevant to the case, even if only through press reports of a discreditable nature towards the defendant,[148] amounts to a legitimate ground for challenging a juror. Prior knowledge of the case is perceived as prejudicial to the accused and, more broadly, as a threat to procedural fairness. This being said, the jury receives the very first account of events from the clerk, who reads the indictment and the plea of innocence at the opening of the trial. If the defendant pleaded guilty to other counts on the same indictment, his or her guilty pleas ought not be disclosed to the jury.

In France, pre-trial investigations are split in two phases: the *enquête*[149] of the police and the *instruction*, directed by the *juge d'instruction* (examining magistrate). The dividing line between the two is marked by the prosecutor's decision to prosecute, which confers on the suspect the status of *personne mise en examen* and commands his or her referral before the examining magistrate. Different procedural formalities and guarantees apply to the two phases of the investigations.[150] Nevertheless, all documents and depositions collected by the police and examining magistrate must be assembled in the dossier for the trial court. As anticipated earlier, exclusions may only result from a ruling of material or virtual nullity by the *Chambre de l'instruction.*[151] For the purposes of the present work, it is useful to underline that the court dossier normally includes the depositions of each and every informant interviewed by the police and the examining magistrate. In the case of a later committal for trial, the dossier is sent to the president of the Assize Court who is required by law to read and study it carefully.

Italian law is based on the compilation of two separate dossiers. All the findings of the preliminary investigations (and committal proceedings) must be

---

[148] *R. v. Kray*, (1969) 53 Cr. App. R. 412 (C.C.C.).

[149] The *enquête* may take two different forms: the *enquête preliminaire* (Arts. 75 to 78 F-CPP) and *enquête de flagrance* (Arts. 53 to 74 F-CPP).

[150] For instance, all acts of *instruction* must be reported in the solemn form of a *procès verbal*, written by the *greffier* and signed by the examining magistrate Accompanying provisions of the French Code set forth very precise rules for the filing and management of documents within the *dossier*, pursuant to Arts. C-143 to C-164 F-CPP.

[151] Parties or the examining magistrate must seek the ruling of the *Chambre de l'instruction* on matters of nullities, since the court cannot intervene *ex officio*.

placed either in the 'court dossier' or the 'prosecution dossier'.[152] The law sets rigorous limits on what may be included in the 'court dossier', since such items count as evidence at trial.[153] All residual findings, including the depositions of informants to the police, prosecution and counsel, are placed in the 'prosecution dossier'. This is only available for consultation by the parties and ought not to be disclosed to the court. The general rule is that a criminal court may base its judgment on both oral evidence and readings of the 'court dossier'. Strict exclusionary rules govern the circumstances in which findings of the prosecution dossier can be transferred in the court dossier, and they will be discussed in more detail in Chapters 5 and 6.

4.3.2 The National Variants of Adversarial Adjudication

It is now time to investigate the true meaning of the terms 'adversarial', *contradictoire* and *contraddittorio* within English, French and Italian law. Far from being translations of one identical legal concept,[154] these terms reveal the beauty of diversity of domestic criminal practice.

The article *preliminaire* to the French Code of criminal procedure does not hand over the inquisitorial tradition when it states that *'la procédure pénale doit être ... contradictoire'*. In essence, this principle – which is described as absolutely fundamental[155] to the criminal proceeding of a democratic society – only calls for the establishment of certain procedural guarantees to the defendant and counsel in the process of evidence adjudication. When French commentators say that the 'hearing must be oral', they convey the idea that the accused and counsel must be given the opportunity to argue and challenge the reliability of all evidence presented to the court. The main implications of the principle are twofold. Firstly, parties should be promptly informed as to the content of the documents and findings that the opposing party seeks to bring to the court's attention. Secondly, they must enjoy adequate time to advance arguments as to the probative force of the admissible evidence. Instead, the *principe du contradictoire* does *not* relinquish the inquisitorial idea that pre-trial materials (including, for the purposes of this work, all previous depositions of informants and witnesses) are indeed admissible evidence.

---

[152] This legal terminology is loose: the 'prosecution dossier' should rather be termed 'investigation dossier', since it also includes the findings of the defence investigations.

[153] By virtue of Art. 431 I-CPP, the court dossier includes the defendant's criminal record, items of real evidence, reports of searches and seizures, evidence collected abroad on commission, transcripts of intercepted communications and conversations and evidence collected at the *incidente probatorio*.

[154] For discussion see J.R. Spencer, *Introduction*, in M. Delmas-Marty and J.R. Spencer (eds), *European Criminal Procedures*, Cambrige Univ. Press, Cambridge, 2002, 1, 45-46.

[155] P. Nicolopoulos, *La Procédure devant les Juridictions Répressives et le Principe du Contradictoire*, [1989] R.S.C. 1-26.

The Italian and English approaches to *contraddittorio* and 'adversarial proceeding' are based upon a completely different assumption. I repeat that in those systems the general rule, albeit intermingled with exceptions and derogations, is that admissible evidence is only what is said at the hearing by testifying witnesses. Readers from a continental background would expect this principle to constitute the opening statement of any discourse on criminal evidence and procedure. This is precisely the case in Italy, where Article 111(4) of the Constitution now declares that the criminal process of evidence adjudication is governed by the *principio del contraddittorio.* In comparison, English law is traditionally short on public announcements of principles.[156] When discussing the law, English commentators take orality for granted and only briefly refer to it when encountering its exceptions.

This being said, it must also be acknowledged that both the English and Italian criminal systems are prepared to allow numerous departures from the process of adversarial adjudication. Contrary to French practice, nevertheless, a perception stands that admissibility in evidence of pre-trial depositions ought to be the exception, not the rule. In Italy the matter is now governed by Article 111(5) of the Constitution. Pursuant to this provision the procedure of evidence adjudication may deviate from adversarial assumptions only (a) when the defendant consents to such deviation, (b) in the case of proved misconduct (e.g. threats or violence against a witnesses to keep him or her away from the courtroom), or (c) when an 'objective impossibility' prevents the collection of oral evidence at trial. In England, this field of the law has been governed for centuries by the idea that out-of-court statements of witnesses were hearsay, and therefore they were inadmissible to prove the matter stated therein, although the hearsay rule has always been subject to multiple penetrating exceptions. Seismic changes to this area of the law, however, have resulted from the coming into force of *C.J.A. 2003*: the Act has adopted an inclusive approach to hearsay evidence (*C.J.A. 2003*, s 114) and has also made prior inconsistent statements of witnesses admissible evidence of any matter stated (*C.J.A. 2003*, s. 119).

4.4 Exclusionary Rules of Evidence

This section briefly considers whether and how exclusionary rules of evidence operate at the stage of trial under French, English and Italian law.

In France, the topic may easily be resolved by reference to the principle of the *liberté de la preuve* (freedom of evidence).[157] The statutory basis of this principle is Article 427 of the Code, according to which a criminal offence may be

[156] J.R. Spencer, *The English System*, in M. Delmas-Marty and J.R. Spencer (eds.), *European Criminal Procedures*, *supra* note 154, 142, 145.

[157] For discussion, cf. H. Leclerc, *Les Limites de la Liberté...*, *supra* note 139, 15-29.

proved by 'any means of proof'.[158] For the purposes of this work, the principle in question has one major implication: the only condition for the admissibility of evidence is that statutory requirements concerning its collection have been respected and parties had been given a chance to comment upon it, as explained in the previous section. Had these procedural formalities been complied with, fairness is automatically ensured. No further exclusionary rules of evidence may put straitjackets upon the *intime conviction* (free will) of a court of justice.[159]

Matters are much more intricate in England and Italy, where some exclusionary rules operate in accordance with adversarial assumptions. These exclusionary rules apply notwithstanding the fact that the information in question *could easily be* or *had in fact been* brought to the attention of the courts and offered for oral discussion to the adverse party. The topic lies at the very centre of the logic of adversarial proceedings: certain evidence must be excluded simply because it is has not been presented orally at trial. As a matter of fact, discussion of the rationale of exclusionary rules remains one of the most fascinating and debatable chapters of evidence law. It is agreed that most of such rules were originally inspired by the objective of enhancing the accuracy of the fact-finding process. It is far more difficult to agree on whether, in practice, this purpose was achieved or, rather, the actual outcome had been to skew it. In order to fully appreciate their purposes, exclusionary rules may be separated into various categories.[160] Firstly, there are rules that exclude slightly probative items of proof. Secondly, some other rules exclude evidence that could be overestimated by the fact-finder (typically, hearsay), on the implied assumption of some kind of cognitive inability on his or her part. Thirdly, certain provisions ban some evidence on the basis that its probative value could be overshadowed by its prejudicial capacity (typically, similar fact evidence), thus predisposing the fact finder to a guilty verdict. Later on, Chapter 5, section 3.3.2 will discuss the details of Italian and English exclusionary rules[161] with specific reference to the testimony of witnesses.[162]

At this stage, a further theoretical distinction should be made. On the one hand, exclusionary rules may be construed so as to *prevent* the disclosure of

---

[158] Although Article 427 F-CPP formally refers only to the procedure before the district courts, the principle is of universal application: P. Conte and P. Maistre Du Chambon, *Procédure Pénale, supra* note 22, §48; M.L. Rassat, *Traité..., supra* note 22, §209.

[159] See below, section 4.5.

[160] These subdivisions are suggested by M.R. Damaška, *Evidence Law Adrift*, Yale Univ. Press, New Haven, 1997, 12-15. Damaška's approach is reviewed and challenged by R.D. Friedman, *Anchors and Flotsam: Is Evidence Law "Adrift"?*, (1988) 107 Yale L.J. 1921-1967.

[161] The traditional English exclusionary rules have been recently amended by *C.J.A. 2003*.

[162] For comparative discussion see J.R. Spencer, *Les Limites en Matière de Preuve – Aspects actuels*, [1992] R.S.C. 42-51 and M Chiavario, *Limites en Matière de Preuve dans la Nouvelle Procédure Pénale Italienne*, [1992] R.S.C. 30-41.

evidentiary material upon which courts are not allowed to rely. The parties are the main recipients of these rules which state what can, and cannot, be presented to the court. If these rules operate properly,[163] the fact finder will sit and deliberate while innocent of any 'non-usable' piece of information information. Common law exclusionary rules tend to be construed in such a way. This feature fits with the presence of the jury as trier of the fact and, furthermore, with the fact that juries give unreasoned verdict. These rules must be enforced promptly by the trial judge, who is in charge of bringing the parties' clashes over questions of admissibility to an end. In this context, inadmissible evidence should not reach the ears of jurors, since they would not be able to disregard it at the time of delivering the verdict. It is precisely for this reason that the ordinary examination of witness is subject to a great deal of interruptions, as it will be shown in Chapter 5, section 3.3.

On the other hand, exclusionary rules may consist of *prohibitions* against the use of certain items of proof that have been offered for consideration to the courts. Here, the rules pose not only a legal but also a moral obligation upon the courts: they must proceed as these non-usable items of proof had never been presented to them. In Italy, this model prevails. Explicit provisions of the Code establish when the evidence is non-usable and any improper reference to non-usable evidence in a court ruling is a legitimate ground for appeal to the Court of Appeal or for judicial review before the Supreme Court.[164] As anticipated, non-usable evidence may well be presented to the Italian criminal courts but it is their duty to discard it. The exclusionary rule concerning hearsay pursuant to Article 195 of the Code, for instance, bans the use in evidence of certain types of oral hearsay but does not prevent the hearsay statements from being made. Although no reference to non-usable hearsay evidence is likely to be made in a criminal judgment, nevertheless some doubts may remain over the influence that such evidence may have played, either consciously or unconsciously, in the mind of the fact-finder.

4.5 Principles of Evidence Evaluation

Matters of evidence evaluation are the cause of some deal of confusion. Readers may be tempted to believe that each case turns on its own facts and no theoretical speculation is profitable. Although this may be partially true, two common principles put some certainty to this topic. They equally apply to English, French and Italian law.

Firstly, no official hierarchy or ranking of evidence sources exists: all admissible means of proof have a potential decisive value and thus may legitimately

[163] When English exclusionary rule fail to operate, the judge would either direct the jury to disregard the evidence or call for a mistrial, see Chapter 5.

[164] Art. 606(1)(c) I-CPP.

ground a conviction. Nowhere it is stated or implied, for instance, that expert evidence should be relied upon more than any other testimony, or that a series of concurring testimonies should necessarily count more than a single one. This principle admits of two sets of minor exceptions that, in any case, must be established explicitly by national law. On the one hand, domestic laws may attach a diminished probative value to some evidence in view of their presumed unreliability, thus requiring corroboration.[165] On the other hand, certain items of proof may be relied upon by preference, until they are formally disproved or their falsity is judicially established.[166]

Secondly, there is no specific evidence that can bind a judge or a jury to convict a defendant. Under the forms of trial considered by the present research, courts can convict an accused person only when they are intimately convinced of his of her culpability. A more difficult problem is to determine what level of certainty is to be reached. The formulas of English ('beyond reasonable doubt'), French (*intime conviction*) and Italian (*libero convincimento*) law have independent historical origins but it is questionable whether they actually mean different things at all.

The 'beyond reasonable doubt' standard was developed by common law courts during the 17th and 18th centuries with a view to setting the directions for the jury in criminal matters.[167] In spite of recurring debates over the exact wording[168] to be employed by the judges in their summing up, there is a wealth of authority of the House of Lords in favour of the 'reasonable doubt' direction.[169] As a rule, judges should not volunteer an explanation of this expression but, where the jury ask for it, they should tell them that 'a reasonable doubt is the sort of doubt that might affect the mind of a person in dealing with matters of importance in his own affairs.[170] At present, the Judicial Studies Board recommends the following standard direction:

> How does the prosecution succeed in proving the defendant's guilt? The answer is: by making you sure of it. Nothing less than that will do. If after considering all

[165] English and Italian rules of corroboration concerning certain groups of witnesses are discussed in Chapter 5.

[166] This is the case for a few groups of official documents (*procés verbaux*) in French law; cf. M.L. Rassat, *Traité..., supra* note 22, §223.

[167] See, with an historical emphasis, B.J. Shapiro, *'Beyond Reasonable Doubt' and 'Probable Cause': Historical Perspectives on the Anglo-American Law of Evidence*, Univ. California Press, Berkeley, 1991.

[168] According to an alternative formula, jury should be told that before they convict they 'must be sure of the guilt of the accused': *R. v. Kritz*, [1950] 1 K.B. 82 (C.A.) approved by *Walters v. R.*, [1969] 2 A.C. 26 (P.C. Jamaica).

[169] P.J. Richardson (ed.), *Archbold Criminal Pleading, Evidence and Practice 2004*, Sweet & Maxwell, London, 2004, §4-384.

[170] *R. v. Gray*, (1974) 58 Cr. App. R. 177 (C.A.), at 183.

> the evidence you are sure that the defendant is guilty, you must return a verdict of 'Guilty'. If you are not sure, your verdict must be 'Not Guilty'.

In France, the formula of *intime conviction*[171] was introduced to replace the system of Roman-canon legal proofs in the *Ancien Regime*. Under that system, convictions and acquittals resulted from a rather artificial arithmetic calculation of the weights to be attached to the items of proof presented to the courts. This landmark reform rested on the belief that the probative weight of evidence is a matter too unruly to obey to the legislator' guidelines and 'too contextual to be captured in a web of categorical norms'.[172] This is why the focus of its expression is traditionally thought to be not only upon the level of certainty that must be met, but also on the freedom of the judge in appreciating the value of evidence. Pursuant to Article 353 of the French Code, the president of the Assize Court should read out the following instruction before the court retires for deliberation:

> The law does not require judges to express the reasons upon which they reached their judgment, (...) the law requires them to interrogate themselves in silence and concentration and think, in the sincerity of their conscience, of the impression that evidence adverse and favourable to the defendant made to their mind. The law asks only one question: are you personally convinced?

Italian jurisprudence refers to the *libero convincimento* (free will) of the criminal courts. Commentators agree that the formula originally ruled out the system of legal proofs but that it does not allow the judge to depart from existing legal rules of admissibility and collection of evidence.[173] Further, the principle was long believed to focus upon the idea that the judge must found the judgment upon his own rational and objective convictions, and should be insulated from any 'external' pressure. Control over the judge's way of reasoning is ensured by the fact that, in Italy, all criminal judgments must be accompanied by written reasons. This makes all criminal judgments challengeable on the ground of 'irrationality' before the Supreme Court. Although the Code of criminal procedure does not explicitly state the principle of *libero convincimento*, the majority of commentators considers it to be encompassed in Article 192.[174] This provi-

---

[171] Cf. Art. 353 F-CPP. The courts constantly recall the paramount importance of this formula: cf. (F) Cass. Crim., 21 November 1991, *Bull crim* n°427, Peyranne. See also (F) Cass. Crim., 29 June 1967, *Bull. crim.* n°199, Heneaux.

[172] M.R. Damaška, *Evidence Law Adrift*, *supra* note 160, 20. The strongest condemnation of the absurdity of the system of *preuve legal* came from the sharp pen of Voltaire, *Prix de la Justice et de l'Humanité*, Ferney, 1778.

[173] M. Nobili, *Il Principio del Libero Convincimento del Giudice*, Giuffrè, Milano, 1974.

[174] E. Amodio, *Libero Convincimento e Tassatività dei Mezzi di Prova: un Approccio Comparativo*, [1999] R.I.D.P.P. 3-9.

sion governs the assessment of evidence and requires courts to give a detailed account of the 'the results achieved and criteria adopted' in grounding their rulings. The Italian standard for conviction, therefore, amounts to a *rationally challengeable* certainty that the accused committed the concerned offence.

It has just been shown that English, French and Italian courts of criminal justice may serve a guilty judgment only when intimately sure of the defendant's culpability. Irrespective of the level of certainty, however, one more factor must be taken into account to compare the systems' approach to the evaluation of evidence. Inevitably, the process of evaluation depends upon the state of mind of those who judge the case. If they incline to believe that no prosecution is brought without a cause they would probably convict on comparatively weaker evidence. At this regard, it has been suggested that professional judges tend to develop a more sceptical attitude toward the defendant than the jury.[175] According to this theory, the jury would normally have a more open mind and, therefore, harden the case for the prosecution. If true, this means that any discrepancy among the jurisdictions under investigation may result not only from the theoretical formulas applied by the law, but also by the respective roles played by lay and professional judges at the time of deliberation.

5 Conclusion

Article 6 of the Convention binds the European States to ensure a fair criminal trial to any accused person and announces the Right to Confrontation, yet it does not specify what testimonial evidence ought to be admitted before the courts. Since evidence law remains in essence a matter for national realms, domestic legal orders in Europe have autonomously developed their own set of rules of evidence and procedure. In doing so, Member States have often walked along the path of two conflicting paradigms, the inquisitorial and the adversarial, which have been described in this chapter. It has been shown that such models can be understood not only as conflicting cultural paradigms in allocating powers and responsibilities between the actors of the criminal process, but also as opposing 'proof-taking' styles.

Focus concentrated specifically on the exclusionary rules of evidence, since the protection of the fundamental Right to Confrontation requires that some unchallenged testimonial evidence is excluded from the adjudication process. Under the inquisitorial variant, evidence is part of procedural law and evidentiary rules of evidence are 'procedural' in nature. In essence, this means that compliance with a set of *procedural* guarantees is the one and only test to which evidence is submitted. If such a test is satisfied, the testimony of witness counts as evidence and the appreciation of the content of such testimony is entirely

[175] J.R. Spencer, *Evidence, supra* note 7, 602.

left to the *intime conviction* of the court. Under the adversarial variant, instead, what matters is also the content of a deposition, since such a deposition may be excluded from evidence on grounds of opinion, hearsay and character. This makes adversarial exclusionary rules *substantial*, as courts are prevented from using them as evidence in the light of their specific content.

Since domestic criminal evidence depends upon the dualism between the inquisitorial and the adversarial paradigms, the choice of Italy, France and England as model European countries could be easily justified. France and the U.K. are prime examples of the said paradigms, while Italy is experiencing a transition from the one to the other. Yet, preliminary comparative analysis has also shown that multi-directional changes characterise the law of criminal procedure across Europe. Italy has attempted to overturned its civil law tradition by enacting an adversarial Code of criminal procedure in which cross-examination, the defence investigation and the rule against hearsay have been established. English law-makers have recently abandoned a long standing commitment against hearsay evidence (*C.J.A. 2003*) and have also enacted a consolidation of *Criminal Procedure Rules 2005* (similar to the U.S. Federal Rules of Criminal procedure), a step that marks departure with centuries of statutory chaos. For its part, France has solemnly announced the equality of the parties to the proceeding, in the context of a far reaching reform of the *Code de procedure pénale* in the year 2000.

Since another present tendency of European jurisdictions is to slide towards a rights-oriented approach, several comparative lessons may be learned from the investigation of the degree of protection afforded in the model Countries to the fundamental Right to Confrontation. This is the ambitious goals of Chapter 5 and 6, in which research will be restricted to criminal trials for the most serious offences in the three model Countries.

CHAPTER 5

Confrontation of Courtroom Accusers

English, French and Italian Criminal Procedure

1 Preliminaries

The most cursory glance at English, Italian and French jurisprudence reveals that testimony is unanimously considered the most important means of proof in criminal proceedings. This approach stems from Bentham's landmark definition of witnesses as *les yeux et les oreilles de la justice.*[1] Italian scholars call testimony the backbone[2] of the law of evidence, while French ones consider it the 'queen amidst contemporary means of proof'.[3] In England, it is more prosaically suggested that the most common vehicle for proof is the evidence of witnesses.[4]

This chapter investigates the ordinary course of testimony in the three model countries. By ordinary, I mean the course of evidence when the witness appears in the courtroom and there is no reason to suggest that he or she may need any protection before, during or after the deposition. Since the focus of this work is on the Right to Confrontation, discussion concentrates on witnesses adverse to the accused: this includes not only prosecution witnesses but also defence witnesses when they turn out to be hostile to the defendant.

2 The Confrontational Paradigm in Action

References to constitutional values and Human Rights are numerous in the national discourse on testimonial evidence. As reported earlier, the European Convention of Human Rights is directly enforceable in the domestic realms of the model countries and defendants may invoke Article 6(3)(d) before the criminal courts.[5] In Italy, since 1999, defendants can also rely upon Article 111(3) of the Constitution, which almost literally duplicates the Confrontation Clause of the Convention.

As suggested in Chapter 1, a testimony is collected in accordance with the Right to Confrontation when the declarant, whose real identity is disclosed to the defence, gives evidence in open court, facing the accused and the trier of fact, under the obligation of truth telling, and the defence has a chance to challenge him or her through contemporaneous adverse-questioning. The standard procedure for the collection of testimonial evidence in the English, French and Italian criminal process complies with this paradigm. Something must be said now about the aforementioned six features in turn.

---

1 J. Bentham, *Traité des Preuves Judiciaires*, Paris, 1823, vol. I, 90.

2 C. Di Martino, *Prova Testimoniale (Diritto Processuale Penale)*, in *Enciclopedia Giuridica Treccani*, Treccani, Roma, 1991, vol. XXV, 1.

3 M.L. Rassat, *Traité de Procédure Pénale*, PUF, Paris, 2001, §247.

4 C. Tapper, *Cross and Tapper on Evidence*, 9th edn., Butterworths, London, 1999, 204.

5 Chap 4, section 3.2.2.

The principle of open justice is England's 'most enduring contribution to the law of other nations'[6] and now applies to all other European jurisdictions. Italian and French criminal trials are public pursuant to Article 471 and Article 306 of the respective Codes of criminal procedure. In theory, some exceptions are tolerated[7] but, in practice, closed doors proceedings are rare, since publicity of trials is regarded as a fundamental principle of law.[8] In England, although at common law there is inherent jurisdiction to sit *in camera* if the administration of justice so requires, only a few trials on indictment are held in such manner,[9] and hardly ever is the press unable to report proceedings. Indeed, it is an oft-quoted dictum that 'the English system of administering justice does require that it be done in public'.[10]

In general, accused persons have the right to be present at the hearings of the proceedings brought against them. In Italy and France, nevertheless, a defendant may waive this right by failing to attend the hearing, when a formal notice was served upon him or her.[11] As a result, convictions can be pronounced against defendants who never appeared in the courtroom. This does not raise a confrontational problem, since the absent defendant does not waive his or her right to legal defence and counsel would be able to represent him or her at the hearing.[12] In England, instead, the rule is that the accused must be present throughout the entire trial of an indictable offence.[13] In practice, a charge may be tried in the absence of the defendant only if he or she has at least appeared to submit his or her plea.[14] In all three jurisdictions the right to be present is also waived by disruptive behaviour during the hearing.[15] This may also include disruptions at the time of the examination of witnesses. Confrontational claims

---

6 G. Robertson, *Freedom, the Individual and the Law*, 7th edn., Penguin, Harmondsworth, 1993, 282.

7 Compare Arts. 471 to 473 I-CPP with Art. 306(2) F-CPP.

8 Compare (I) Corte cost., judgment No. 373/1992, [1992] Giur. Cost. 2977 with (F) Cass. crim., 10 July 1974, *Bull. crim.* n°253, Court and (F) Cass. crim., 4 February 1985, *Bull. crim.* n°53, Fournet.

9 *Official Secrets Act 1920*, s. 8(4).

10 *Att-Gen v. Leveller Magazine Ltd.*, [1979] A.C. 440 (H.L.) at 450 (Lord Diplock) quoting *Scott v. Scott*, [1913] A.C. 417 (H.L.). With regard to magistrates' courts, the principle of public justice is enshrined in *M.C.A. 1980*, s. 121(4).

11 The practice is legitimate under ECHR law, provided that (1) the concerned State acted diligently in serving notice of the hearing and (2) the accused is afforded the opportunity to obtain a fresh determination of the merits of the charge, when he can demonstrate that he was unaware of the proceeding brought against him or her; cf. *Colozza v. Italy*, Series A No. 89, (1985) 7 EHRR 516 at paras 27 s.

12 The rules for criminal trials *in absentia* are significantly different in Italian and French criminal procedure; compare Arts. 420bis to 420quinquies and 484 I-CPP with Arts. 627 to 641 F-CPP.

13 See *Lawrence v. R.*, [1933] A.C. 699 (P.C.) at 708.

14 *R. v. Browne*, (1906) 70 J.P. 472.

15 See *R. v. Jones*, [2003] 1 A.C. 1 (H.L.).

may thus arise if the decision to remove the accused from the courtroom is allegedly disproportionate or illegitimate under ECHR or national law.

Similar rules apply as to the presence of the fact-finder at the time in which oral evidence is given. In Italy, a judgment is *de iure* void if pronounced by a judge other than those who attended the hearings.[16] It is a settled principle of English law that evidence given in the course of the trial on indictments must be tendered in the presence of the jury.[17] Since Article 307 of the French Code requires that trials before the Assize Courts be held with no interruptions from the beginning to the end, changes in the panel at the stage of the final deliberation are cause for procedural nullity.

In all jurisdictions under investigation, testifying witnesses are asked to state their full name at the outset of the examination. While Article 497(2) of the Italian Code is satisfied with the disclosure of name and surname, Article 331(2) of the French Code requires further personal details such as 'age, occupation and address of temporary or permanent residence'. In England, address needs not be disclosed unless indispensable for evidentiary purposes,[18] but the standard practice of asking witnesses their occupation at the outset of the examination is unobjectionable.[19] Subject to specific statutory exceptions, national press are normally entitled to publish the name and address of court witnesses.

In Italy and France, witnesses are expected to affirm their commitment to truthful depositions.[20] Similarly, in England witnesses must be sworn in open court in accordance to the manner of administration of the oath, governed by *Oaths Act 1978*, s. 1 or, alternatively, *Oath Act 1978*, ss. 5, 6 (for those who object to being sworn on the Bible). It will be later[21] shown that no obligation to tell the truth is placed in France and Italy (with the sole exception of the 'assisted witness') upon the testifying defendant, even when he or she gives evidence against a co-defendant.

Methods of adverse questioning are discussed in more detail as my discussion unfolds. At this stage, it is worth recalling that in Italian[22] and English proceedings, questioning of unfavourable witnesses takes the form of cross-

---

16 Art. 525 I-CPP.

17 *R. v. Reynolds*, [1950] 1 K.B. 606 (C.C.A.).

18 This rule has been laid down in July 1996 by Lord Bingham CJ in the 'Criminal Justice Consultative Council's Trial Issues Group's Statements of National Standard of Witness Care in the Criminal Justice system' (see P.J. Richardson (ed.), *Archbold Criminal Pleading, Evidence and Practice*, 51st edn., Sweet & Maxwell, London, 2003, 1069) Nevertheless, this specific document was never been published as a practice direction in any of the English law reports.

19 *R. v. D.S.*, [1999] Crim. L.R. 911 (C.A.); for further discussion see F.G. Davies, *Preserving the Anonymity of Witnesses*, (1997) 161 J.P.&L.G.L. 351-354.

20 See Art. 497(2) I-CPP and Art. 331(3) F-CPP.

21 See below, section 3.2.3.

22 Pursuant to Arts. 499 and 500 I-CPP.

examination by counsel, after the person has given evidence-in-chief to the party who summoned him or her. Although the style of Italian and English cross-examinations varies considerably,[23] their scope is similar: opposing parties attack the credibility of the declarant and the reliability of his or her account in a rather antagonistic manner, before a judge acting as an umpire, rather than an inquisitor. Until 2001, the rule in French proceedings was that the president of the Assize Courts alone would lead the examination and play the role of the intermediary between the parties and the declarant. Tradition was broken by the statutory reform in the year 2000: pursuant to the amended Article 312 of the procedural Code[24] prosecutors and counsel may now directly question the witnesses with the president's leave.

3 Variants of Confrontation: The Beauty of Diversity

Although the collection of the evidence of testifying accusers in England, France and Italy *prima facie* conforms to the confrontational paradigm described in Chapter 1, a host of difference may also be found in domestic law and practice. National variants do not necessarily raise confrontational concerns; on the contrary, they express the beauty of diversity of national approaches to the process of evidence adjudication. In the following sections, discussion will run through several evidentiary and procedural matters, such as the witnesses' status, the legitimacy of pre-trial contacts with counsel, the oral performance and the principles of evidence evaluation. It will be argued that many of these differences are still rooted in the inquisitorial or adversarial inspiration of the respective proceedings.

3.1 Investigation Stage

3.1.1 Status of Informants and Pre-trial Depositions

The present section considers the depositions given by potential witnesses at the investigation stage. Testimonial statements may be collected in a variety of ways and by several judicial authorities: the main ones are the police, prosecutors and other professional or lay magistrates. Specific rules of evidence dictates what the status of the declarant is at this stage, what his or her obliga-

[23] By way of illustration, Italian law does not allow cross-examination of the 'hostile witnesses' (i.e. a person that does not appear desirous of telling the truth at the instance of the party calling him) although it consents to the use of previous inconsistent statements in both direct and cross-examination.

[24] As amended by Art. 36, Law No. 516/2000 (the scope and purposes of this far-reaching reform are discussed in Chapter 4, section 3.3).

tions are, whether the defence is allowed to attend at the taking of the deposition and ask questions, and in what manner statements are to be recorded and retained for future reference.[25]

In a purely adversarial environment, out-of-court depositions could be collected informally, since they are not evidence of the matter stated and could only serve very little evidentiary purpose. Matters are much more complicated in England and Italy, where out-of-court statements may stand as evidence at trial in a number of cases specified by statutory law: this may happen when none of the parties object to the statements being tendered in evidence,[26] when the evidence given at trial differs from what the person previously said[27] and, sometimes, even when no court examination takes place at all.[28] In comparison, French law follows the inquisitorial assumption according to which an out-of-court deposition ought to be included in the court dossier and can always be relied upon along with a court testimony.

In Italy and England, individuals with a purported knowledge of circumstances relevant to the case are considered 'informed persons',[29] not witnesses, at the investigation stage. In France, the persons interviewed by the police are 'informants'[30], while those summoned before the *juge d'instruction* have a full witness status. This reflects in the presence, or absence, of an obligation to speak truthfully. In France, while depositions given to the police at the time of the *enquête* are unsworn,[31] those interviewed by the *juge d'instruction* must give evidence under oath.[32] In England, citizens are under no obligation to answer to the enquiries of the police, and written depositions are normally unsworn. In Italy, informed persons can be summoned to the police station or the prosecu-

[25] In Italy and France, depositions of witnesses must be reported in formal documents (*procès verbaux*) in accordance with detailed statutory requirements (cf. Art. 373 I-CPP and Arts. 63, 106 F-CPP). Art. 429(2) F-CPP, as amended by Law No. 516/2000 specifies that the *procès verbaux* of an interview must record not only the answers given by the witness, but also the questions posed to him or her. In England, depositions of informants are recorded under the requirements of *C.J.A. 1996*, s. 2(a), 2(b) in order to allow proof by written statements, in the case the parties later agree to such a procedure.

[26] In England, cf. *C.J.A. 1967*, s. 9; in Italy cf. Art. 500(7) I-CPP.

[27] The use in evidence of prior inconsistent statements is discussed at some length below, section 3.3.4.

[28] The evidence of absent witnesses is considered in Chapter 6, section 2.

[29] *'Persone informate sui fatti'* (Art. 362 I-CPP).

[30] According to the terminology of the French Code of criminal procedure, their technical status is that of *personnes susceptibles de fournir des renseignements*. Nevertheless, commentators tend to ignore this definition and simply refer to such early informants as 'witnesses', cf. R. Merle and A. Vitu, *Traité De Droit Criminel – Procèdure Pénale*, 5th edn., Cujas, Paris, 2001, 215-16; J. Susini, *Le Témoin, le Témoignage et la Police*, [1980] R.S.C. 499.

[31] Identical rules apply to the ordinary form of *enquête* (Art. 78(1) F-CPP) and to the *enquête de flagrance* (Art. 62(2) F-CPP).

[32] Art. 103 F-CPP.

tor's office. Only in the latter case, however, they are under the obligation to tell the truth, although no formal oath or affirmation is taken by the declarant.[33]

Normally, early interviews with potential witnesses are held unilaterally by police, prosecutor or other magistrates, while counsel have only a limited opportunity to participate. In France, for instance, defence counsel may only attend the interviews of those witnesses who he or she had explicitly required to be examined by the *juge d'instruction*.[34] Such an examination, however, is still presided by the *juge d'instruction* and counsel is not entitled to question the witness. Similarly, in England defendant and counsel have no right to attend the taking of the deposition by police. They also have no right to attend the testimonial hearings held by magistrates with a view to committal proceedings pursuant to *M.C.A. 1980, s. 97A*,[35] and if they do attend they have normally no right to cross-examine the witness.

National laws also set out some opportunities for an early collection of testimonial evidence in a confrontational manner. When this is the case, depositions stand as evidence at trial. In Italy, for example, parties may require the collection of testimony in a dedicated hearing named *incidente probatorio*. This type of hearing may be held when there are reasons to believe that the witness will be unavailable at a later stage, or when the quality of his or her evidence is likely to deteriorate.[36] Examination of witnesses at the *incidente probatorio* conforms to adversarial principles: witnesses are sworn, examined by the summoning party and cross-examined by the adverse party. Nonetheless, the hearing takes place *in camera* before the judge of the preliminary investigation, not the trial judge. The examination is recorded and included in the court dossier in the case of a later committal for trial. Similar rules apply to the depositions collected at

[33] Cf. Art. 371bis I-CP. This provision was introduced in the I-CP by Art. 11, Law No. 356/1992.

[34] A traditional feature of French law was the absolute discretion enjoyed by the *juge d'instruction* in summoning witnesses on his or her own behalf. Art. 101(1) F-CPP still states that the examining magistrate may call any persons whose hearing may be useful for the purposes of the investigation. Parties can also call for the examination of certain witnesses before the *judge d'instruction* but, until 2002, he or she had no obligation to give reasons for a refusal to do so. Following the coming into force of the Law No. 516/2000, reasons must now be given for a refusal by virtue of Art. 82-1(2) F-CPP. A refusal to call a witness is subject to the judicial review of the *Chambre d'instruction*.

[35] Pursuant to *C.P.I.A. 1996*, s. 68 and Sch. II, these statements may be stand as evidence at trial, even if the maker of the statements is available to be called as a witness at that stage and is not afraid to give oral evidence.

[36] Cf. Art. 392 I-CPP. Parties may apply for the collection of evidence at the *incidente probatorio* when the witness has poor health or when he or she may be intimidated or bribed to avoid a judicial examination or to give false evidence. Suspects may also be examined at the *incidente probatorio* when their depositions incriminate a co-defendant, in order to prevent future pressure against the declarant. Furthermore, the evidence of a children under the age of 16 may be collected at the *incidente probatorio* in the case of prosecution for certain sexual offences.

the committal hearing, to which counsel are entitled to attend.[37] In England, pre-trial examinations and cross-examination of vulnerable witnesses have been envisioned by *Y.J.C.E.A. 1999, s. 28* – a provision that has not yet entered into force – for which more discussion is provided in Chapter 6.

3.1.2 Contacts between Informants and Counsel

Parties to adversarial trials are expected to prepare the witness for the court performance: there, testimonies are often rehearsed in the offices of lawyers and prosecutors. Not only are pre-trial contacts between counsel and witnesses allowed, but they are also regarded as indispensable ingredients of an effective defence strategy. Moreover, rules concerning the oral examinations are laid down under the assumption that the parties summoning the witness are familiar with the evidence he or she intends to give.

In this respect, the U.S. criminal justice system closely conforms to the adversarial archetype. In the U.S., the constitutional right of the accused to call evidence in his or her favour is interpreted as including the 'right to prepare for trial, which, in turn, includes the right to interview material witnesses privately and to ascertain truth from them'.[38] At the beginning of the twentieth century a principle was established whereby defendants in a criminal prosecution may interview 'as many as possible of the eyewitnesses to the facts in controversy'[39] and personally or by counsel verify what their testimony may be. Any interference by the prosecution in the private investigation of the defence is forbidden, as well as any pressure to potential witnesses so that they refuse an interview by the opposing counsel.[40] Nonetheless, informants may still refuse to be interviewed by counsel prior to trial[41] and may also dictate the circumstances under which they accept to submit to an interview.[42] It is the skill of the attorney to approach and coach witnesses favourable to the case so that, under certain circumstances, an action for malpractice can even be brought against those who fail to brief or prepare the witnesses for the trial hearing.[43]

---

37 Arts. 422, 500 I-CPP.

38 *Bobo v. Com.*, 48 S.E. 2d 213 (Va. 1948).

39 *State v. Papa*, 80 A. 12 (R.I. 1911). This opportunity must be granted to the defendant even if the prospective witness is held in custody; cf. *Com. v. Balliro*, 349 Mass. 505, 209 N.E.2d 308 (Mass. 1965); *U.S. v. McCarthy* 292 F. supp. 937 (S.D.N.Y. 1968).

40 *Gammon v. State*, 506 S.W.2d 188 (Tenn. Cr. App. 1973); *State v. York*, 632 P.2d 1261 (Or. 1981). The same principle applies to co-defendants; cf. *White v. State*, 52 Miss. 216 (Miss. 1876).

41 *Dover v. State*, 296 S.E.2d 710 (Ga. 1982).

42 *U.S. v. Dryden*, 423 F. 2d 1175 (5th Cir. 1970).

43 *Woodruff v. Tomlin*, 616 F.2d 924 (6th Cir. 1980). While the determination of whether to call a particular person as a witness at trial is a tactical decision involving the exercise of professional judgement, the same cannot be said of the failure to interview a potential witness brought to the attention of an attorney by the client: cf. D.J. Beck, *Nature of Legal Malpractice*, (1991) 43 Baylor L.R. 43-90.

In comparison, in the inquisitorial world pre-trial contacts between counsel and witnesses are perceived as suspicious: parties are not supposed to influence, let alone to prepare, the oral testimony. The assumption is that the collection of evidence should be restricted to official interviews before the public authorities, while informal contacts are dismissed as if they were attempts to impair the genuineness and spontaneity of depositions. Approaching informed persons comes dangerously close to the offence of perverting the course of justice.[44]

Let us now turn to the current state of English, French and Italian law. In comparison with U.S. law, the solution adopted in England is complicated by the separation of the legal profession into barristers and solicitors. It is true that a rule of etiquette forbids any barrister to 'interview or discuss the case with any witnesses or permit them to be present at any consultation or conferences with him'.[45] This does not mean, however, that contacts between witnesses and counsel are forbidden. In fact, the instructing solicitor will have normally interviewed the favourable witness and will have prepared a proof of evidence which sets out what the witness is likely to report at trial. This proof will be with counsel's brief, and counsel will use it for the court examination.

In the year 2000,[46] the Italian Parliament passed a comprehensive reform of the private investigations in an attempt to promote 'equality of arms' even at the early stages of the criminal proceeding.[47] Counsel may now file requests for documents to the offices of the public administration documents and, with some limitations, may also access private premises to take notice of their conditions. More importantly, counsel may approach informants, interview them and collect their depositions.[48] The reform brought about a dramatic change for the legal profession: the provisions of the Bar Code of conduct that previously treated out-of-court meetings between lawyers and witnesses as disciplinary

---

[44] Cf. M. Garçon, *L'Avocat et la Morale*, Bouchet-Chastel, Paris, 1963, 59-82, according to which any activity other than legal assistance is an impairment of the independence and dignity of the legal profession.

[45] R.E. Megarry, *Lawyer and Litigant in England*, Stevens, London, 1962, 46. The present rule is to be found in the *Written Standards for the Conduct of Professional Work in the Code of Conduct of the Bar*, para 6.3.1, according to which it is 'wholly inappropriate for a barrister' to interview any potential witness.

[46] Law No. 397/2000. For discussion see G. Di Chiara, *Le Linee Prospettiche del 'Difendersi Cercando': Luci e Ombre delle 'Nuove' Investigazioni Difensive*, [2002] Leg. Pen. 1-28; M. Nobili, *Giusto Processo e Indagini Difensive: Verso Una Nuova Procedura Penale?*, [2001] Dir. Pen. Proc. 5-14.

[47] In 1988, the right to perform private investigations was acknowledged in the supplementary provisions of the Code, although very little was said about the procedures to be followed for the collection of information and its subsequent use in evidence. As a result, the Supreme Court rigidly limited the judicial use of such investigations between 1988 and 2000: see (I) Cass. crim., 18 August 1992, Burrafato, [1993] Cass. Pen. 1502; (I) Cass. crim., 31 January 1994, Vincenti, [1994-III] Giust. Pen. 586; (I) Cass. crim., 16 March 1994, Cagnazzo, [1995] Cass. Pen. 115.

[48] Arts. 391bis and 391ter I-CPP. Such depositions may be used in evidence at the exact same conditions as those collected by the police and prosecution.

matters were repealed,[49] and private investigation agencies promptly extended their services as to include such 'criminal' investigations. As anticipated, in Italy the defence is now fully entitled to approach an informant. If the informant agrees to answer questions, he or she undertakes the obligation to be sincere, subject to criminal sanction. If the informant refuses to answer, counsel may require his or her summoning to the prosecutor's office. An interview will then take place there, and the defence will be entitled to initiate it.[50] Clearly, counsel will not always pursue this option, since it may be hazardous to disclose a potentially unfavourable source of evidence to the prosecution. What matters, nevertheless, is that Italian counsel have been granted an enforceable opportunity to collect relevant information from potential witnesses at the investigation stage. Depositions collected in the defence investigation are to be included in the 'prosecution dossier'[51] if the case is later committed for trial.

Unsurprisingly, the French *Code de procédure pénale* still makes no reference to the defence investigations. Nor does a single reference exist on this topic in the criminal procedure doctrine, even in the aftermath of the recent statutory reform, which allegedly pursued the enhancement of equality of arms between the parties to the criminal process.[52] As mentioned above, counsel may well require – and now also obtain[53] – that the investigating judge summons certain witnesses before him or her. This right, however, is exercised sparingly because there is a always a risk that the informant may become a weapon in the hands of the prosecution. Pre-trial contacts between counsel and informants may only occur in a context of utter informality, and the related conversation cannot be included in the court dossier and used in evidence.

3.2 Trial Stage

3.2.1 Status of Witnesses

Under the adversarial variant parties are expected to call and summon their own witnesses, in order to elicit information favourable to their own case. English and Italian laws follow this theoretical framework. In these jurisdictions, it is for the summoning party to conduct the first segment of the

---

49 Cf. *Codice Deontologico degli Avvocati*, s. 52.

50 Art. 391bis(10) I-CPP.

51 The allocation of evidentiary material in two separate dossiers is a typical feature of Italian law: see Chapter 4, section 4.3.1.

52 According to Commission Justice Pénale et Droits de l'Homme, *La Mise en Etat des Affaires Pénales. Rapports*, La Documentation Française, Paris, 1991, 57, 'counsel cannot perform any investigation' in the French legal order. After 15 years, this rule continues to apply to the present state of French procedure.

53 See footnote n 34, and text thereat.

oral examination of witnesses. This has major implications for the style and limits of the related questioning. Furthermore, the prosecution witnesses are to be presented and examined before those summoned by the defence.[54]

Under the inquisitorial variant, there are no separate witnesses for the prosecution and defence: both are seen as sources of evidence for the bench. This is why, in France, the president may set out the specific order of the examinations as he or she deems appropriate.[55] By convention, witnesses called by the prosecution are normally heard first, but departures from this practice do not amount to nullity and are by no means sanctioned as violations of the rights of the accused.[56]

3.2.2 Summoning

Adversarial style implies that it is for the parties to call the witnesses they believe may assist their case. Instead, trials of an inquisitorial inspiration present the courts with the opportunity to call any witness they wish to question. In the adversarial context, the decision of a judge to step into the arena and issue a witness summons can easily be viewed as a potential threat to impartiality. By contrast, inquisitorial discourse would argue that the courts' power to call witness on their own motion is purely functional to the pursuance of the truth.

It is certainly true that the summoning of a witness on the part of the court may benefit any party of the proceeding, depending on the content of her testimony. Nevertheless, it may also be argued that, of all parties, the defendant is the one who has most to fear from an extensive use of this power. In fact, the decision to summon 'supplementary' witnesses on behalf of the bench is often reasoned upon some kind of 'insufficiency' of proof in the prosecution case. The presumption of innocence requires that the prosecution prove the defendant's guilt[57] and when the evidence of the prosecution witnesses fails to convey reasonable certainty over the facts at issue, the defendant has a legitimate expectation of being promptly acquitted.

These considerations are of some assistance in the scrutiny of national laws. In Italy, Articles 190(1) and 468(1) of the procedural Code govern the matter:

---

54 As for the examination of the defendant, under English law he or she must take the stand at the end of the prosecution case, before any other defence witness (*P.A.C.E. 1984*, s. 79; *C.E.A. 1898*, s. 1(g)) on the rationale that he or she should not be able to adjust his or her evidence to theirs. The rule is subject to exceptions under very special circumstances: cf. *R. v. Smith*, [1968] 2 All E.R. 115 (C.A.). In comparison, the defendant is the very last person to enter the witness box in Italian criminal trials, pursuant to Art. 496 I-CPP.

55 Art. 331(1) F-CPP. Case law does not usually challenge the exercise of this discretion: (F) Cass. crim., 26 February 1992, *Bull. crim.* n°90, Barbot.

56 (F) Cass. crim., 6 February 1980, *Bull. crim.* n°49, Bischwiller.

57 Cf. Chapter 4, section 4.1.

witnesses are summoned on the parties' behalf only at the opening of the trial. In England, a very similar rule is slightly complicated by the obligation on the prosecution to serve summons upon certain witnesses. According to the authority of *R. v. Russell-Jones*,

> The prosecution must have at court all witnesses whose statements have been served as witnesses on whom the prosecution intends to rely, if the defence wishes those witnesses to attend. [...] The prosecution enjoys a discretion whether to call, or tender, any witness it requires to attend, but this discretion is not unfettered and must be exercised in the interests of justice, so as to promote a fair trial. In practice the prosecution ought normally to call or offer to call all the witnesses who can give direct evidence of the primary facts of the case.[58]

The crucial point is that Italian and English courts are entitled to call witnesses on their behalf only at a late stage of the proceeding, and under exceptional circumstances. In England, although judges theoretically have a discretion to summon witnesses ex officio,[59] case law recommends that this power be exercised sparingly[60] and only when strictly necessary to ensure trial fairness and promote the interests of justice. In practice, it is restricted to instances in which, at the end of the case for the defence, 'no injustice or prejudice could be caused to the defendant and some matters arose ex improviso'.[61] Under no circumstances may this power be used to circumvent the restrictions on the prosecution reopening their case. In Italy, instead, further witnesses may be summoned on behalf of the court at the end of the case for the defence, when the presentation of their evidence appears to be 'absolutely necessary'.[62] Both the Constitutional and the Supreme Court have broadly construed the concept of 'absolute necessity' in an attempt to expand the area of the courts' discretion. Criminal courts are allowed to invoke the related provision (Article 507 I-CPP) as a remedy against the deadlines for summoning and disclosure, which the public party or any other party may have failed to meet.[63] Further, witnesses can be called by the court even when a negligent prosecutor office had presented no evidence at all to support the case against the defendant.[64] This questionable case law is the emblem of the reluctance of the Italian judiciary to accept

---

58 [1995] 3 All E.R. 239 (C.A.) 244, 245.

59 *R. v. Wallwork*, (1958) 42 Cr. App. R. 153 (C.A.). This discretionary power applies to both the magistrates' and the Crown Court: *R. v.* Wellingborough *Justices Ex p. Francois*, (1994) 158 J.P. 813 (D.C.).

60 *R. v. Roberts*, (1985) 80 Cr. App. R. 89 (C.A.) 94.

61 *R. v. Cleghorn*, [1967] 2 Q.B. 584 (C.A.).

62 Art. 507(1) I-CPP.

63 Cf. (I) Cass. crim., 10 October 1991, Paolini, [1992] Cass. Pen. 1258.

64 (I) Cass. crim., 6 November 1992, Martin, [1992] Arch. Nuova Proc. Pen. 685; endorsed by (I) Corte cost., judgment No. 111/1993, [1993] Giur. Cost. 901.

the leading role of the parties in the process of evidence adjudication and it has been openly contested by the champions of the new adversarial spirit of Italian criminal procedure.[65]

In comparison, courts in trials of an inquisitorial inspiration are free to summon anybody who may provide useful information. In France, witnesses are summoned in the first place on behalf of the parties. At any time during the trial, however, the president of the Assize Court may require the attendance of any individual who may contribute to the 'disclosure of the truth' (Article 310 F-CPP).[66] To be more accurate, individuals summoned on the courts' behalf bear a peculiar legal status. On the one hand, they are not expected to swear on oath to tell the truth. On the other hand, their statements are termed *renseignements* (information), not testimonies.[67] This may lead to some confusion. The reader might jump to the conclusion that the French criminal process acknowledges two separate classes of witnesses: an 'ordinary' class, including those who are summoned by the parties, and a 'exceptional' class, consisting of those who are called to take the stand ex officio. Instead, case law firmly states that this distinction is purely an historical remainder of the former system of legal proof.[68] At present, not only can statements of ex officio witnesses be relied upon in the final decision, but their evidentiary value may also exceed, under the circumstances of the case, that of ordinary testimonies.[69] The aforementioned distinction affects the course of testimony exclusively with reference to the presence, or absence, of the obligation of the declarant to speak truthfully.[70] Finally, the president of an Assize Court may also invoke his or her powers under Article 310 of the Code in order to set aside some of the procedural provisions concerning competence to testify. By way of illustration, parties to the proceedings are entitled to file an opposition against the summoning of *incapables*[71] or *reprochables*[72] witnesses on behalf of the opposing party. Even when the Assize Court

---

65 L. Marafioti, *L'Art. 507 CPP al Vaglio delle Sezioni Unite: un Addio al Processo Accusatorio e all'Imparzialità del Giudice Dibattimentale*, [1993] R.I.D.P.P. 829-849. *Contra* F. Cordero, *Procedura Penale*, 7th edn., Giuffrè, Milano, 2003, 940-941.

66 This is a strictly personal attribution of the president; the other members of the Assize Court have no say in this matter; (F) Cass. crim., 9 December 1998, *Bull. Crim.* n°337, Chaouad; (F) Cass. crim., 20 December 2000, X. [2001-IV] J.C.P. 1449.

67 Cf. Art. 310(3) F-CPP.

68 M.L. Rassat, *Traité de Procédure Pénale*, *supra* note 3, §262.

69 B. Bouloc, G. Levasseur and G. Stefani, *Procédure Pènale*, 17th edn., Dalloz, Paris, 2000, 115.

70 In any case, the judge cannot hear *ex officio* those who were summoned by the parties but refused to take the oath, as witnesses must not be given a chance to get round the legal sanctions against false depositions: (F) Cass. crim., 26 November 1980, *Bull. crim.* n°318, Baradel.

71 Art. 335 F-CPP. This category includes the relatives and the spouse of the defendant, as well as the civil party and all children aged under 16.

72 According to Art. 131-26(4) F-CP, convicted persons who have been disqualified from civil and political rights are *incapable* to submit a testimony – but not simple *renseignements* – to a court of justice.

endorses such an opposition, the president retains a personal discretion to call them ex officio to take the stand.

3.2.3 The Accused as a Witness

An accused person may also be an 'accuser', in the case he or she gives evidence against one or more co-defendants, who in turn may be tried jointly or separately for the same or related offences. At this point, some remarks must be made on the accused as a source of testimonial evidence at the trial hearing. In Chapter 6 discussion will focus on the accused as an 'absent witness', in the case he or she makes out-of-court admissions implicating a co-accused but then refuses to give oral evidence.

Contemporary western culture acknowledges that the accused persons are at liberty not to say a word at criminal proceedings mounted against them: *nemo tenetur se detegere*.[73] This means, on the one hand, that silence is not punishable as a criminal offence[74] and, on the other hand, that convictions cannot be grounded simply on the failure to testify.[75] Although these are uncontroversial principles of law, their implementation may be pursued in rather different manners.

The inquisitorial model perceives the interrogation of the defendant as both a means of judicial investigation and a procedural guarantee. This is the reason why, in France, an attempt of interrogation must always be made.[76] Nevertheless, the accused has the right to remain silent[77] and may legitimately refuse to answer any of the questions posed to him or her. Lies before a court of justice are also not punishable, because the accused is entitled to pursue his or her

---

73 ECHR law on the right to silence was briefly considered in Chapter 3.

74 It must be recalled that pursuant to Art. VII, Tit. XIV of the 1670 *Ordonnance Criminelle* (Chapter 1, section 2.3) the principle *nemo tenetur se detegere* did not apply in the Ancien Regime: the accused person was legally bound to answer truthfully to all the questions put to him (or her) during the interrogation.

75 This does not necessarily exclude, however, that the trier of the fact could draw some inferences from the accused's failure to provide an explanation for the charges brought against him or her. It is beyond the scope of this research to investigate under which precise circumstances national courts are allowed to do so. In England, *C.J.P.O. 1994*, ss. 34 to 38 govern the subject while in France commentators suggests that courts have a right to infer from silence 'every useful indication for their intimate conviction': R. Merle and A. Vitu, *Traité de Droit Criminel*, *supra* note 30, 236.

76 Art. 328 F-CPP. Limited exceptions apply when the accused had already presented his or her case to the court: (F) Cass. crim., 16 March 1971, *Bull. crim.* n°90, Guerlot; (F) Cass. crim., 29 April 1971, *Bull. crim.* n°129, Bossuyt.

77 Although no statutory provision requires the court to inform the defendant of such a right during the course of the trial; cf. (F) Cass crim, 1 June 1995, *Bull. crim.* n° 202, Touvier.

strategy of defence through any possible means.[78] No exceptions apply when the defendant is tried jointly or separately with others.

In comparison, the English rule states that an accused is incompetent as a witness for the prosecution.[79] An accused charged jointly with somebody else is also incompetent for the prosecution.[80] In other words, it is only the defendant who can waive the right to silence and opt to submit to a court examination.[81] In this case, he or she is examined-in-chief by the defence and cross-examined by the opposing parties, under the obligation to answer truthfully to all admissible questions. This does not mean, however, that the accused who gives evidence is in the exact same position as any other witness. Ordinary witnesses, in fact, enjoy the privilege against self incrimination while defendants may be asked any question in cross-examination notwithstanding that they would tend to incriminate them as to the offence charged.[82] Further, defendants may be required to answer, under oath, to questions concerning *other* offences, in the case they give evidence of a good character or cast imputation on the prosecutor or the witnesses for the prosecutions.[83]

Italian defendants have more strategic options at disposal: 1) they may refuse to testify at all; 2) they may take the stand on their own behalf; 3) they may accept to be called on to the stand by the prosecution or a co-accused.[84] In the cases sub b) and c), the course of evidence follows the usual sequence of examination-in-chief, cross-examination and re-examination. Nevertheless, the declarant may not be compelled to answer any question and is under no obligation to tell the truth. This 'departure' from the confrontational paradigm is obviously prejudicial to co-defendants who are tried jointly but is partially compensated by the fact that the oral evidence of a co-accused always needs supporting evidence.[85]

Since 1977,[86] the right to silence has been granted in Italy not only to defendants in their own trials, but also to defendants who were tried for related offences in separate proceedings. The rule was that these peculiar co-defendants

---

78 Cf. (F) Cass. crim., 6 January 1923, *Bull. crim.* n°7; (F) Chambre corr., 23 November 1960, Clavaud et Prunaud, [1961-II] J.C.P. n° 11952.

79 *C.E.A. 1898*, s. 1; *R. v. Rhodes* [1899] 1 Q.B. 77 (C.C.C.R.).

80 *R. v. Payne* (1872) 1 L.R.C.C.R. 349 (C.C.C.R.); *R. v. Grant* [1944] 2 All E.R. 311 (Ass.); *R. v. Sharrock*, [1948] 1 All E.R. 145 (Ass.).

81 See *C.E.A. 1898*, s. 1.

82 *C.E.A. 1898*, s. 1(e).

83 *C.E.A. 1898*, s. 1(f).

84 Cf. Art. 503 I-CPP. If this is the case, prosecution would obviously perform the examination-in-chief, instead of the cross-examination.

85 See below, section 3.4.

86 Law No. 534/1977; cf. M. Bargis, *Incompatibilità a Testimoniare e Connessione di Reati*, Giuffrè, Milano, 1980, 97-110.

(so called *imputati in procedimenti connessi*) could be summoned to give evidence in an accomplice's trial, but could not be compelled to answer under oath. The argument was that such compellability could be prejudicial to their own defence, since the requested testimony would likely cover the very same facts at issue in the proceedings brought against them.

In 2001, this area of the law was restructured in an attempt to reduce the area of the right to silence for certain co-defendants who made prior allegations against an accomplice. Suppose that Mr. A's admission to the police implicated Mr. B. When Mr. A and Mr. B are jointly tried, they both enjoy the panoply of options described above. Let us now consider what happens when Mr. A and Mr. B are tried separately. A distinction must be made according to the intensity of the connection between the respective charges and the state of such proceedings. When Mr. A is being tried with the same or 'closely linked'[87] offences, he can be summoned in Mr. B's trial, but cannot be compelled to answer any question and has no obligation to speak truthfully. The evidence of Mr. A can be used against Mr. B, if duly corroborated. Conversely, when Mr. A is being tried with a 'remotely linked offence',[88] he may be summoned in Mr. B's trial in the peculiar capacity of an 'assisted witness'.[89] This rule also applies when a final judgment has been reached in Mr. A's separate proceeding for the same or a closely linked offence. The status of 'assisted witness' entails the obligatory assistance of a lawyer at the time of the examination and the obligation to speak truthfully, although only to questions concerning the responsibility of other people, not one's own.[90] The evidence of an assisted witness also needs corroboration.[91]

To sum up, it appears that in Italy and France the rights of the defendants who give evidence in court take priority over the Right to Confrontation of those who are implicated by their oral testimony. There, in fact, court allegations are often made by co-defendants who have a statutory right to lie. In Italy, nevertheless, this is counterbalanced by the statutory corroboration requirement for the evidence of co-defendants and 'assisted witnesses'. In comparison, no confrontational challenge may be brought against this area of English law, since the accuser co-defendants who accepts to testify is examined in full accordance with the 'confrontational paradigm' outlined in Chapter 1.

---

87 Art. 12(1)(a) I-CPP.

88 By virtue of Art. 12(1)(c) I-CPP, offences are 'remotely linked' when they have been perpetrated in order to ensure the successful performance, or conceal the outcome, of each other.

89 For discussion see M. Daniele, *La Testimonianza 'Assistita' e l'Esame degli Imputati in Procedimenti Connessi*, in R.E. Kostoris (ed.), *Il Giusto Processo tra Contraddittorio e Diritto al Silenzio*, Giappichelli, Torino, 2002, 196.

90 Art. 197bis(4) I-CPP, inserted by *Law No. 63/2001*.

91 Art. 197bis I-CPP.

3.2.4 Obligations and Privileges

Upon receipt of a summons on behalf of the parties, witnesses are expected to appear in court at a required day and time, swear on oath or other equivalent affirmation to state the truth, and give evidence. To ensure attendance, national laws allow the courts to issue enforceable orders and to compel the witness to testify. In England, both disobeying a witness summons[92] and refusing to be sworn, affirmed[93] or to answer admissible questions[94] amount to contempt of court. In France, a witness that fails to come to court or refuses to swear[95] or give her evidence is liable to a € 3750 fine.[96] In Italy, she may be punished with imprisonment for a term not exceeding six-months and a fine up to €516,46.[97]

Lying in court amounts to the offence of perjury or false testimony, which carry comparable sentences in the three model countries: up to seven years imprisonment and/or a fine in England,[98] between two and six years in Italy,[99] seven years and a €100.000 fine in France.[100] Some diversity can be found with regard to the depositions given at the investigation stage. As anticipated, in France informants have full witness status at the time of the *instruction* and thus false testimony applies to the depositions given to the *juge d'instruction*.[101] In Italy, separate offences punish those who give false statements to prosecuting authorities or counsel.[102] In England, perjury only punishes the false testimony in a court of law. On closer inspection, these differences may be regarded as symptoms of the diverging assumptions of the concerned jurisdictions on the process of evidence adjudication. It is agreed that the offences of perjury and false testimony are established to protect the veracity of the evidence tendered before a courts of justice. Let us consider English law first. Since evidence only

---

92 *Criminal Procedure (Attendance of Witnesses Act) 1965*, s. 3.

93 *Hennegal v. Evance*, (1806) 12 Ves. 201, 33 E.R. 77.

94 Unless a claim of privilege is made; cf. *Att-Gen. v. Clough* [1963] 1 Q.B. 773 (Q.B.D.).

95 Unless the law explicitly requires the testimony to be unsworn.

96 Cf. Arts. 437, 438 and 536 F-CPP. Under Art. 434-15-1 F-CP, the same penalty applies to those who refuse to swear or testify before the investigating magistrate or police officers at the investigation stage.

97 Art. 366 I-CP.

98 *Perjury Act 1911*, s. 1.

99 Art. 372 I-CP.

100 This is the sentence for *crimes*, pursuant to Art. 434-14 F-CP. When the alleged offence is qualified as a *délit* or *contravention*, triable respectively before the *tribunal correctionnel* and *tribunal de police*, a penalty of 5-year imprisonment and €75.000 fine apply (Art. 434-13 F-CP).

101 Under French law, the *juge d'instruction* may require the police to perform certain acts of official investigation on his behalf; in these cases, the formal order is given in a written document termed *commission rogatorie* (Art. 151 to 155 F-CPP).

102 Arts. 371bis and 371ter I-CP, respectively.

includes what is said at the public hearing, pre-trial depositions of witnesses fall, in principle, outside the ambit of application of the aforementioned criminal offences. An opposite solution is applied by French law, where statements collected by the *juge d'instruction* count as evidence. It is no wonder, therefore, that false testimony applies to these depositions as well as to court testimonies.

In comparison, the Italian approach is striking for its inconsistency. As reported above,[103] the Code of criminal procedure confines the status of witness to the trial stage of the proceeding. Therefore, the offence of false testimony only refers to lies that are spoken in open court.[104] This was the state of the law in 1989, at the time of the coming into force of the new Code. In 1992, amid dramatic criminal emergencies[105] and public calls for more effective investigations, a further offence was inserted in order to incriminate the false depositions given in the interviews with the prosecutor.[106] The recent statutory reform concerning the private investigations of the defence restored equality between the parties at the investigation stage by inserting a third offence,[107] which now also punishes false statements to counsel.

Witnesses also benefit of an array of privileges under national law. At this stage, I will only briefly touch upon the standard measures established by national laws to reduce interference in the process of collection of their evidence and the claims that may be raised by the witness in order to avoid examination and/or submission of certain sensitive information. No major differences in these matters derive from the adversarial or inquisitorial inspirations of the respective proceedings.

In all model jurisdictions, any attempt to influence or manipulate the deposition of a witness is equivalent to an attempt to pervert the course of justice. A typical endeavour is the subornation of witnesses or informed persons so that they provide no evidence, or false evidence. In practice, the author of such a subornation may be liable for various offences, according to the means employed

---

103 See discussion above, section 3.1.1.

104 And, additionally, in the peculiar hearing termed *incidente probatorio* (above, footnote 36 and text thereat).

105 Reference is to the assassinations of prosecutors Giovanni Falcone and Paolo Borsellino, in 1992 (above, Chapter 4, footnote 53 and text thereat).

106 Art. 371bis I-CP (*False informazioni al pubblico ministero*). Note the use of the term 'information', instead of 'testimony'. Italian commentators have sharply pointed out the inconsistency between this provision and the original adversarial assumptions of the I-CPP; cf. G. Frigo, *Dalla Tutela Penale della Prova alla Tutela Penale dell'Indagine*, [1995-3] Crit. Dir. 210-214.

107 Art. 371ter I-CP (*False informazioni al difensore*). It must be noted that any person approached by counsel outside the courtroom has no obligation to answer their enquiries. Nevertheless, if the informant decides to submit a deposition to counsel he or she is legally required to state the truth and is also liable for the offence in question.

to sway the declarant: bribes[108], threats or menaces.[109] Chapter 6 will later consider the impact of witness intimidation in national laws, with regard to both witnesses absent via fear and anonymous witnesses.

As anticipated, some witnesses may also be granted the privilege of refusing (a) to respond to certain questions or (b) to take the stand at all. These privileges are being progressively reduced, in an attempt to enhance the accuracy of the adjudication process. In the perspective adopted in the present work, the two aforementioned matters should be kept separate. On the one hand, provisions according to which the witness has the right to disregard certain questions (on grounds such as the privilege against self-incrimination[110] or other professional privileges)[111] fall outside the scope of this research, as they do not raise confrontational concerns. These provisions, in fact, only apply to 'testifying' accusers that are subject to confrontation. In comparison, when the witness is free to take the stand or not, and in fact refuses to do so, a confrontational problem may arise if the courts may employ his or her previous depositions as evidence (in such cases, the person is in fact an 'absent witness').

3.3 Witnesses on the Stand

The conflicting nature of adversarial and inquisitorial proof-taking styles materialises at the time of the court examination. The art of taking testimony is notably different under the two variants, and correspondingly so are the skills required of lawyers and judges to make the best of it. The topic may be profitably approached by staging the opposition between *fluency* and *interruptions*.[112]

In France, before any question is put to a witness, he or she must be given a chance to freely report his or her personal experience. Pursuant to Article 331(4) of the procedural Code, at the initial stage of the examination witnesses ought

---

108 Attempt to bribe a witness amounts to contempt of court in England, pursuant to *Perjury Act 1911*, s. 7(1). Compare also Art. 377 I-CP (*Subornazione*) with Art. 434-15 F-CP.

109 These constitutes separate offences in England and Italy: cf. *R. v. Kellett*, [1976] Q.B. 372 (C.A.) and Art. 377bis I-CP.

110 According to which a witness is not compelled to answer a question if there is a risk that the answer will expose him (or her) to proceedings for a criminal offence or recovery of a penalty; cf., in England, the authority of *Blunt v. Park Lane Hotel*, [1942] 2 K.B. 253 (C.A.) and, in Italy, Art. 198(2) I-CPP. No. privilege of this type exists in France.

111 *E.g.* typical of all jurisdictions are the privileges of the communications between lawyer and client, physician and patient, clergyman and those who give a religious confession.

112 As suggested by W.T. Pizzi, *Trials without Truth: Why Our System of Criminal Trials Has Become an Expensive Failure and What We Need to Do to Rebuild It*, N.Y. Univ. Press, New York, 1999, 5-24. The author draws a parallel between these features of the American and the (Continental) European styles of criminal procedures and the rules of their national sports: i.e. 'American football' and 'soccer'.

not be interrupted: an assumption stands that the best evidence is what unfolds from their spontaneous recollection. Intrusions by the bench may only be aimed at assisting the witness in expressing his or her views or at steering him or her back from irrelevancy. Only at a later stage may the interrogation from the court and parties begin. From the point of view of bystanders, however, the questioning style resembles a conversation much more than a strict sequence of questions and answers. This cannot by any means be equated to the firmly structured three-staged examination (examination-in-chief, cross-examination, re-examination) of English and Italian law. There, the witness is expected and required to limit his or her answers to the scope of the related questions, and any departure may, and indeed should, be objected to by the parties.

3.3.1 The Interviewer

Under the inquisitorial variant, it is the judge, not the parties, who bear the primary duty of collecting testimony. By virtue of the attributions under Article 310 F-CPP, the president of the Assize Court may ask any question that he or she deems useful for the discovery of the truth. In fact, the president is in an excellent position to do so effectively: he had full access to the court *dossier* and should therefore be aware of the investigative framework as well as the prior depositions of all court declarants. Side judges and jurors may also pose question by virtue of Article 311, but they had no prior access to the dossier and their questions are normally less incisive and numerous. Traditionally, parties could only put questions with the mediation of the presiding judge. The recent statutory reform, however, amended Article 312 of the Code so that prosecutors and defence counsel may now directly question the witnesses, with the president's leave. The president's intervention, however, is still required for any interrogation posed by the defendant in person and by the civil party.

In comparison, English and Italian laws follow adversarial assumptions: it is primarily for the parties to elicit the evidence of witnesses. Parties conduct the examination-in-chief, the cross-examination and the re-examination of all witnesses. Further elaboration is nevertheless necessary to fully appreciate what role the presiding judges can play during the witness's deposition. Although it is certainly true that the adversarial presentation of evidence can be moderated, intrusions from the bench should necessarily be limited.[113] Indeed, it is exceedingly hard for a judge to ask meaningful questions, innocent as he (or she) is of any comprehensive knowledge of the case.

This principle is strictly applied by English law since excessive intervention by the trial judge is a common ground of appeal. The Court of Appeal, however, agrees that in certain circumstances intervention may be justifiable.

[113] Cf. M.R. Damaška, *Presentation of Evidence and Fact-finding Precision*, (1975) 123 Univ. Pa. L.R. 1083, 1090.

For instance, this is often the case when the answers given were ambiguous, inaudible or, broadly speaking, when a particular question cried out to be asked and the parties failed to do so. The judge is also expected to curb prolixity and repetition and exclude discursiveness from the part of the witnesses.[114] On the other hand, the adversarial inspiration of the law of evidence also suggests that:

> It is a fundamental principle of an English trial that an accused giving evidence must be allowed to do so without being badgered and interrupted by the judge. Interventions by the judge will lead to a conviction being quashed, when they invite the jury to disbelieve evidence for the defence so strongly that the effect cannot be cured by telling the jury that they are the judges of fact, when they prevent defence counsel from conducting his case, or the defendant or a witness from telling his story in his own way.[115]

Although this emerges as a landmark ruling on the matter, slightly different nuances may be found in other judgments. In *Jones v. National Coal Board*, for instance, the Court of Appeal held that:[116]

> The judge sits to hear and determine the issues raised by the parties, not to conduct an investigation or examination on behalf of society at large as happens, we believe, in some foreign countries. Even in England, however, a judge is not a mere umpire to answer the question 'How's that?'. His object, above all, is to find out the truth, and to do justice according to law.

In practice, it would be difficult to justify the conduct of a judge who broke the sequence of questions and answers, especially at the time of the cross-examination.[117] A perception remains that, when the judge steps into the arena, the defendant could be left with a sense of injustice on the ground that his (or her) case has not been fairly put before the jury. Therefore, a judge must not intervene with such frequency and hostility as to convey to the jury a disbelief of the witness's evidence[118]. Furthermore, case law has also recently suggested that, although a member of the jury is entitled to formulate questions during the cross-examinations of witnesses, this is a 'dangerous practice not to be encouraged' by the court.[119]

---

114 *R. v. Whybrow*, (1994) 144 N.L.J. 124 (C.A.).

115 *R. v. Hulusi* (1974), 58 Cr. App. R. 378 (C.A.) 385 (L.J. Lawton).

116 *Jones v. National Coal Board*, [1957] 2 Q.B. 55 (C.A.).

117 Cf. *R. v. Wiggan*, The Times, 22 March 1999 (C.A.); *R. v. Leggett*, [1970] 1 Q.B. 67 (C.A.); *R. v. Clewer*, (1953) 37 Cr. App. R. 37 (C.A.).

118 The matter has once been brought to Strasbourg: the related ruling, however, suggests that the intensity and nature of interruptions are in principle matters for the appreciation of domestic courts; cf. *C G. v. U.K.*, App. No. 43373/98 (19 December 2001), (2002) 34 EHRR 789.

119 *R. v. Barnes*, [1991] Crim. L.R. 132 (C.A.).

In Italian law, the matter is governed under Article 506(2) of the Code of criminal procedure: the president of the court may question all court declarants (including the co-defendant and the civil party) after the cross-examination by the opposing party. Counsel enjoys the right to bring to a close the oral performance of their witnesses by means of the re-examination. In practice, judges are reluctant to abandon their long-standing habit of leading the examination. Their justification would normally be that the evidence elicited up to that moment had been ambiguous, or insufficient. No case law has ever suggested that an overactive role of the court could lead to the quashing of a criminal conviction on appeal.

A final question to be answered here is whether the accused may be granted permission to *personally* interview his or her accusers in the courtroom. The state of the law in the model countries is considerably diverse. At common law, the defendant has a right to represent himself[120] and this obviously includes the right to cross-examine all witnesses against him. In England, however, statutory reforms have increasingly restricted the ambit of application of this right in order to prevent intimidation in circumstances in which it is purported that the witness would find a personal altercation with the accused extraordinarily distressful. *C.J.A. 1991* introduced for the first time a prohibition on cross-examination by the accused in person, with regard to certain child witnesses and complainants in sexual cases.[121] This provision was later repealed and replaced by the broader *Y.J.C.E.A. 1999*, ss. 30-40. A general prohibition on personal cross examination is now established in any case involving the complainant of a sexual offence[122] and children victims or witnesses of a sexual offence.[123] In addition, a new provision has given the court a wide discretion to prohibit cross-examination by the accused in person in any case, even of its own motion: this may lead to conclude that the right to a personal cross-examination has virtually been abolished in English law.[124] In comparison, no right to cross-

---

[120] In the United States, the right to the *pro se representation*, although not absolute, has a constitutional foundation (*U.S. v. Dougherty* 473 F.2d 1113 (D.C. Cir. 1972)) and rules of evidence, procedure and substantive law are applied in the same way to all parties to a criminal trials, whether they are represented by counsel or they are acting pro se (*Williams v. State*, 549 S.W.2d 183, 187 (Tex. Crim. App. 1977)).

[121] *C.J.A. 1991*, s. 55(7) inserted a new s. 34A into the *C.J.A. 1988*.

[122] *Y.J.C.E.A. 1999*, s. 34.

[123] *Y.J.C.E.A. 1999*, s. 35.

[124] *Y.J.C.E.A. 1999*, s. 36. This power may be exercised if the court is satisfied that (1) the quality of the evidence given by the witness is likely to be diminished by a cross examination in person, or (2) the evidence is likely to be improved if such cross examination were prohibited, and that it would not be contrary to the interests of justice to do so. According to Part 31 of the *Criminal Procedure Rules 2005*, in these cases 'the court shall explain to the accused as early in the proceedings as is reasonably practicable that he a) is prevented from cross-examining a witness in person; and b) should arrange for a legal representative to act for him for the purpose of cross-examining the witness'.

examine adverse witnesses in person ever existed in French law where, as it has been anticipated, the president's mediation is required for any questioned advanced by the defendant.[125] In Italy, the matter has only recently emerged, following the reformation of Article 111 of the Constitution. Article 111(4) now states that the accused may not be found guilty of the charged offence 'on the basis of the evidence given by those who have always avoided confrontation *with the defendant or his counsel*'. In the light of this phrasing, some commentators[126] have promptly argued that a personal right to cross-examine has now been introduced and that this provision should obviously prevail over Article 498(1) of the Code, which restricts to the prosecutor and counsel the procedural right to perform examination-in-chief and cross-examination. Although this view has also found the endorsement of a local criminal court,[127] the majority of Italian commentators are strongly opposed to it.[128]

3.3.2 The Questions

This section will disclose how great a gulf separates inquisitorial and adversarial methods for the collection of testimonial evidence in the courtroom. Whilst the solutions adopted by French and English law are emblems of their differing models, Italian criminal procedure is experiencing a rather confusing transitional phase.

As far as French law is concerned, the matter can be satisfactorily dealt with in a single paragraph. Pursuant to Article 331(5) of the Code, witnesses are expected to give their evidence 'on the facts brought against the defendant, his morality and his personality'. One may wonder what legal provision could allow more liberty for the questioning of a person in a court of justice. The principle of *liberté de la preuve*, mentioned earlier in this work,[129] finds full implementation here. To be accurate, a few basic limitations on the scope and manner of questioning may be found, but, in practice, they play only a marginal role. Firstly, the president and court may not disclose their opinion on the accused's guilt.[130] Secondly, case law forbids French counsel from commenting upon the evidence

---

[125] See (F) Cass. crim., 26 January 1994, Hamchaoui, [1994] Gaz. Pal. Crim. 164.

[126] C. Taormina, *Riforme Da Riformare*, [2000-I] Giust. Pen. 1; S. Maffei, *Il Diritto al Confronto con l'Accusatore*, CELT, Piacenza, 2003, 307-309.

[127] (I) Tribunale di Cagliari, judgment of 9 June 2000, Porcu, [2000] Dir. Pen. Proc. 1235.

[128] P. Ferrua, *Una Garanzia 'Finale' a Tutela del Contraddittorio: il Nuovo Art. 526 comma 1bis CPP*, in P. Tonini (ed.), *Giusto Processo: Nuove Norme sulla Formazione e Valutazione della Prova*, Cedam, Padova, 2001, 522; G. Di Chiara, *La 'Nuova' Istruttoria Dibattimentale: Attuazione del 'Giusto Processo', Metodo del Contraddittorio e Prova Rappresentativa*, [2001-V] Foro Ital. 295; P.P. Paulesu, *Giudice e Parti nella 'Dialettica' della Prova Testimoniale*, Giappichelli, Torino, 2002, 242.

[129] Cf. Chapter 4, s 4.5.

[130] (F) Cass. crim., 4 June 1984, *Bull. crim.* n°201, X.

or from 'manipulating' it while it is given.[131] Thirdly, the president may object to the questions posed by the parties, pursuant to the discretionary powers under the terms of Article 310 of the procedural Code. Since parties may require the court to state formal reasons for a refusal of this type,[132] however, denials tend to be confined to striking examples of dilatory[133] or aggressive conduct by counsel.

By contrast, analysis of the same topic under English law would require the exposition of the most technical, difficult and controversial chapters of the law of evidence. In Chapter 4, it was argued that the main function of evidence law in an adversarial context is precisely to establish some exclusionary rules. Professor Tapper describes these exclusionary rules as 'provisions declaring that certain matters which may well be accepted as evidence of a fact by other responsible inquirers will not be accepted by the courts, rules declaring, in other words, what is not judicial evidence'.[134] As far as the examination of witnesses is concerned, exclusionary rules establish which questions can be put before them at the time of their examination-in-chief, cross-examination and re-examination. While a comprehensive account of these matters is far beyond the scope of this work, a few considerations are nevertheless functional to the arguments that are made later.

In very simplified terms, restrictions on questioning in English law may be grouped in two main categories.

The first category comprises the questions that are forbidden due to their specific formulation. Leading questions at the stage of the examination-in-chief are an example. Leading questions are normally defined as questions framed in such a way as to suggest the answer sought or to assume the existence of facts yet to be established. 'Leading', however, is a relative[135] concept, and the determination of whether a question is leading or not has created long-standing disputes among the authors of manuals of trial techniques. It may also be observed that strict adherence to the rule is neither desirable nor possible; in fact, it is settled that leading questions relating to introductory or undisputed matters are unobjectionable. Notwithstanding the theoretical uncertainties and these minor exceptions, the class of leading questions appears to be fully established within English law. The rationale of this rule is twofold. Firstly, it is reasoned upon the assumption that the witness may be biased in favour of the party bringing him (or her) to court. Secondly, it is fair to say that the party calling a witness has an advantage over the adversary, since the former generally knows beforehand what evidence the witness is likely to say. In any case, conducting an examination-in-chief out of the blue is a hazardous strategy: the summoning party would run

[131] (F) Cass. crim., 5 March 1986, *Bull. crim.* n°92, Rodrigues.

[132] Under the procedure of the so-called *incident contentieux*, Art. 316 F-CPP.

[133] (F) Cass. crim., 21 July 1993, *Bull. crim.* n°251, Bidart.

[134] C. Tapper, *Cross and Tapper on Evidence*, 9th edn., Butterworths, London, 1999, 1.

[135] W.M. Best, *The Principles of the Law of Evidence*, 12th edn., Sweet & Maxwell, London, 1922, 562.

the risk of placing a weapon in the hands of the opponent. It is also important to stress that evidence elicited by leading questions during examination-in-chief is not per se inadmissible, albeit its weight may be substantially reduced.[136] Exceptions to the rule are also established to confront the situation where a witness provides evidence unfavourable to the party that summoned him or her: for this reason, special procedures apply in England for the examination of hostile[137] and unfavourable[138] witnesses.

The second – extremely broad – category consists of questions that are banned because they elicit 'irrelevant' or inadmissible evidence. In order to thwart irrelevancy, for instance, counsel are prevented from contradicting the answer given by witnesses in cross-examination on matters which go merely to the credit but which are otherwise irrelevant to the issues in the case. This rule, known as 'rule of finality of answers to questions on collateral matters', is reasoned upon the desirability of avoiding the multiplication of collateral issues.

The major adversary exclusionary rules are 'hearsay', 'opinion' and 'character'. Something must be briefly said about them in turn. The rule against hearsay states that an assertion other than one made by a person while giving evidence in the proceedings is inadmissible as evidence of any fact asserted.[139] The opinion rule is based on the idea that a witness should not be allowed to give an estimation on matters which the court considers call for the special skill or knowledge of an expert. Hence, witnesses may only give evidence of facts that they have personally perceived and not evidence of the inference they have drawn from such facts. The rule stands on the assumption that a clear cut line divides facts from opinion, a matter that appears to have given rise to little litigation in England compared to the United States.[140] Finally, the exclusionary rule concerning character prevents the prosecution from adducing evidence of the personality of the accused in any form. The broad nature of this rule may be inferred from the fact that it covers previous convictions –the so called 'similar facts evidence' – misconduct, disposition towards wrongdoing or immoral-

---

136 *Moor v. Moor,* [1954] 1 W.L.R. 927; *R. v. Wilson* (1913) 9 Cr. App. R. 124 (C.A.).

137 A witness may be deemed 'hostile' by the trial judge when he or she appears not desirous of telling the truth and bears a hostile animus towards the party calling him or her. Hostile witnesses can be cross-examined but the party producing them is never allow to impeach their credit by general evidence of bad character; cf. *C.P.A. 1865*, s. 3. For discussion, R. Pattenden, *The Hostile Witness,* (1992) 56 Journal Crim. Law 414-425; M. Newark, *The Hostile Witness and the Adversary System*, [1986] Crim. L.R. 441-454.

138 'Unfavourable' are deemed all those witnesses who fail to give the evidence that was expected from them: they cannot be discredited or cross-examined by the party calling them but other evidence can be called to 'repair the damage done'; cf. *Ewer v. Ambrose,* (1825) 3 B.&C. 746.

139 C. Tapper, *Cross and Tapper on Evidence, supra* note 134, 530, adopted by *R. v. Kearley,* [1992] 2 A.C. 228 (H.L.).

140 In the U.S., the matter is governed by F.R.E. 701. For discussion cf. C.B. Mueller and L.C. Kirkpatrick, *Evidence*, 2nd edn., Aspen Law & Business, Gaithersburg, 1999, 688-696.

ity, or even bad reputation. The three rules are subject to an array of technical exceptions whose exact determination involves careful legal scrutiny and give rise to endless and animated disputes between the parties. The most invoked common law exceptions to the hearsay rule in criminal cases include dying declarations,[141] spontaneous statements,[142] and statements concerning contemporaneous mental[143] or physical state.[144] Statutory exceptions include first hand documentary hearsay as defined under *C.J.A. 1988*, s. 23 and trade, business and related documents, pursuant to *C.J.A. 1988*, s. 24. As for the opinion rule, it is settled that it does not apply when the impression is derived from facts that are too complicated to be separated and distinctly narrated'.[145] The parameter upon which similar fact evidence ought to be admitted is also highly controversial: evidence of character can be brought to a jury when its probative force, due to instances of striking similarities,[146] outweighs the prejudice against the accused.

It is a typical feature of the English trial that a question posed to the witness attracts the objections from the adverse party. Objections reasoned upon the formulation of a purported leading question may sometimes create sometimes heated disputes. Objections relating to hearsay, opinion and character will almost invariably do so. In order to decide whether to allow or exclude the question, the judge will often need to predict whether the forthcoming answer of the witness might amount to admissible or inadmissible evidence. At this stage, complexity is both inevitable and essential, as the entire corpus of evidence law is intended to operate *before* the witness jumps the gun and gives the answer. As noted earlier, a perception remains that once inadmissible evidence has been elicited, 'the damage is done' as the jury will inevitably be influenced by it.

In practice, the English judge may not understand the thrust of the objection, ignorant as he or she is of what the witness is expected to say, or may need more time to hear the arguments from counsel. This is the purpose of the

---

[141] A declaration may not be caught by the hearsay rule if given by a person under a settled and hopeless expectation of death and adduced in evidence, in murder cases, to prove the cause of the declarant's death; *Mills v. R.*, [1995] 1 W.L.R. 511 (P.C. Jamaica) 521.

[142] It is settled that evidence of a hearsay statements made spontaneously by a participant in, or a observer of, an event may be admissible as part of the *res gestae*, cf. the landmark decision *R. v. Bedingfield*, (1879) 14 Cox C.C. 341.

[143] Cf. *R. v. Blastland*, [1986] A.C. 41 (H.L.).

[144] Statements concerning contemporaneous physical sensations are admissible in evidence to prove the existence of those sensations

[145] J.H. Wigmore, *Evidence in Trials at Common Law*, J.H. Chadbourn Rev., Little Brown, Boston, 1978, vol. VII, §1918, quoting the opinion of Gibson J. in the ancient case of *Cornell v. Green*, 10 S.&R. 14, 16 (Pa. 1823).

[146] English law has got itself in a multitude of difficulties in the attempt to put exact boundaries to this expression. The leading case on the 'sufficient probative force' required to admit evidence of character is *D.P.P. v. P.*, [1991] 2 A.C. 447 (H.L.).

'sidebar' or 'bench conferences' in the U.S. legal system. Most of these conferences are on record but they occur outside the jury's hearing, in order to keep the jury from overhearing what is debated. Sometimes these discussions may by animated, leaving the jury, the witness and the public puzzled on what is going on and why. In England, by comparison, the idea is that where an issue arises as to the admissibility of evidence, there should be no discussion of the matter in front of the jury. When a decision cannot be taken on the spot, the judge may order the jury out of the courtroom and allow the parties to fully argue their cases. There can even be a proper hearing within the trial (*voir dire* hearings)[147] in which the judge may preview the proposed testimony from the witness in relatively relaxed circumstances. This may help the judge to assess if all or parts of the testimony are appropriate for the jury's consideration.

It should now be apparent that interruptions are the defining feature of the course of evidence in the Anglo-American world. The skill of the U.S. attorney and English barrister consists precisely of the management of the aforementioned exclusionary rules, in order to maximise favourable information and to attack effectively the reliability of adverse testimonies and the credit of their authors.

In line with its contemporary adversarial assumptions, Italian evidence law also prevents the parties from posing a significant number of questions to testifying witnesses. In practice, however, exclusionary rules are not always effectively enforced as litigants and judges appear to a certain extent reluctant to adapt to the recently enacted reforms.[148] As in England, certain questions are banned for their very formulation, while others for the fact that they may elicit non-usable[149] evidence. The actual impact of these two sets of rules on the style of questioning, however, is much less significant than in England. I will now discuss them in turn.

Pursuant to Article 499(2) I-CPP any question that 'may hamper the sincerity of the related answers' is banned at all stages of the examination. The rather vague formulation of this provision has led commentators to construe narrowly this class of the 'damaging questions', so as to rule out only extreme instances of improper, aggressive or deceitful conduct by counsel. Leading questions are banned during the examination-in-chief, although no remedies are established for the case in which a witness turns adverse to the party that summoned him

---

[147] The rules for *voire dire* hearings are set out in *R. v. Mitchell*, [1998] A.C. 695 (P.C. Bahamas). At the conclusion of the *voire dire*, the judge should not mention to the jury the merit of the decisions taken: the jury could be lead to believe that, in the light of such rulings, the judge has formed a particular view on the facts in issue.

[148] I have briefly touched upon the cultural and historical reasons for this resistance in Chapter 4, section 3.2.3.

[149] The features of the category of *inutilizzabilità* (non-usability) in Italian criminal procedure have been discussed in Chapter 4, section 4.4.

or her.[150] In addition, there has not yet been any conceptualisation of the nature of the 'leading question', and the matter is only incidentally dealt with in the textbooks of criminal procedure.

Some other questions are banned because they may elicit non-usable information. The matter requires a preliminary remark. As argued in Chapter 4, rules of non-usability mainly speak to the courts, not the parties. These rules are complied with if no reference is made to non-usable evidence in the judgment, but do not necessarily prevent the parties from eliciting the related evidence. It is now time to observe one of these rules in operation. In principle, first hand hearsay evidence is non-usable under Italian law. Questions eliciting hearsay, however, may not attract objection, since the exclusionary rule of Article 195[151] of the Code operates only *after* the hearsay statement is tendered into evidence. The rule states that the assertion of Mr. B, as reported by the testifying Mr. A, may not be used in evidence *unless* Mr. B comes to court and testifies on the issue. It is clear that the question of summoning Mr. B[152] only comes into the picture once Mr. A has given the hearsay declaration to the court. Italian criminal courts, therefore, may legitimately hear the substance of such 'non-usable' source of information. Only one 'hearsay question' is objectionable under Italian law pursuant to Article 195(4): police agents and officers cannot be asked to report the content of the depositions that they collected from an informant at the time of the investigation.

Opinion evidence from a non-expert witness is also non-usable under Italian law. Prompt objections from counsel may here put off the answer since, pursuant to Article 194(3) of the Code, witnesses are to be examined 'on matters of fact only'. Personal impressions and beliefs, however, may be elicited if intimately affiliated with a fact in issue. As for character, Italian law allows criminal records to be included as documentary evidence in the court dossier; nevertheless, witnesses cannot be questioned generically on the 'morality' of the defendant.[153]

To summarise, more than a decade after the introduction of the new procedural Code, examinations in Italian courts of criminal justice bear little resemblance to the dynamics of the Anglo-American tradition. Interruptions are, therefore, much less frequent than in an English trial. Besides, no evidentiary sanctions are enforced against the pursuance of damaging and leading lines of

---

150 Under Italian law, however, the use of previous inconsistent statements to impeach the witness is not confined to cross-examination, cf. below section 3.3.4.

151 This provision sets out the legal conditions for the admissibility of 'indirect testimony' (*testimonianza de relato*). Article 195 refers to the case in which Mr. A, a testifying witness, reports what Mr. B told him. The provision only applies when the truth of Mr. B's assertion is in issue, and clearly overlaps with the common law theory of hearsay.

152 The summons of Mr. B may be served on behalf of the parties or the court *ex officio* (Art. 195(2) I-CPP).

153 Pursuant to Art. 194(1) I-CPP.

questioning. In addition, some non-usable evidence may legally be elicited from testifying witnesses. The assumption is that a professional judge is always able to disregard any item of non-usable evidence, despite the fact that he or she may have come across much of such evidence during the adjudication process.

3.3.3 The Answers

Under French law, freedom of questioning corresponds to freedom of answering. The fluency of the witnesses' account will seldom be interrupted and testimony would be intermingled with hearsay and opinion.[154] It is for the Assize Court to intimately assess the evidentiary value of such depositions, in line with the principle of the *liberté de la preuve*.

By comparison, the very purpose of English evidence law is to prevent inadmissible evidence from being elicited in the first place. However, it is not always possible for counsel and judge to interpose and make their objections in time to stop the witness from giving answers. Exclusionary rules may be – and indeed often are – bypassed by mere accident and may thus cause 'accidental prejudice'. Over the centuries, the law has developed an array of remedies to deal with accidental prejudices, in order to adjust flexibly to their specific gravity. Normally, the judge will promptly announce in solemn terms that the answer is 'no evidence'. The answer will then be struck from the record and the jury will be ordered to disregard it. If this is the case, trust is placed on the fairness of jurors in moving that issue away from their minds. Whenever necessity arises, the English judge may also discharge the jury and order a new trial. This often occurs when a witness spontaneously reports the accused's bad character at a trial in which character is not in issue.[155] The idea is that under certain circumstances, a direction to disregard some evidence will not suffice to compensate for the prejudice against the accused or, from a different angle, that the jury are incapable of dismissing certain items of evidence from their minds, at the time of deliberation.[156]

By definition, 'non-usable' evidence (such as hearsay or opinion) that was elicited – legitimately or by accident – from testifying witnesses before Italian courts cannot be relied upon to ground a judgement. Matters of non-usability may be reviewed in appeal or before the Supreme Court, pursuant to Article 191(2) of the Italian Code of criminal procedure. It must be repeated that the

---

[154] French case law allows the witnesses to freely express their opinion (*sentiment*): cf. (F) Cass. crim., 28 February 1979, *Bull. crim.* n° 90, Birague, according to which 'the words spoken spontaneously by the witness at the hearing do not affect to any extent the validity of the procedure'.

[155] *R. v. Weaver*, [1968] 1 Q.B. 353 (C.A.).

[156] Although, in principle, the decision to discharge the jury remains a matter for the judge's discretion, the Court of Appeal has sometimes agreed to overrule decisions taken in trials at first instance; cf. *R. v. Palmer*, (1935) 25 Cr. App. R. 97 (C.A.).

sanction of non-usability operates so long as the court makes some reference to non-usable pieces of evidence in the written reasons. The fact that Italian courts may come across various types of non-usable evidence, however, casts some doubts over the effectiveness of these exclusionary rules. Similar considerations will also apply to the rules governing the use of prior inconsistent statements, for which extensive discussion is provided in the following section.

3.3.4 Prior Inconsistent Statements

The court testimony of a witness may differ from what he or she reported to police, prosecutors or defence counsel at pre-trial stage. This section explores the evidentiary value of prior inconsistent statements and the procedures to be followed to bring them to the attention of the courts.

French law adheres to the inquisitorial archetype: prior statements of witnesses to investigating authorities are included in the court *dossier* and are made available for consultation to the president of the Assize Court. At the time of the oral examination, the president (and now also the parties)[157] may challenge the witnesses with their prior inconsistent statements. Any inconsistency in the multiple accounts of a witness is to be recorded in the *procès verbal.* The *principle du contradictoire,* as interpreted by the French legal theory,[158] only requires that the reading[159] of the prior deposition *follows* the oral deposition.[160] If this formality is complied with, prior statements may then count as evidence.[161]

Italian laws, instead, follow adversarial assumptions. Criminal courts are innocent of the previous statements of a testifying witness,[162] until one of the parties introduces them in the course of evidence, to impeach his or her credibility. As a general rule, previous inconsistent statements merely impugn the oral testimony and, therefore, may not be employed as evidence of the facts stated. The present rule re-embraces a principle that had been put forward by the original version of the Code in 1989, and later suffered of shifting statu-

---

157 See above, section 3.3.1.

158 See discussion in Chapter 4, section 4.3.

159 The reading of prior depositions ought to be performed in the presence of all concerned parties: (F) Cass. crim., 9 April 1986, *Bull. crim.* n° 120, Klasa.

160 (F) Cass. crim., 8 January 1992, *Bull. crim.* n°4, Weber.

161 This accords with ECHR law: when witnesses are examined in accordance with the confrontational paradigm, no violation of Art. 6(3)(d) may be invoked if their previous depositions are used in evidence, in spite of their inconsistency with the oral testimony. As suggested in Chapter 3, the assumption is that, in these circumstances, previous statements become part of a confrontational process of adjudication; cf. *Camilleri v. Malta*, App. No. 51760/99 (16 March 2000).

162 With the exception of the evidence collected at the special hearing termed *incidente probatorio*; cf. above, section 3.1.1.

tory reforms.[163] The new amended version of Article 500(2)[164] establishes that previous inconsistent statements included in the prosecution file may be read in court only to impeach the credibility of the witness, unless it is proved that the witness has been bribed or threatened to change his or her deposition. All parties to the proceeding may impeach the witness with prior inconsistent statements, as statutory provisions do not confine this procedure to the stage of cross-examination. This feature may be seen as a compensation for the absence, in the Italian code, of remedies concerning hostile witnesses. It is crucial to note, however, that prior statements tendered in evidence to impeach the witness are transferred from the prosecution dossier into the trial dossier.[165] Here, a few practical problems may arise. Normally, the entire document in which the previous depositions have been recorded is transferred from one dossier into the other, with the consequence that all of it, not only the passages quoted by the impeaching party, becomes available for consultation to the courts. The assumption, once again, is that the courts will only take account of the paragraphs read out by the impeaching party. Improper reference to prior statements can be challenged before the Supreme Court, pursuant to Article 606(1)(c) of the Code of criminal procedure.

A separate comment is required for English law, in which seismic changes to well-established principles of law have been brought about by the entry into force of *C.J.A. 2003*. Before April 5, 2005, when prior inconsistent statement were put in evidence under *C.P.A. 1865*, ss. 4-5, they went only to the credit of the witness,[166] except to the extent that the maker adopted any part of it as true. Several options were open to the parties as to the manner to challenge the person on the stand. First, cross-examination on the general content of previous statements was allowed without it being shown to the witness. However, counsel must have had the statement at their disposal, in case the judge required it to be produced for inspection.[167] Secondly, previous written statements could be shown to the witness without putting them in evidence. The witness could be directed to read the relevant part of it to himself, and would have then be asked whether he wished to adhere to his testimony. If he did so, there was no need to contradict him and put the document in evidence. Thirdly, if the party

---

[163] The principle of non-usability of prior inconsistent statement as evidence of the matter stated was overturned in 1992, following a Constitutional Court ruling against the original version of Art. 500 I-CPP; this provision was amended accordingly by virtue of Law No 356/1992.

[164] As amended by Law No. 63/2001.

[165] Cf. Art. 511(5) I-CPP.

[166] Illustration of the common law is provided by *R. v. White*, (1922) 17 Cr. App. R. 60 (C.A.).There is no need to give proof of previous statements when the witness himself (or herself) admits to having made a previous oral or written statement inconsistent with the present testimony cf. *R. v. P. (G.R.)* [1998] Crim. L.R. 663 (C.A.).

[167] *R. v. Anderson*, (1929) 21 Cr. App. R. 178 (C.A.); *R. v. Yousry*, (1914) 11 Cr. App. R. 13 (C.A.).

had wished to contradict the witness, he was required to put the document in evidence by reading out aloud the contradictory statement.[168] After a request fro an explanation to the defendant, it was open to the judge to decide which part of the written document should have gone before the jury. In other words, the judge could prevent the jury from hearing sections of the previous statements other than those upon which the cross examination had been based.[169] In any case, it was also a duty of the judge to inform the jury of the peculiar evidentiary value of prior inconsistent statements.[170] After April 5, 2005, however, the law changed. *C.J.A. 2003*, s. 119 now establishes that prior inconsistent statements proved by virtue of *C.P.A. 1865* are routinely admissible in England as evidence of the matter stated therein[171]. In such cases, it is for the judge to direct the jury as to the appropriate weight to be attached to the statement. Such prior statements, however, may only be introduced in evidence by the opposing party, during the cross examination.

3.4 The Evaluation of Testimony

The Bible required the evidence of two or three witnesses for capital punishment.[172] By contrast, analysis of English, Italian and French contemporary law reveals that the evidence of one witness alone may prove any issue and ground a criminal conviction even for the most serious offences. The principle is subject only to minor exceptions.[173] Hence, one prosecution witness may well be relied upon in preference to several witnesses lined up by the defence, and the opposite is equally true. This state of affairs does not violate ECHR law.[174] The Italian and English legal orders, however, are sensitive to the

---

[168] *R. v. Riley*, (1866) 4 F.&F. 964 (Guildford Crown Court), *R. v. Wright*, (1866) 4 F.&F. 967 (Guildford Crown Court).

[169] *R. v. Beattie*, (1989) 89 Cr. App. R. 302 (C.A.); *R. v. Longden*, The Times, 31 May 1995 (C.A.).

[170] *R. v. Askew*, [1981] Crim. L.R. 398 (C.A.); *R. v. Jarvis*, [1991] Crim. L.R. 374 (C.A.). For an early authority see *R. v. Birch*, [1924] 18 Cr. App. R. 26 (CA).

[171] To be accurate the letter of *C.J.A. 2003*, s. 119 reads as follows: the prior inconsistent statement is admissible as evidence of any matter stated of which oral evidence by [the witness] would be admissible.

[172] Deuteronomy 17:6, 19:15-18 (King James); these passages also imply that the depositions had to be given in public.

[173] For some French references, see (F) Cass. crim., 27 March 1931, *Bull. crim.* n°93, Batthyany and (F) Cass. crim., 13 January 1960, *Bull. crim.* n°17, Ferrandi. In Italy, the principle is absolutely unquestioned, since corroboration is required for the evidence of co-defendants only, pursuant to Art. 192(3) I-CPP. As far as England is concerned, the principle is affirmed in *D.P.P. v. Hester*, [1973] A.C. 296 (H.L.) and *D.P.P. v. Kilbourne*, [1973] A.C. 729 (H.L.). However, two narrow statutory exceptions to the rule apply: perjury (*Perjury Act 1911*, s. 13) and treason (*Treason Act 1795*, s. 1, a provision to be repealed from a day to be appointed, *Crime and Disorder Act 1998*, s. 36) for which the evidence of one witness does not suffice.

[174] *X. v. U.K.*, App. No. 6208/73 (29 September 1975), 2 Digest Strasbourg 389.

idea that, in certain circumstances, it may be unwise to allow too much reliance on a court declarant, even if he or she has been subject to an orthodox confrontational examination. No such restrictions may be found in French law, owing to its engrained reluctance to place straitjacket upon the *intime conviction* of the court.

Historically, the common law developed several rules of corroboration, either because of the nature of the allegation or because the witness fell into a particular class. The corroboration requirements applied to the depositions of (1) complainants in sexual cases, (2) accomplices of the defendants when summoned by the prosecution and (3) children. In these cases, the judge warned the jury that it would have been dangerous to give full credit to the concerned depositions, unless they were accompanied by some other supporting evidence. In recent times, the law of corroboration became extremely technical and was thus criticised on various grounds. Firstly, it was widely believed that a typical corroboration direction bordered on the unintelligible to the ordinary person.[175] Secondly, a change of perception consolidated as for the purported inherent unreliability of the child witness. Thirdly, the corroboration direction in sexual cases was perceived as offensive to women. Following the publication of a Law Commission report[176] that argued that the corroboration rules had made the law 'arcane, technical and difficult to convey to juries',[177] legislation abolished them at once.[178] English statutory reform, however, has not entirely eradicated the issuing of judicial warnings on the weight to be attached to the evidence of certain witnesses. Beyond the three aforementioned categories, common law had also developed the idea that in some exceptional cases, usually referred to as 'analogous cases', justice demanded that the jury be warned of a special need for caution. Regrettably, these occurrences have never been accurately defined and the matter has raised conflicting opinions among commentators. Some guidance on the circumstances that might merit a judicial warning can be found in the case law concerning the evidence of co-defendants,[179] mental patients[180] or witnesses tainted by improper motive.[181] Although no obligation to warn the jury about the dangers of convicting on the basis of this evidence alone exists, the judge retains the discretion to do so.[182] No specific wording is recom-

---

[175] *D.P.P. v. Hester, supra* note 173, 328 (Lord Diplock).

[176] Law Commission, *Corroboration of Evidence in Criminal Trials*, Law Com. No. 115, 1990.

[177] *R. v. Cheema*, [1994] 1 W.L.R. 147 (C.A.) 158.

[178] This reform was passed in two stages: *C.J.A. 1988*, s. 34 (referring to children) and *C.J.P.O. 1994*, s. 32 (referring to the other aforementioned categories of witnesses).

[179] *R. v. Prater*, [1960] 2 Q.B. 464 (C.A.); *R. v. Loveridge*, (1983) 76 Cr. App. R. 125 (C.A.); *R. v. Knowlden*, (1983) 77 Cr. App. R. 94 (C.A.).

[180] *R. v. Spencer*, [1987] A.C. 128 (H.L.); *R. v. Bagshaw*, [1984] 1 W.L.R. 477 (C.A.).

[181] This is the so called 'suspect witness'; cf. *R. v. Beck*, [1982] 1 W.L.R. 461 (C.A.).

[182] This view is challenged by C. Tapper, *Cross and Tapper on Evidence*, supra *note* 134, 228. The author argues that there exists an obligation, not a mere discretion, to give warning of caution with regard to all witnesses 'involved in some way in the commission of the crime with which the accused is charged'.

mended, so long as the direction is suitably and fairly tailored to the circumstances of the case.[183] The Court of Appeal is extremely reluctant to interfere with the exercise of this discretion.[184]

In Italy, corroboration is required for the evidence of co-defendants who are tried jointly or separately (Article 192(3) I-CPP), as well as for the evidence of the 'assisted witness' (Article 197bis(6) I-CPP). In other words, the law sets out a presumption of unreliability[185], on the rationale that the deposition of an accomplice is always tainted by his or her intent to set the charges aside or to minimise the involvement in the concerned offence. Although the rule of corroboration applies to all criminal proceedings, it is especially significant in mafia trials, in which the statements of an (alleged) former clan member are often the only available evidence. In a theoretical perspective, it must also be said that the rule has caused some discomfort among commentators, who struggled to align it with the principle of the court's free evaluation of usable evidence.[186] Contrary to ECHR discourse, however, Italian case law has established over the years a remarkably solid concept of 'corroboration'. A three-staged test for the assessment of corroboration has been developed in several rulings of the Supreme Court on mafia proceedings.[187] Firstly, the court should focus on the credit of the declarant and consider his or her personality, previous convictions as well as motive for the decision to take the stand against a former associate. Secondly, the courts should assess the reliability of the account on the basis of certain parameters, such as precision, spontaneity and consistency over time. Thirdly, the evidence must be appreciated in the context of all other 'external' sources that may support, or else challenge, its reliability. Only when these three steps are taken and the court is satisfied that the evidence is worthy of belief, may the deposition of a co-accused legitimately ground a criminal conviction. The evaluating process must be accurately explained in the reasons of the judgments: failure to do so would most likely result in the quashing of the conviction by the Supreme Court.[188]

---

[183] P. Murphy (ed.), *Blackstone's Criminal Practice 2004*, Oxford Univ. Press, Oxford, 2003, §F5.8; C. Tapper, *Cross and Tapper on Evidence, supra* note 134, 228.

[184] *R. v. Makanjuola*, [1995] 1 W.L.R. 1348 (C.A.).

[185] See (I) Cass. crim., 19 January 1990, Cardaropoli, [1991] Archivio Nuova Procedura Penale 129. This opinion is endorsed by V. Grevi, *Le Dichiarazioni Rese dal Coimputato nel Nuovo Codice di Procedura Penale*, in L. De Cataldo Neuberger, *Chiamata in Correità e Psicologia del Pentitismo nel Nuovo Processo Penale*, Cedam, Padova, 1992, 7-46.

[186] This principle was discussed in Chapter 4, section 4.5. According to F. Cordero, *Procedura Penale*, 7th edn., Giuffrè, Milano, 2003, 624, Article 192(3) of the Code 'attempts to codify what cannot be sensibly codified'.

[187] The landmark decision is (I) Cass. crim., 21 October 1992, Marino, [1993] Cass. Pen. 1939.

[188] Cf. Art. 606(1)(e) I-CPP.

4 Conclusion

Facts do play an important role, of course, in the drama of a criminal case, and among those facts the face-to face confrontation between the accused and his or her accuser is likely to have an impact that goes far beyond the technicalities of the law. The courtroom is the ideal stage for such confrontation. There, the opponents are placed the one in front of the other, before the attentive eyes of the public, the judge and the jury. Every detail may be noticed, every answer may be challenged by the opponent, every question may leave a trace in the mind of the trier of the fact. It is at this very moment that the fate of the accused is often decided, and ritualism is thus essential. The public expects the prosecution to present the accuser in an attempt to elicit the evidence directly from his or her lips. The clerk calls the witness's name, he or she enters the courtroom, he or she takes the stand, the oath, and then the challenge begins.

It comes as no surprise to discover that these crucial – and emotional – moments are fully governed and regulated by procedural law. In this chapter, the process of courtroom confrontation was investigated with regard to Italian, French and English criminal practice. The status of 'informants' and 'witness' have been discussed, together with the duties and obligations of court declarants. Something was said on the questions that may be asked, the answers that may be given, the objections that may be brought forward by the parties and the use in evidence of prior inconsistent statements.

The chapter has shown the *beauty of diversity* of national laws in ensuring the 'confrontational paradigm' described in Chapter 1. More specifically, three sets of conclusions have been reached.

Firstly, it was argued that a series of differences among the rules of the three model Countries is based on their adversarial or inquisitorial assumptions. In Italy and England, for instance, pre-trial contacts between witnesses and counsel are encouraged and perceived as essential means to prepare the parties for direct and cross-examination. In France, instead, pre-trial deposition may only be collected by the police and the investigating judge. An opposition between *fluency* and *interruptions* was also staged with regard to the style of the oral debate. In the adversarial variant, the depositions of witnesses are lead by counsel who are also bound to comply with a number of exclusionary rules. This is the reason why in England and Italy witnesses are bound to answer specifically to the questions brought forward by the parties and are not allowed to give a free account of their experience. Instead, in France, the witness is invited to speak freely, and no interruption from the parties is tolerated until the declarant has completed his or her description of the events. Secondly, it was suggested that some more differences among the model Countries are the product of unique national traditions. This is the case for the legal rules concerning the 'accuser co-defendant', exposed in section 3.2.3, and for the corroboration rules, which were recently abolished in England after decades of criticism and were instead imported in Italy with a view to proceedings for mafia crimes. Thirdly, some significant similarities among the Model Countries have also been found. In France, Italy and England, the sanctions for false testimony are practically identical, and the evidence of one adverse witness alone may prove any issue and ground a criminal conviction even for the most serious offences.

It is now time to move on to investigate the extent of the departures from the confrontational paradigm in the model Counties. In the following chapter, the analysis of the categories of absent, anonymous and vulnerable witnesses will indeed show to what extent the English, Italian and French legal systems are willing, and capable, to take the Right to Confrontation seriously.

CHAPTER 6

Absent, Anonymous and Vulnerable Witnesses in English, French and Italian Criminal Procedure

1 Preliminaries

This work now turns to investigate the extent of the departures from the confrontational paradigm in England, France and Italy. In this comparative effort, the categories of absent, anonymous and vulnerable witnesses serve as functional equivalents. This should ensure an advanced understanding of the legal rules governing the topic and a critical evaluation of the similarities and differences among the systems. More broadly, comparative analysis should cast some light upon the manner in which the values of fundamental rights and 'public interest' are prioritised in the model countries. For each category of witness, an attempt is made to assess whether national laws comply with the minimal requirements of ECHR law and whether certain national rules or court practices may bring an additional meaningful contribution to a common theory of confrontation.

2 The Evidence of the Absent Witness

Earlier, this work argued that the Right to Confrontation comes into relevance whenever a *testimonial* statement is presented in evidence. Contrary to the U.S. – where the prior depositions of an absent witness are governed solely by the statutory law of hearsay – ECHR discourse acknowledges that national laws ought to place some limits against the use of such evidence, for its impact on the fairness of the proceeding. ECHR law, however, fails to set specific restrictions against the *admissibility* of the evidence of an absent witness and only calls for its corroboration: national convictions are unfair under Artcile 6(3)(d) of the Convention, if they are based solely or mainly upon absent testimonial statements.

This work has taken a more stringent approach on admissibility, under the assumption that incursions into a fundamental right can be tolerated only if (a) the values protected by the original right are not really at stake in the case, or they are at stake only in some attenuated form; (b) some competing and equally fundamental rights are at stake; or (c) costs to society in protecting the right are of a degree 'far beyond' what the society originally intended to pay to ensure it.[1] Following this approach, the evidence of an absent witness ought to be admitted in evidence only when the declarant is dead or in poor health at the time of the trial, or when he or she is kept out of the way against his or her will by the accused or other person acting on his behalf, or by some other compelling reason.

---

1 See Chapter 1; this approach is based on the rights theory developed by R.M. Dworkin, *Taking Rights Seriously*, Duckworth, London, 1977, 200.

It is now time to discuss the permeability of the English, French and Italian principles of orality to 'departures' concerning absent testimonial statements. Discussion focuses primarily on pre-trial depositions given to a judicial authority (*juge d'instruction*, prosecutor, police officer) by informants and co-defendants. A separate section deals with oral hearsay and other testimonial documents.

2.1 Pre-Trial Depositions of an Informant

2.1.1 In France

In France, when a witness does not come to testify at the requested hearing, the court may issue a witness warrant to be served immediately or adjourn the hearing to a later date.[2] The court may also disregard such absence and proceed (*passer outre*). When a party objects against the judicial decision to *passer outre*, an incidental proceeding termed *incident contentieux* begins. Parties may file written briefs with the court and the court must provide a reasoned decision on the matter at issue. The decision to proceed despite the absence cannot be grounded simply on the argument that the court testimony would be superfluous because that particular witness had already been interviewed at the investigation stage. Such a reasoning amounts to a violation of the principle of orality according to abundant and consistent case law.[3] In comparison, claims that the witness could not be traced despite the effort to serve the summons,[4] or that he or she was absent due to intimidation by the defendant,[5] are accepted by the Supreme Court as legitimate reasons to *passer outre*. Elsewhere, the Supreme Court has suggested that the decision to proceed in spite of the absence of a prosecution witness can also be grounded upon the argument that the oral testimony would not be 'useful for the discovery of the truth'.[6]

Once the decision to proceed is taken, it is then for the president of the Assize Court to determine whether the prior depositions of the *témoin defaillante* can be read out in court, or not. This aspect is crucial for this work, since the process of reading makes a prior deposition 'evidence of the matter stated' and, in effect, generates a 'departure' from the confrontational paradigm. While statutory law sets no predetermined criteria at this regard, the decision to read

---

2 Art. 326 F-CPP.

3 This reasoning amounts to a violation of the principle of orality, according to abundant French case law: (F) Cass crim., 18 May 1983, *Bull crim* n°146, Pensarini; (F) Cass. crim., 21 January 1987, *Bull. crim.* n°35, Recco; (F) Cass. crim., 1 April 1992, *Bull. crim.* n°137, Voinot.

4 (F) Cass. crim., 23 January 1991, *Bull. crim.* n°40, Akobe.

5 (F) Cass. crim., 12 January 1989, *Bull. crim.* n°13, Randhawa.

6 (F) Cass. crim., 13 June 1991, *Bull. crim.* n°252, Calvy; (F) Cass. crim., 3 April 1991, Lambert, [1991-7] Droit Pénal n°213.

prior depositions was traditionally left to the president's discretion.[7] This was a corollary of his or her leading role in the judicial pursuance of the truth (Article 310, French Code of Criminal Procedure). More recently, the Supreme Court has established certain straitjackets upon such discretion, in an attempt to align domestic law with the ECHR discourse on confrontation.[8]

In the 1991 leading case *Dobbertin*, the Supreme Court held that, in principle, a court of appeal must ensure the appearance of all informants who had not been previously confronted with the defence. Reading of the prior deposition of an absent witness is permissible only when it is 'impossible' to obtain the presence of the declarant in the courtroom.[9] While this phrasing certainly covers the dead or seriously ill witness, one could argue that it leaves out the absconding informant. In French case law as in ECHR law, nonetheless, the concept of 'impossibility' has been broadly construed and bears only limited selective value. Prior statements are read out not only when it is proved that the informant was kept out of the way,[10] but also when it is impracticable to make him or her attend the trial. In practice, reading takes place when a basic attempt to serve the summons was unsuccessful, even if the reason of such failure was purely that the residence of the declarant was 'unknown'[11] to the authority responsible for summoning. In other words, the law considers 'impossible' to ensure the attendance of any 'unavailable' witness, and 'unavailability' automatically justifies the use in evidence of prior depositions.

Moreover, out-of-court statements may be read out when the decision to *passer outre* had been grounded on the claim that a court testimony would have not been 'useful for the discovery of the truth'.[12] This is even more perplexing. If the court testimony of Mr. A. is not useful, then why should the deposition given by him in secret to a prosecutor or examining magistrate count as evidence against the accused? French evidence law is still construed on the assumption that the reliability of a statement can be inferred from the role and function

---

7 (F) Cass. crim., 4 June 1969, *Bull. crim.* n°187, Jouany; (F) Cass. crim., 16 October 1985, *Bull. crim.* n°318, Soroge.

8 For discussion see H. Angevin, *Incidences de la Convention Européenne des Droits de l'Homme sur la Procédure Pénale Française et Plus Spécialement sur celle de la Cour d'Assises*, [1991-7] Droit Pénal 3-5.

9 (F) Cass. crim., 6 March 1991, *Bull. crim.* n°115, Dobbertin, confirmed by (F) Cass. crim., 25 May 1992, *Bull. crim.* n°208, Maurice and (F) Cass. crim., 4 June 1998, *Bull. crim.* n°184, Gausserand.

10 (F) Cass. crim., 26 October 1994, *Bull. crim.* n°343, Manhallah (evidence of ongoing intimidation against a witness who was detained in the same prison as the defendant); (F) Cass. crim., 29 November 1989, *Bull. crim.* n°457, Checchi (witness detained abroad).

11 (F) Cass. crim., 13 June 1991, *supra* note 6. See also *Rachdad v. France*, App. No. 71846/01 (13 November 2003), at para. 25 (claim of 'unknown' residence of an absent witness made by the French authorities was criticised by the Strasbourg Court, although the violation of the Confrontation Clause was eventually grounded on the lack of corroboration).

12 (F) Cass. crim., 9 October 1991, *Bull. crim.* n°336, Lecoq.

of the person to which such statement is made. Since informants before the *juge d'instruction* are 'witnesses' and have an obligation to tell the truth, the reasoning goes, it would be unreasonable to deprive a court of justice from such (reliable) source of information. An official effort to gather testimonial evidence, in other words, is as much conducive to the truth as the process of an open confrontation with the opposing party. Following this view, it would be against the 'public interest' to exclude prior official depositions from evidence, and in fact these depositions are routinely read out and stand as evidence. The false assumption is that, in this way, the Right to Confrontation is diminished from a *fundamental* right of the accused person to a mere *procedural* right. As a *procedural* right, it would then be subject to curtailment whenever the summoning procedure was formally followed, but no additional effort was made to ensure the attendance of the adverse witness. Earlier in this work it was argued that individuals with a positive interest in avoiding face-to-face confrontation can escape a summons with little difficulty. A serious commitment to confrontation requires that the society be prepared to pay 'an extra cost' when the summons of a prosecution witness is ineffective: such cost is precisely the inadmissibility in evidence of the prior depositions of that declarant.

French law follows the footsteps of ECHR law insofar it sets almost no barriers to the admissibility of the evidence of an absent witness. Contrary to ECHR law, however, no discourse on corroboration can be found in the relevant case law. To be accurate, in a few occasions the courts of first instance argued that prior statements of certain prosecution witnesses had not been employed as evidence, but purely as a source of 'information'.[13] The difference between evidence and *renseignements* in French law, however, is purely a formalistic one; no pirouettes of legal reasoning can conceal the fact that a French court of justice can simply disregard the former in favour of the latter. While the French principle of *intime conviction* hardly tolerates the constraints of a corroboration requirement, this area of the law appears to be a good candidate for successful challenges before the Strasbourg Court.

2.1.2 In England

In England, pre-trial depositions of informants to the police are the subject of various common law and statutory exceptions to the hearsay rule and may also be admissible under *Criminal Justice Act 1988*, s. 23 or s. 24. It is a frequent occurrence in English law that the exceptions to the hearsay rule overlap to a perplexing extent, and that safeguards applicable to one exception are absent from exceptions dealing with rather similar matters.[14] *Criminal Justice*

---

[13] (F) Cass. crim., 25 June 1996, *Bull. crim.* n°273, Fabien.

[14] Examples of over-complexity, arbitrariness and incoherence of the law, concerning the admissibility of the prior depositions of informants were enumerated by J.R. Spencer, *Orality and the Evidence of Absent Witnesses*, [1994] Crim. L.R. 631-634.

Act 2003 is meant to simply this area of the law: since the new hearsay provisions have come into force in 2005, the whole of Part II, Sch. 2 and Sch. 13 paras 2-5 of the 1988 Act was repealed and only certain common law exceptions to the hearsay rule are preserved (*e.g. res gestae*, public documents, confessions).

At the outset, it must be said that neither the Law Commission's Report on hearsay in 1997[15] nor the *C.J.A. 2003* makes any explicit and overt concession to the Confrontation Clause of the European Convention on Human Rights. Presumably, they both relies on the underlying soundness of the proposed treatment of the hearsay rule in criminal cases to comply with the requirements of Article 6(3)(d) of the Convention. Before the new legal regime is briefly considered, account must be taken of the law as it still stands.

Pre-trial depositions of informants to the police are potentially admissible as evidence of the matter stated, despite the fact that the defendant could not cross-examine the maker[16] of the statements, when any of the following five conditions are met: the maker is dead[17] or unfit to attend as a witness;[18] he or she is outside the United Kingdom and it is not practicable to secure his or her attendance;[19] all reasonable steps have been taken to trace the declarant, but unsuccessfully;[20] the maker is kept away through fear;[21] or he or she may not be expected to recall the matter dealt in the prior statements.[22] Some of these conditions have been broadly construed by the courts over the years. By way of illustration, 'unfitness' to attend the court includes any mental condition giving rise to anxiety and failure to recall while under stress.[23] Although the fact that a witness was absent through fear must be proved by admissible evidence,[24] the

15 Law Commission, *Evidence in Criminal Proceedings: Hearsay and Related Topics*, Law Com. No. 245, 1997.

16 In practice, pre trial depositions are usually drafted by police constables, not the informant himself. This, however, does not affect the application of *C.J.A. 1988*, s. 23, 24 since it would be 'artificial, when considering whether the statements should be admitted whether the *writer*, rather than the *provider of the information*, is dead, abroad or unavailable for other reasons'(emphasis added): *R. v. Derodra*, [2000] 1 Cr. App. R. 41 (C.A.).

17 A further common law exception covers the so called 'dying declarations'. This exception is briefly considered later in this chapter, since such declarations are admissible also as oral hearsay. Had they been documented in writing, they would instead be admitted under *C.J.A. 1988*, s. 23: cf. *R. v. Kennedy*, [1994] Crim. L.R. 50 (C.A.).

18 *C.J.A. 1988*, s. 23(2)(a).

19 *C.J.A. 1988*, s. 23(2)(b).

20 *C.J.A. 1988*, s. 23(2)(c).

21 *C.J.A. 1988*, s. 23(3).

22 *C.J.A. 1988*, s 24(4)(iii).

23 *R. v. Setz-Dempsey*, (1994) 98 Cr. App. R. 23 (C.A.).

24 *Neill v. North Antrim Magistrates Court*, [1992] 1 W.L.R. 1220 (H.L.); *R. v. Belmarsh Magistrates Court, ex. p. Gilligan*, [1998] 1 Cr. App. R. 14 (Q.B.D.).

requirement of 'fear' does not connote any objective requirement that the fear be reasonable, nor that it must be caused by something said or done after the crime.[25] In *Martin*, the Court of Appeal suggested that the cause of fear is *per se* irrelevant.[26] As a result, adverse statements may be used in evidence also when the accused or his associates played no part in the intimidation of the prosecution informant.[27] Absence through fear also includes the refusal to answer question during court examination, when the court is satisfied that such behaviour occurred because of fear.[28] Further, the words 'reasonably practicable' to secure attendance were interpreted as to involve consideration over the 'standard' procedure of summons, while prior depositions may be read also when it appears that the witness was deliberately absconding herself.[29] A process of extension characterises also further exceptions to the hearsay rule. The House of Lords once considered statements to the police in the immediate aftermath of the crime to fall within the *res gestae* exception,[30] which was traditionally intended only for 'what people spontaneously shouted out while the offence was taking place'.[31] In proceedings for sexual offences, the 'recent complaint' exception is also relevant in enabling the court to hear the terms in which the witness (normally the victim) originally reported the offence.[32]

This being said, one could arguably come to the conclusion that English law opens the doors to the evidence of an absent witness far beyond the strict limits that are imposed by a serious commitment to the Right to Confrontation. Yet, such conclusion would be, at least to some extent, inaccurate. It must be noted that depositions to the police qualify as statements 'made for the purposes of pending or contemplated criminal proceedings' pursuant *Criminal Justice Act 1988*, s. 26. Therefore, they are not admissible unless the court grants a specific

---

25 *R. v. Acton Justices, ex p. McMullen*, (1991) 92 Cr. App. R. 98 (Q.B.D.).

26 *R. v. Martin*, [1996] Crim. L.R. 589 (C.A.): the witness has been allegedly intimidated by the appearance of a silent stranger outside his home. Despite the fact that there was no evidence that the stranger said or did anything, and that he could not be related directly to the offence, the Court of Appeal held that the witness's understandable fear was enough. For more discussion cf. A. Samuels, *Reading the Statement of the Witness Absent through Fear*, (1999) 163 J.P.&L.G.L. 50-51.

27 The phrasing of the law is criticized by P. Murphy, *Evidence*, 8th edn., Oxford Univ. Press., Oxford, 2003, 348. The author acutely points out that, taken *ad literam*, s. 23 would also permit to adduce hearsay evidence from an informant whom the police have kept out of the way, even for reasons they consider valid, such as the witness's own protection.

28 *R. v. Ashford ex p. Hilden*, [1993] Q.B. 555 (Q.B.D.); *R. v. Waters*, (1997) 161 J.P. 249 (C.A.).

29 *R. v. James*, [1996] 2 Cr. App. R. 38 (C.A.).

30 *R. v. Andrews*, [1987] A.C. 281 (H.L.).

31 J.R. Spencer, *Orality..., supra* note 14, 628. Similar conclusions have been reached in the U.S., in relation to the 'excited utterance' exception under F.R.E. 803(2): see *White v. Illinois*, 502 U.S. 346, 112 S. Ct. 736 (1992).

32 *R. v. Jarvis*, [1991] Crim. L.R. 374 (C.A.).

leave. The Court of Appeal has specified that the whole purpose of the discretion under s. 26 is to assess the interests of justice by reference to the risk of unfairness against the accused.[33]

Especially after the coming into force of *Human Rights Act 1998*, the English courts have increasingly made use of the discretion under s. 26, although it remains to be seen whether such practice entirely aligns English law to the principles of ECHR case law.[34] For instance, there is no general rule that a statement that is crucial to the party tendering it must be excluded. On the contrary, the significance of the evidence is a factor which may tell in its favour,[35] despite the fact that the Court in Strasbourg may reasonably argue that the subsequent conviction was based 'mainly' upon such evidence. If the evidence of a crucial witness is to be read to the jury, however, it is not enough to warn them in general term that there has been no cross-examination. The judge should instead explain, if necessary with examples and illustrations, the effects that the absence of cross-examination may have, and also underline that the jury 'might feel quite unable to attach anything like as much weight to the evidence in the statement',[36] as if it had been tested. Although it does not formally amount to a 'corroboration' requirement, a robust direction calling for caution is likely to meet approval at Strasbourg. Conversely, failure to direct jury's attention to the matter in question is fatal to a conviction.

The English courts have also developed a stringent approach for the admissibility of prior statements of informants who live abroad at the time of the trial. In *Radak*, the prosecution filed an application under *C.J.A. 1988*, s. 23, even though it might have been possible, had arrangements been made in time, to hear the person on commission. The Court of appeal held that the failure to explore this alternative was a factor to be consider under s 26, and concluded that such evidence should not have been admitted.[37] In *R. v. Chalmers*,[38] the Crown Prosecution Service was criticised for failing to assess whether the declarant's fear that her application for a green card could be jeopardized if she returned to England was founded. Since no formal enquiry was sent to the

---

33 *R. v. Gokal*, [1997] 2 Cr. App. R. 266 (C.A.). This reflect what was previously said in *R. v. Cole*, [1990] 1 W.L.R. 865 (C.A.), in relation to the whole statutory scheme (including s. 25(2)(d)) and not just s. 26.

34 This is despite the optimistic view taken by the Court of Appeal in *R. v. Radak*, [1999] 1 Cr. App. R. 187 (C.A.) – a case of an absent witness abroad – according to which the proper application of the Convention 'coincides' with the proper application of the concerned statutory under investigation.

35 *R. v. Batt and Batt*, [1995] Crim. L.R. 240 (C.A.).

36 *R. v. McCoy*, [2000] 6 Archbold News 2 (C.A.).

37 *R. v. Radak, supra* note 34. As to the step that may reasonably be required from the prosecution to stage a confrontational examinations of informants who live abroad see also *R. v. Bray*, (1988) 88 Cr. App. R. 354 (C.A.); *R. v. Gonzales de Arango*, (1993) 96 Cr. App. R. 399 (C.A.). For further discussion see J.A. Coutts, *Written Statements of Witnesses Abroad*, (1998) 62 J. Crim. L. 68-69.

38 *R. v. Chalmers*, [2000] C.L.Y. n°945 (Crown Court (Maidstone)).

United States immigration office, the Crown Court held that C.P.S. had failed to take all reasonable steps to secure her attendance and excluded her prior depositions from evidence.

In comparison, the law concerning the signed depositions[39] tendered by the prosecution at committal proceeding has the potential to deprive the accused unfairly of his or her Right to Confrontation. Under *MCA. 1980*, s. 5A to 5F, as inserted by *CPIA 1996*, written statements and depositions that have been admitted at committal are automatically admissible at trial as a further exception to the rule against hearsay. For reason of compliance with ECHR law, the Law Commission recommended the repeal of these provisions in 1997,[40] and they have in effect been abolished in April 2005, when *CJA 2003* fully came into force.

As anticipated, this area of the law is affected by *C.J.A. 2003*. It is not yet possible to describe the new provisions in detail, or to predict what approach will be taken by the courts in applying them. With specific reference to the out-of-court depositions of an informant to the police, the conditions set by *C.J.A. 2003*, s. 116, however, do not diverge significantly from those established by *Criminal Justice Act* 1988, s. 23.[41] The only difference is that admissibility is no longer be subject to a specific leave of the court, save from the case of absence through fear.[42] Beyond the statutory provisions and the preserved common law rules, however, hearsay has become admissible also whenever a criminal court is satisfied 'that it is in the interest of justice to do so'.[43] This is a radical, and potentially dangerous provision, which may effectively render any hearsay evidence admissible at the discretion of the judge. On the other hand, *C.J.A. 2003*, s. 125(1)(a) also gives to the court the power to stop the trial if the case against the accused is based wholly or partly on a statement not made in oral evidence. In conclusion, the fate of the pre-trial depositions of an absent witness will be most likely abandoned to the discretionary rulings of the English courts: it will be their primary responsibility to accord the practice of future trials with the Confrontation Clause of the European Convention.

2.1.3 In Italy

It is anticipated that, following the 1999 fair trial constitutional amendment, Italian law set rigorous boundaries against the use in evidence

---

39 *M.C.A. 1980*, s. 5A.

40 Law Commission, *Evidence in Criminal Proceedings, supra* note 15, at paras 8.108-8.113.

41 Instead, the real revolution is that for the first time in the history of the English criminal trial, also *oral hearsay* is generally admissible under the provisions equivalent to *C.J.A. 1988*, s. 23, in the same way as statements contained in documents.

42 *C.J.A. 2003*, s. 116(4).

43 *C.J.A. 2003*, s. 114(1)(d).

of out-of-court depositions gathered unilaterally by the police or prosecution. By virtue of Article 111(4) of the Constitution, an accused person may not be convicted 'on the basis of evidence given by those who have always *voluntarily* avoided confrontation with the defendant or his counsel'. Article 111(5) specifies that a deviation from the principle of adversarial adjudication is nevertheless acceptable when an 'objective impossibility' prevents the collection of oral evidence at trial. The determination of the exact meaning of these clauses has caused some controversy in Italian jurisprudence and deserves further clarification.

While many provisions of the Code of criminal procedure were re-written in order to accommodate the novel constitutional framework, some others, although formally untouched by the 2001 statutory reform, were re-interpreted accordingly. Included in the latter group is Article 512, which governs the reading of prior depositions of informants to prosecutor, police and defence counsel.[44] The said provision states that when a witness fails to come to court, such depositions may be read out if, and only if, the absence is the consequence of 'unforeseeable circumstances that make it impossible to stage a oral examination'.[45]

In the past, the concept of impossibility was broadly construed. In 1994, the Constitutional Court argued that reading of a prior deposition was legitimate also in instances of 'subjective impossibility': that is, when the absence was the consequence of the refusal of a non-compellable accuser to take the stand. The early adverse depositions of a wife could then be used against the husband defendant, if she came to court and invoked the statutory privilege of silence.[46] This reasoning met the firm objections of the Italian doctrine. Commentators rightly argued that, in essence, the 1994 ruling subjected the Right to Confrontation to the arbitrary determinations of certain accusers who could make incriminatory allegations at the time of the investigations and then 'hide' behind the shield of non-compellability.[47] This state of affairs could not longer be justified after Article 111 of the Constitution mentioned *objective* impossibility as one of the legitimate reasons for departure from the principle of adversarial adjudication. In 2000 the Constitutional Court reversed its prior ruling and acknowledged that Article 512 does not apply to non-compellable witnesses[48] but only to the dead, seriously ill or untraceable informant.

---

44 These depositions are assembled in the 'prosecution dossier' and may not be disclosed to the court unless their reading is permitted under a specific statutory provision.

45 Art. 512, I-CPP.

46 Art. 199, I-CPP; see (I) Corte cost, judgment No. 179/1994, [1994] Giur. Cost. 1589.

47 A. Giarda, *La 'precaria' facoltà di non testimoniare dei prossimi congiunti dell'imputato*, [1994] Corr. Giur. 963.

48 (I) Corte cost, judgment No. 440/2000, [2000] Giur. Cost. 3306.

Even if the declarant is dead, ill or untraceable, nonetheless his or her prior evidence may not be read in courtroom if such conditions could be reasonably foreseen when he or she gave the pre-trial deposition. This condition is established by Article 512 in an attempt to encourage the parties to apply for an *incidente probatorio* at the investigation stage. When there is a material risk that the informant might not be available for trial confrontation, prosecution and defence are entitled to apply for such confrontational hearing to be held in camera before the pre-trial judge. As reported earlier, the hearing entails disclosure and the parties are free to set aside such option for strategic reasons. If they do so, however, they may not put in evidence the depositions collected unilaterally from that declarant.

While reading of the out-of-court statements of an 'untraceable' informant is possible under Article 512, the specific usability of such statements is also subject to Article 526(1bis). This provision – which duplicates Article 111(4) of the Constitution – prevents the use *against* the defendant of the depositions given by those who 'had always *voluntarily* avoided confrontation'. Such phrasing leaves no room for speculation: whenever a failure to appear in court qualifies as a voluntary behavior on the part of the declarant, his or her prior depositions may not be used *against* the accused to which they refer. It is then for the prosecution to demonstrate that the informant was kept out of the way against his or her own will.

On the one hand, the prosecution may present evidence of corruption, threats and intimidation against the absent witness. If the author of such conduct is the defendant or an associate acting on his or her behalf, the Right to Confrontation may not be invoked, since it is the accused, not the accuser, who deliberately impinge the confrontational paradigm. It is unclear what the rule is when the threat or intimidation comes from a third party. Technically, in such cases the absence of the witness does not qualify as 'voluntary' under Article 526(1bis) and prior depositions could then count as evidence against the accused. It is nonetheless arguable that a defendant should not suffer any substantial prejudice from the independent behavior of somebody who is likely serving his or her illegal purposes.

On the other hand, the prosecution may try and demonstrate that the declarant was not allowed to leave the foreign country and return to Italy to take the stand. In such cases, the declarant cannot be said to have *voluntarily* avoided confrontation and his or her prior depositions may then be read by virtue of Article 512bis. In comparison, the claim that failure to appear was due to the unsustainable costs of the journey cannot satisfy a court that the conduct of the declarant was involuntary, and thus cannot make prior statements 'usable' evidence against the accused.

This being said, the Italian approach to the out-of-court depositions of an untraceable informant is extremely attractive for a general theory of confrontation. The previous sections have shown that English and French law are construed around the concept of 'witness unavailability'; as a consequence, reading of prior statement is possible when it is proved that public authorities made an effort, albeit unsuccessful, to bring the prior declarant in open court. In comparison, Italian law has now abandoned any reference to such effort: commendably, absence is *in itself* considered as an attempt of the prior declarant to avoid a public confrontation with the accused person. The burden to prove that such absence was instead 'involuntary' lies with the office of the prosecution.

It must also be noted, however, that in the very limited cases in which the deposition of an absent witness can be used against a defendant (namely, unforeseeable death or poor health, residence abroad), no statutory requirement of corroboration applies. Due to the direct enforceability of ECHR law in Italian law, however, the Italian criminal courts appear extremely reluctant to serve a conviction if this evidence was indeed central to the case for the prosecution.[49]

2.2 Pre-trial Depositions of a Co-defendant

In all model countries, a confession or admission made spontaneously by an accused person which is lawfully admitted in evidence counts as evidence against him or her.[50] Instead, the question to be addressed here is whether such evidence (or other prior depositions of a suspect) may be *evidence against others* implicated in it, in the case the maker of the statement refuses to give oral evidence at trial. According to the assumptions of this work, this scenario raises confrontational concerns in so far the accuser co-defendant is, in effect, an absent witness. While English and Italian law acknowledge the potential threat against the Right to Confrontation and are construed accordingly, French law approaches the subject purely as a procedural matter.

In England, the rule is that confessions are not evidence against co-defendants unless they are made in the presence of that person and he or she acknowledges the incriminating part, so as to make them his or her own.[51] Also, the Court of Appeal once held that, when a jury hear a confessions that implicates a co-accused, 'it is the duty of the judge to impress the jury that the statement of one prisoner not made on oath in the course of trial is not evidence against the other and must be entirely disregarded'.[52] This is to be contrasted with the evidence on oath of a co-accused in a joint trial, which is obviously evidence for all purposes, including the purpose of being evidence against the

49 (I) Cass. crim., 12 July 2002, Biagioni, [2001] Giur. Ital. 791.

50 In England cf. *P.A.C.E. 1984*, s. 76(1); in Italy cf. Art. 503 I-CPP. In France, such rule may be inferred from consistent case law suggesting that, pursuant to the discretionary powers under Art. 309 F-CPP, the president may order the reading of any *procès-verbaux* concerning the prior statements of the accused person: cf. (F) Cass. crim., 5 January 1978, *Bull. crim.* n°7, Hedin.

51 *R. v. Rhodes*, (1959) 44 Cr. App. R. 23 (C.C.A.).

52 *R. v. Gunewardene*, [1951] 2 K.B. 600 (C.C.A.).

accused. This state of the law is in line with the theory of confrontation established in Chapter 1; when the accused elects to testify in an English trial on indictment, the 'confrontational' paradigm is complied with: he gives evidence publicly, under oath and before the judge, and is liable to cross-examination by the co-defendant's counsel.[53] This is not to deny that in a joint trial the risk of prejudice against a co-defendants is high when the whole prior confession is put to the jury: the hope that a jury will ignore inadmissible evidence about Mr. A. at the same time as accepting it in relation to Mr. B. may be 'unrealistic'.[54] Nonetheless, recent case law[55] seems to exclude the suggestion made earlier[56] that the judge has a discretion to edit a confession as to deprive one defendant of relevant defence evidence in order to minimise injustice to another. In exceptional circumstances, the existence of a confession by one accused which seriously prejudices another may be ground for ordering separate trials although, in England, this is rarely[57] granted if defendants are alleged to have participated in the same offence. Further complications are posed by the use in evidence of the plea of guilt of a co-defendant in a separate proceeding. For the purposes of this study, such plea may arguably be seen as a 'testimonial statement' with possible adverse implications against those who took part in the offence. While it is settled that no direct use of such plea can be made against another defendant, it is also true that where the evidence of a Mr. A. is a pre-requisite to the conviction of Mr. B. the jury may regard A's guilt as proved when they consider the case against Mr. B.

In Italy, protection against the incriminatory pre-trial depositions of a silent co-accused, in the same or related proceeding, is now provided for directly in the Constitution. The topic was the cause of a heated controversy between the Parliament and the Constitutional Court in the 1990s. In two separate rulings, in 1992 and 1998, the Constitutional Court held that the exclusionary rule concerning the pre-trial depositions of a silent co-defendant caused of an unreasonable 'loss of reliable evidence'.[58] After the coming into force of the fair trial amendment, Article 111(4) of the Constitution now states that a criminal conviction may not be grounded on the evidence of those who have always voluntarily avoided confrontation with the accused or counsel. The amendment finds is reflected in Article 513 of the Code, pursuant to which the prior statements of a silent co-defendant may be used against other defendants tried jointly or

---

53 Pursuant to *C.J.A. 1982*, s. 72, the accused has no longer a right to make unsworn statements from the dock.

54 A promoter of this view is P. Thornton, *The Prejudiced Defendant: Unfairness Suffered by a Defendant in a Joint Trial*, [2003] Crim. L.R. 433.

55 *Lobban v. The Queen*, [1995] 2 Cr. App. R. 573 (P.C. Jamaica).

56 *R. v. Rogers*, [1971] Crim. L.R. 413 (C.A.).

57 *R. v. Lake*, (1977) 64 Cr. App. R. 172 (C.A.), at 175.

58 (I) Corte cost, judgment No. 361/1998, [1998] Giur. Cost. 2083.

separately only when they consent to such use.[59] Defendants will arguably give consent only when the statements are favourable to their case.

Faced with the troubling prospect of discarding all the allegations made to the police and prosecutors by a suspect in investigations concerning multiple offenders, Parliament made two corrections to such principle. It is anticipated that neither of them violates the Right to Confrontation.

Firstly, Article 513 makes an exception for the cases under Article 500(4): when evidence of threat, intimidation or corruption aimed at keeping a co-defendant silent is presented to the court, a prior deposition may be used as evidence against the author[60] of such misconduct (or his associates). This accords with the theoretical foundation of this work: no confrontational claim may be invoked by an accused who directly or indirectly takes action to avoid a face-to-face confrontation with the accuser. Secondly, some restrictions have been introduced against the right to silence of certain prior declarants, who are being tried in separate but related proceedings.[61] Prior to 2001 such declarants could not be compelled to testify: the argument was that the requested testimony would have likely covered the same facts at issue in their own trial and could have been therefore prejudicial to their own defence. Now, in comparison, defendants for 'remotely linked offences' who are being tried separately and made prior allegations against an accomplice are bound to take the stand in the latter's trial, albeit in the peculiar status of 'assisted witnesses'.

What is crucial for this work, however, is that in English and Italian law the Right to Confrontation is not surrendered against the right to silence of a co-defendant. In other words, the silence of an accused person in the courtroom does not automatically make his or her prior depositions admissible evidence against a co-accused. This state of affair causes obvious concerns to the prosecution. It would be hazardous to base the decision to prosecute mainly on the evidence of an accomplice, since there is always a risk that those who made prior allegations will later refuse to take the stand to pursue their own strategic purposes.

---

59 For a comment see E. Amodio, *Giusto Processo, Diritto al Silenzio e Obblighi di Verità dell'Imputato sul Fatto Altrui*, [2001] Cass. Pen. 3587.

60 Although Art. 500(4) I-CPP does not specify that pre-trial depositions of informants may be used in evidence *only* against the author of such threats and intimidation (or his associates), such narrow reading appears to be imposed by the phrasing of Art. 111(4) of the Italian Constitution.

61 The novel limitations to the right to silence have caused mixed emotions among Italian commentators. While discomfort for an alleged impairment of the constitutional right to defence is voiced by E. Amodio, *Giusto Processo, Diritto al Silenzio...*, *supra* note 59, at 3595, others have recommended the transplant of the Anglo-American rule whereby the accused may take the stand as a witness only on his own behalf: P. Tonini and P. Ferrua, *Testimonianza Volontaria dell'Imputato e Diritto al Contraddittorio. Progetto di Modifica del Codice di Procedura Penale*, [2000] Cass. Pen. 2868.

In comparison, this area of French law wholly disregards confrontational concerns. While it is true that all defendants must be interrogated at the opening of the trial pursuant to Article 328 of the French Code of Criminal Procedure, it is also true that they may simply refuse to answer to all questions. In any case, prior depositions of the declarant are read out[62] after the interrogation. No statutory rule prevents the use in evidence of such depositions against other individuals tried in the same proceeding, and no jurisprudence have yet challenged this state of affairs as an apparent infringement of their Right to Confrontation.

2.3 Oral Hearsay and 'Testimonial' Documents

While the national discourse surrounding the pre-trial depositions of an informant is to a considerable extent influenced by the principles of ECHR law, the jurisdictions under scrutiny are rather unresponsive to the claim that the Right to Confrontation may also be violated by the use in evidence of 'testimonial statements' reported as oral hearsay or incorporated in other written documents. If abused, these means of proof can impinge the primacy of orality, and silently circumvent the restrictions against the use in evidence of out-of-court depositions. In a conspiracy theory scenario, a police officer could secretly suggest that an informant give his or her account to a third party – or write it down as part of a personal diary – only to 'substitute' oral hearsay, or the document, to oral testimony.

In the legal tradition of common law, certain limits against the admissibility of these kinds of *derivative* evidence are traditionally established by the rule against hearsay. Although intermingled with a panoply of exceptions, such rule prevents in principle the use in evidence of an assertion made by a person other than a court witness, as evidence of the matter asserted. In England, however, the dissatisfaction for the inconsistencies and over-complexity of the rule has led to its abolition in civil cases by *Criminal Evidence Act 1995*, while *C.J.A. 2003* has re-defined hearsay in criminal proceedings with a view of broadening its admissibility. In comparison, the hearsay rule is simply absent from French law while only a limited version of it operates in Italy since 1988.

Imagine that Mr. B. comes to court in a trial for causing death by dangerous driving and reports what Mr. A., a bystander, alleged to have seen at the scene of the accident. Since hearsay logic is foreign to French criminal procedure and testifying witnesses may not be interrupted at the time of their depositions, the court will then hear Mr. A.'s 'indirect' account and will be free to base the judgment upon it. This is not to deny that French judges might be aware of the typical dangers of hearsay and could reasonably attach little weight to such evidence. What matters is that no statutory provision or case law ruling set any straitjacket

[62] (F) Cass. crim., 14 March 1984, *Bull. crim.*, n°111, Loviconi.

on the manner in which French court evaluate admissible evidence. In Italy, the case is governed by Article 195(5) of the Code: the hearsay statements of Mr. B. are non-usable if a party expresses the intention to summon Mr. A. Instead, they are usable if the court is satisfied that Mr. A. cannot be brought in court because he is 'dead, in poor health or untraceable'. As anticipated, the exclusionary rule only becomes operational after the hearsay declaration is given (and the court heard it). Although any explicit reference to non-usable evidence in the judgment's reasons will cause its reversal in appeal, nothing can guarantee that the court will wholly disregard it.

Matters are much more complicated in England. In the case described above, hearsay could be admissible as *res gestae*, if the allegations were given as an uncalculated outburst in the heat of the moment. Further testimonial statements may also be admissible under other common law exceptions to the hearsay rule. In trials for homicide, for instance, oral hearsay is admissible under the exception for dying declarations, if the author of the statement was the alleged victim of murder or manslaughter.[63] This area of the law is now governed by statute as the new hearsay provisions of *C.J.A. 2003* have come into force in April 2005.[64] Oral hearsay is now admissible at the same conditions as documentary hearsay: that is, whenever the author of the concerned statement is considered 'unavailable' to testify, for any of the several reasons described above. Furthermore, additional oral hearsay is also admissible when the courts is satisfied that 'it is in the interest of justice for it to be admissible'.[65]

Even fewer barriers are established at national level against the use in evidence of 'testimonial' documents (*e.g.* diaries, letters). In France, all documents are admissible insofar they are relevant and no confrontational concern has ever been voiced at this regard. In Italy, in the aftermath of the coming into force of the 1988 Code, scholars paid some attention to private documents including 'testimonial' declarations. Despite the silence of the Code on this specific matter, it was remarkably argued that a distinction should be made between the use of such documents as 'evidence of the matter asserted' in the statements and as evidence that such statements had in fact been made. This distinction clearly echoed the Anglo American hearsay logic and was precisely intended to prevent the use of any document as surrogate for oral testimonies. Regrettably, in the 1990s both the Constitutional Court[66] and the Supreme Court[67] dismissed this view as lacking any legal foundation in the sources of Italian law. These rulings have settled the matter, and the issue of testimonial

---

63 When the only evidence comes from a deceased, however, the jury should be warned of the dangers of convicting on untested evidence: *Scott v. The Queen*, [1989] A.C. 1242 (P.C. Jamaica).

64 P. Murphy, *Evidence, supra* note 27, 334-336.

65 *C.J.A. 2003*, s. 114(1)(d).

66 (I) Corte cost., judgment No. 142/1992, [1992] Giur. Cost. 1170.

67 (I) Cass. crim., 11 July 1997, Lutfija-Saiti, [1998] Dir. Pen. Proc. 994-97.

documents has not re-emerged even after the 1999 fair trial amendment to the Constitution. In England, several documents of a 'testimonial' nature are admissible in evidence under certain statutory exceptions to the rule against hearsay (i.e. *C.J.A. 1988*, s. 24). Under the new definition provided by *C.J.A. 2003*, letters should remain hearsay for the most part, and thus admissible under the – rather broad – terms of the 2003 Act. Diaries, instead, would seem to fall completely outside the definition of hearsay in the Act,[68] and thus would be in principle admissible to the extent to which they are relevant. This does not necessarily mean that domestic approaches to written testimonial documents are completely indistinguishable. In France and Italy relevant documents are invariably admitted and fully employable as evidence of the matter stated, and no corroboration requirement applies. In England, strong preference for oral testimony and hearsay logic will still most likely inspire the court's reasoning even after the relevant provisions of *C.J.A. 2003* have come into force. Furthermore, proceedings against a defendant based purely on such absent testimonial statements would be immediate candidate for the application of *C.J.A. 2003*, s. 125(1)(a).[69]

3. The Evidence of the Anonymous Witness

In ECHR law the admissibility of anonymous evidence is limited to exceptional circumstances – in which there appears to be a serious risk of threat and intimidation against the declarant – and it is also subject to a rather stringent test of corroboration. The following sections examine whether such evidence is admissible in English, Italian and French proceedings. In line with the earlier definition of the testimonial statement, discussion will touch upon not only the collection of evidence from unnamed court witnesses, but also the anonymous statements reported as hearsay by court declarants (*e.g.* a police officer who testifies that Mr. X., who is not named, saw the accused commit the offence) and anonymous documents.

3.1 The Restrictive Case Law of the English Courts

Although a defendant has a 'fundamental right'[70] under English law to see and be informed of the identity of all his accusers, it is undisputed that judges at common law also have the power to take reasonable steps to protect and reassure the witnesses so that they will not be deterred from coming

68 The definition of hearsay under *C.J.A. 2003*, s. 115 covers statements that appear to have been made to 'cause another person to believe the matter'.

69 This provision gives to the court the power to stop the trial if the prosecution case relies wholly or partly on a statement not made in oral evidence.

70 *R. v. Taylor*, [1995] Crim. L.R. 253 (C.A.).

forward.[71] When the risk of threats and reprisals is significantly high, it is not uncommon for an order to be made preventing the public disclosure of the identity of a court witness: indeed, this is precisely what the *Contempt of Court Act 1981*, s. 11 facilitates. The interests of justice may also require the public gallery of the court to be cleared when a witness is uncomfortable and unwilling to give evidence, even in cases where there is no immediate evidence of fear or intimidation.[72]

The question to be answered here, however, is what valid cause may lead an English court to go further and make an order precluding the defendant and counsel in a criminal proceeding[73] from knowing the identity of a testifying adverse witness.[74] Although, in the absence of any statutory guidelines, the judge's rulings on the matter have been described to be a 'model exercise of discretion',[75] the common law power to grant anonymity has been exercised only sparingly and appears to be subject to a number of restrictive tests.

In 1989, in *R. v. D.J.X.*,[76] Lord Lane said that, where there was a question of withholding the identity of a witness, the trial judge had a duty to see that justice was done, in the sense that the criminal process must operate fairly not only to the defendant but also to the prosecution and witness. The judgment, however, was vague as to the counterbalances that should be established in order

---

[71] Special measures, other than the granting of anonymity, for intimidated witnesses have also been implemented in English law following the publication of Home Office, *Speaking Up for Justice: Report of the Interdepartmental Working Group on the Treatment of Vulnerable or Intimidated Witnesses in the Criminal Justice System*, London, Stationery Office, 1998.

[72] *R. v. Richards*, [1999] Crim. L.R. 764 (C.A.).

[73] I will not investigate the question of the admissibility of anonymous evidence in applications for anti-social behaviour orders under *Crime and Disorder Act 1998*, s. 1, since these proceedings are identified from the outset as preventative in character rather than punitive or disciplinary, and must therefore be considered 'civil', not 'criminal' (*R. (on the application of McCann) v. Manchester Crown Court Court*, [2003] 1 A.C. 787 (H.L.)). Similarly, no attention can be paid in this work to the issue of the anonymity of witnesses who were called to testify before Tribunals established under the *Tribunal of Inquiry (Evidence) Act 1921* since these Institutions are by no means comparable to criminal courts of justice (cf. *R. v. Lord Saville of Newdigate, ex p. A. and others*, [2000] 1 W.L.R. 1855 (C.A.), quashing the decision of the tribunal set up to inquire into the circumstances of the 'Bloody Sunday' shootings in 1972 to withdrew anonymity from individual soldiers who had either admitted firing, or were alleged to have fired, live rounds, since the public nature of the inquiry would be preserved despite the maintenance of anonymity).

[74] Anonymous witnesses are to be referred to by letter or numbers (cf. *Att-Gen. v. Leveller Magazine Ltd.*, [1979] A.C. 440 (H.L.) 464) or colours (*R. v. Watford Magistrates' Court ex p. Lenman*, [1993] Crim. L.R. 388 (Q.B.D.)).

[75] *R. v. Taylor*, supra note 70, at 254, see also *R. v. Watford Magistrates' Court ex. p. Lenman*, *supra* note 74, at 389.

[76] (1990) 91 Cr. App. R. 36 (C.A.).

to compensate for the inevitable prejudice for the accused and the procedural guarantees that had to be met in order to admit the anonymous testimony.

In 1992, at a trial for murder, anonymity was granted to three prosecution witnesses who expressed fear and indicated that they would rather prefer to be held in contempt of court than give public evidence.[77] The judge alluded to the possibility that prior statements of these witnesses could be admitted under *C.J.A. 1988*, s. 23 and concluded that that would result in the defendant being placed in a far worse position, since anonymous witnesses could still be cross-examined in court, while sitting behind visual barriers. The argument overlooks the fact that out-of-court depositions can be challenged in some of the usual ways by which one may challenge court testimony, while no attack on credibility is possible if the declarant remains anonymous. In addition, it is to be expected that significant limitations on the admissible questions – to prevent the disclosure of the declarant's identity – would significantly impair the effect of cross-examination.

In 1994, *R. v. Taylor* provided more comprehensive authority on the matter. There, Evans L.J. enumerated several factors to be considered in assessing whether anonymity should be granted to witnesses in criminal trials.

Firstly, there must be real grounds for fear of the consequences if the evidence were given and the identity of the witness revealed. In practical terms, it might well be sufficient to draw a parallel with section 23(3)(b) of the *C.J.A. 1988*, which concerns the admissibility of statements where the witness did not wish to give oral evidence through fear, but in principle it might not be necessary for the witness himself to be fearful or to be fearful for himself alone. There could be cases where concern is expressed by other persons, or where the witness is concerned for his family rather than himself.

Secondly, the evidence must be sufficiently relevant and important to make it unfair to make the Crown proceed without it. However, since the greater the importance of the evidence, the greater the potential unfairness to the accused, a distinction could be drawn between cases where the creditworthiness of the witness is in issue and others where the issue for the jury is the merely the accuracy and reliability of his account, not his credit.

Thirdly, the Crown must satisfy the court that the creditworthiness of the witness had been fully investigated and disclosed to the defence, insofar this is compatible with anonymity. Judicial assurance ought to be given to the defence that all the relevant enquiries had been made and there was nothing known about the witness (*e.g.* previous convictions for perjury or other offences of dishonesty and previous occurrences of discreditable conduct) of which fairness requires disclosure.

---

77 *R. v. Brindle*, 28 April 1992 (C.C.C.), unreported (reference to this case my be found in P. Fennell and others (eds.), *Criminal Justice in Europe: A Comparative Study*, Clarendon, Oxford, 1995, 291.

Fourthly, the court must be satisfied that there would be no undue prejudice to the accused, some prejudice being inevitable if leave for anonymity is given.

Further and foremost, the court is entitled to balance the need for protection of the witness, including the extent of that protection, against unfairness or the appearance of unfairness. Earlier in this work it has been suggested that balancing tests may not always be good protectors of fundamental rights.[78] More recently, a more stringent attitude has emerged in a family law case, in which it has been held that anonymous testimony should be extended no further than in cases of 'absolutely necessity'.[79]

Anonymous witnesses would normally give their evidence from behind a screen and with their voice disguised. It has been suggested that this could be prejudicial to the accused, as the jury could jump to the conclusion that the defendants had already in some way intimidated the witness. The argument is not persuasive in the light of the present law, since video links and visual barriers between the defendant and the witness are increasingly becoming a common occurrence in the criminal process, especially when the declarant is a vulnerable witness.

Despite the wide discretion enjoyed by English courts on the matter, however, it is undisputed that, in the last decades, anonymity has been granted in very few criminal trials, mainly in cases of blackmail victims, national security and individuals who permit their premises to be used as observation posts.[80] In these limited occurrences, the options for complaint by the defence are very limited. The most obvious tactic is to apply for disclosure of the name of the informants. A successful application would usually persuade the prosecution to entirely abandon the informant's evidence. Alternatively, an application for a stay on the grounds of abuse of process may be made on the ground that if the credit of the informant is a substantial issue then no fair trial is possible.[81]

No corroboration test is referred to in *R. v. Taylor* or any other more recent authority, despite the long-established ECHR case law on anonymous witnesses. In *Taylor*, in fact, the evidence of the witness was decisive,[82] as it provided the only evidence that the victim's body had been removed from the premises where the murder allegedly occurred. Although this reflects the present ingrained disfavour of English law for placing corroboration constraints upon the courts of criminal justice, it also collides with the requirements established by the case law on Article 6(3)(d) of the European Convention of Human Rights.

---

78 S. Enright, *The Anonymous Witness*, [1996] N.L.J. 1032.

79 *Re. W. (Children) (Care Proceedings: Witness Anonymity)*, The Times, 1 November 2002.

80 *R. v. Rankine*, [1986] Q.B. 861 (C.A.).

81 A refusal to disclose certain material held by the prosecution may be successfully challenged before the Strasbourg Court: cf. *Edwards and Lewis v. U.K.*, App. No. 39647/98 (22 July 2003). See also *R. v. H.*, [2004] 2 W.L.R. 335 (H.L.).

82 D. Cheney, *Criminal Justice and the Human Rights Act 1998*, 2nd edn., Jordans, Bristol, 2001, 142.

Weaker standards for allowing anonymity were applied at committal proceedings with consideration of evidence prior to 1996. There, the purpose was to assess whether the Crown had established a prima facie case against the accused and magistrates were expected to be mindful that a refusal of the application may have pre-empted the decision of a judge of the Crown court, who may have taken a different view in the light of the whole of committal statements before him.[83] Similarly, anonymous evidence has been recently been deemed admissible in the proceedings to detain suspect terrorists pending the extradition decision.[84]

Despite the fact that the comparison carried out in this work is limited to the law of England and Wales, it is worth mentioning the employment of anonymous sources of evidence in the prosecution of serious crimes in Northern Ireland in the Diplock courts,[85] since the practice of these courts has been brought to the attention of the Strasbourg organs with reference to matters of confrontation.[86] The use of emergency powers in Northern Ireland has a long and troubled history that cannot be investigated in this work. It is sufficient to recall that the non jury trial system for Northern Ireland included also special evidence procedures that were precisely intended to overcome the pervasive atmosphere of intimidation due to the violent actions of paramilitary groups. Special powers also include the granting of anonymity to a court declarant, if the court 'reasonably believes it to be necessary in order to serve the ends of justice'.[87] This authorises the courts to give greater weight to the public interest against the protection of individual fundamental rights. Unsurprisingly, the facility with which the Diplock courts have sometimes allowed the anonymity of the witnesses and their physical shielding from the defendant have been described as 'disquieting'[88] by some commentators.

Instead, a threat to the Right to Confrontation may derive from anonymous hearsay, which is not automatically inadmissible under English law. Although there will always be, in practice, a great deal of pressure to reveal the name of the direct source, statutory provisions do not absolutely require such a disclo-

83 *R. v. Liverpool City Magistrates Court, ex p. D.P.P.*, (1997) 161 J.P. 43. Under the system established by *CPIA 1996*, committal proceedings with consideration of evidence have been amended so that out-of-court depositions statements are now read out but the witnesses no longer attend the hearing.

84 Cf. *R. (on the application of Al-Fawwaz) v. Governor of Brixton Prison*, [2002] 1 A.C. 556 (H.L.).

85 The courts were set up after Lord Diplock published a report in 1972 recommending non-jury trials and the easier use of confessions to convict suspected guerrillas; Home Office, *Report of the Commission to Consider Legal Procedures to Deal with Terrorist Activities in Northern Ireland (Cm. 5185)*, London, Stationery Office, 1972.

86 *R. v. Murphy and another*, [1990] N.I. 306 (C.A.). The case before the Strasbourg Court is *A.M. v. U.K.*, App. No. 20657/92 (2 December 1992), (1993) 15 EHRR CD 113.

87 *R v Murphy and another, supra* note 86.

88 G. Marcus, *Secret Witnesses*, [1990] P.L. 207-223.

sure, and even contemplate that the ultimate maker of the statement which may be used 'testimonially', may be unknown and unknowable (especially in case of some business records).[89]

3.2 Italy: A Nearly Absolute Statutory Ban

The Italian Code of criminal procedure places no reliance on information from unknown sources. Not only is this type of evidence perceived as prejudicial to the defendant, but it is also detrimental to an accurate judicial decision-making process. Various provisions of the Code explicitly declare anonymous evidence non-usable, regardless of the gravity of the concerned offence, the risks of reprisals and intimidation against the declarant or the alleged anti-social behaviour of the defendant.

Noticeably, the statutory prohibition of anonymous evidence refers not only to the trial phase, but also to the preliminary investigations. In this respect, Italian law is fully aware that one of the hallmarks of totalitarian societies is the anonymous accusation based on rumour.[90] Contrary to the previous 1930 Code, anonymous complaints cannot be relied upon by the police to launch an official enquiry,[91] and, in addition, anonymous hearsay may not be referred to in the decision concerning the remand of the suspect in pre-trial custody.[92] Anonymous testimonial evidence is also excluded from committal proceedings.

At trial, court declarants are required to state their name and surname at the outset of their testimonies. In practice, however, the identity of all adverse witnesses is disclosed to the defence no less than seven days before the trial hearing, when the deadline for the submission to the court of the list of all witnesses to be heard and summoned expires, pursuant to Article 468 of the Code. Out-of-court depositions collected by prosecuting authorities, counsel, and private investigators, which are included in the prosecution dossier, may be read under the conditions mentioned above, only if the identity of the declarant has been duly recorded at the time of the interview and later disclosed to the opposing party by virtue of Article 415bis(2).

Under no circumstances is anonymous hearsay usable, pursuant to Article 195(7). As a consequence, the evidence of secret service agents is often of no utility to criminal courts, as they are not compellable to disclose the identity of their informants.[93]

---

89 C. Tapper, *Cross and Tapper on Evidence*, 9th edn., Butterworths, London, 1999, 587.

90 Witnesses are strictly forbidden from testifying on rumour, pursuant to Art. 194(3) of the Code of Criminal Procedure and documents referring to rumour are excluded under Art. 234(3).

91 Art. 333(3) I-CPP.

92 Art. 274(1bis) I-CPP.

93 Art. 203 I-CPP.

Anonymous documents may not be used in evidence, unless they constitute real evidence of the offence under prosecution or they have been introduced in evidence by the defendant (Article 240). Leading doctrine reads the provision as applying both to (a) written documents whose author is unknown and (b) documents from known authors in which anonymous statements are reported. The reason for anonymity is irrelevant; Article 240 applies both when the source intended to remain anonymous and when anonymity is the result of an accident (*e.g.* partial burn of the document).

It is open to debate whether the present state of the law is conflicting with the Strasburg case law according to which the interests of witnesses (and victims) are central to the criminal process and Member State are under the positive obligation to organise their proceedings 'in such a way that those interests are not unjustifiably imperilled'.[94] Nevertheless, Italian commentators have so far firmly dismissed the temptation to re-establish an evidentiary function for anonymous accusations in the criminal process.[95] In comparison, they have instead suggested that instruments other than anonymity (primarily, administrative witness and victim protection programs) may well achieve comparable results, and avoid departures from the confrontational paradigm.

3.3 Multiple Anonymity Tools in French Criminal Procedure

French criminal procedure is traditionally reluctant to establish exclusionary rules of evidence, which are perceived as obstacles to the proper judicial task of pursuing the discovery of the truth. Although the admissibility of anonymous testimonial evidence was not directly governed by the *Code de procédure pénale* until 2001, the judicial use of it was implicitly permitted by certain statutory provisions, case law, and certain rules of practice concerning the performance of preliminary police enquiries.

Firstly, it must be reiterated that no statutory provision declares anonymous hearsay submitted by testifying witnesses inadmissible. As suggested earlier, witnesses are in principle allowed to speak freely and without interruptions pursuant to Article 331(4) of the Code and it is thus not unusual for the courts to hear accounts of what other individuals told them or what was said in their presence. It may well happen that the direct source of the information remains unknown, and this does not per se render the evidence inadmissible or the testimony void, although it is expected that the courts would place only limited reliance on it.

---

94 *Doorson v. The Netherlands*, [1996-II] RJD 446, (1996) 22 EHRR 330, at para 70.

95 M. Vogliotti, *La Logica Floue della Corte Europea dei Diritti dell'Uomo tra Tutela del Testimone e Salvaguardia del Contraddittorio: il Caso delle Testimonianze Anonime*, [1998] Giur. Ital. 851; S. Maffei, *Le Testimonianze Anonime nella Giurisprudenza della Corte Europea dei Diritti dell'Uomo*, [2003] Cass. Pen. 1700.

Secondly, the *Cour de Cassation* has come up with an atypically restrictive concept of *anonymous evidence*, in an attempt to ensure the efficient collection of information from State departments and other public authorities. In this regard, it has been suggested that written documents submitted by representatives of a public body or organisation are not anonymous in nature, even if the official who provided the evidence and/or was the direct source of it cannot be located. In the Court's view, the related information still 'originates' within the concerned organisation and, therefore, must be deemed equivalent to evidence submitted by named informants.[96]

Thirdly, a limited use of anonymous statements has always been permitted at the investigation stage. Lacking statutory guidelines, police have developed a rather informal practice for the collection of evidence from informants at the stage of the *enquête*. This practice also calls for the collection of forms of 'disguised' or 'diminished' testimony. It is therefore common for the police officers to report the content of the interview with a potential witness, to omit his personal details,[97] and, instead, to add the customary phrase that 'the statement comes from a reliable source who expressed his desire to remain anonymous'.[98] Anonymous statements of this type, however, may only serve the purpose of initiating proceedings and bear no evidentiary value at trial,[99] although they may still be included in the trial dossier. In comparison, during the formal phase of the *instruction*, the collection of anonymous information before judicial authorities results in a procedural nullity because reports of depositions must necessarily include the personal details of the witness[100] (Articles 103, 107 F-CPP). This rule, however, has not always prevented the most zealous examining magistrates from collecting anonymous testimonial evidence in the diminished form of *renseignements*, to which the aforementioned statutory provisions do not apply.[101]

Fourthly, no specific rule exists in relation to anonymous written documents submitted by parties other than the prosecution. This may raise confrontation concerns when these documents include unchallenged testimonial statements prejudicial to an accused person that have been submitted by the civil party or a

---

96 (F) Cass. crim., 30 May 1991, *Bull. crim.* n°192, Elliot.

97 (F) Cass. crim., 4 June 1997, *Bull. crim.* n°222, Souillie (a case of indecent exposure at a motorway toll station, in which anonymity was granted to the toll person).

98 R. Legeais, *L'Utilisation de Témoignages sous Forme Anonyme ou Déguisée dans la Procédure des Juridictions Répréssives*, (1998) R.I.D.C. 711, 714.

99 M. Guerrin, *Le Témoignage Anonyme au Regard de la Jurisprudence de la Cour Européenne des Droits de l'Homme*, (2002) R.T.D.H. 45, 51.

100 See Art. 103 F-CPP. Similar consideration apply to codefendants; cf. (F) Cass. crim., 22 March 1988, *Bull. crim.* n°141 (collection of anonymous statements from an accomplice at the phase of the *instruction* in a murder case is prejudicial to the right of the defence).

101 (F) Cass crim, 9 June 1998, *Bull. crim.* n°187, X.

co-defendant. The matter is for the discretion of the presiding judge, who may admit or refuse the inclusion of documents of this kind in the *dossier* by making use of his powers under Article 309 of the Code.[102]

This being said, it is remarkable that until very recently court declarants were always requested to disclose their name, surname and residence at the outset of their depositions. The obvious rationale was that, since trials are public reviews of the preliminary investigation, the identity of the accusers had to be disclosed to the defendant so that he could contest their creditworthiness. In the past, strategies of witness protection[103] had focused on the need to restrict unnecessary exposure of criminal witnesses to the general public. For this reason, since 1995, witnesses in fear of reprisals and intimidation can apply for a 'virtual' residence at the local police station in order to hide their true address from the public and the defendant for the entire course of the related proceedings.

In 2001, only a few months after the approval of the statutory reform on the presumption of innocence, the French Parliament cleared the way for the institutionalised use of anonymous testimonies. Comprehensive provisions concerning the protection of witnesses have been introduced in the Code of criminal procedure by Law No. 1062/2001,[104] in a fresh effort to promote *sécurité quotidienne*[105] ('day by day security'), which is just another catchphrase for the affirmation of values of 'public interest' and 'social defence' over individual fundamental rights. The Act in question also gave full legitimacy to anonymous testimonies in the various stages of the criminal process. Pursuant to Article 706-63 of the Code, the actual implementation of the related provisions was initially subject to the conditions specified in a supplementary decree of the *Conseil d'Etat*, which was eventually approved in March 2003.[106]

Article 706-58 of the Code states that applications for the collection of anonymous evidence may now be filed by the prosecutor or the investigating magistrate with reference to those informants who are assigned a virtual residence at the local police station, for the reasons mentioned above.[107] Conditions for the

---

[102] (F) Cass. crim., 19 March 1981, *Bull. crim.* n°100, Maurice (refusal to admit anonymous letter is within the powers of the presiding judge).

[103] For a more extensive analysis of the matter see M. Lemonde, *La Protection des Témoins devant les Tribunaux Français*, [1996] R.S.C. 815.

[104] Law No. 1062, 15 November 2001 *'relative à la sécurité quotidienne'*.

[105] On the concept of *sécurité quotidienne* and its theoretical implications see H. Causse, *Le Principe de Sûreté et le Droit à la Sécurité*, [2001] Gaz. Pal. Doct. 2007.

[106] Art. 2, Decret en Conseil d'État No. 455, 16 May 2003: for a comment see A. Maron, *'Principales Dispositions du Décret du 16 Mai 2003, Relatif à la Protection des Témoins et à l'Utilisation de Moyens de Télécommunication*, [2003-7/8] Droit Pénal n°23.

[107] Codefendants may not be anonymous witnesses, since suspects for the offence under investigation do not qualify for the aforementioned virtual residence under the terms of Art. 706-57 of the Code of Criminal Procedure.

award of anonymity are: (a) that the crime under prosecution is punished with more than three years imprisonment, and (b) that open testimony may seriously endanger the life and personal safety of the declarant, his family and close relatives. Leave for anonymity is given by the *juge de la liberté et de la detention*, whose decision is only subject to limited judicial review before the *Chambre de l'instruction*, in the terms of Article 706-60. Depositions under conditions of anonymity may be collected by the prosecutor, the *juge d'instruction* or the *juge de la liberté et de la detention*.

Certain minimal guarantees for the defence have also been established. Firstly, the personal details of the informants must be disclosed to the relevant judicial authorities and recorded in a special register, and unlawful disclosure to the public or the defence amounts to a criminal offence punished with five years imprisonment (Article 706-59 F-CPP). Secondly, the defendant is still allowed to obtain an examination of the anonymous witness at trial. Testimony will be collected via a video-link, and the voice of the declarant will be suitably disguised. Thirdly, Article 706-62 states that 'no criminal convictions may be based only on the evidence' collected under the terms described above. Although the phrasing of this provision attempts to echo the requirement of corroboration of ECHR law on anonymous witnesses, it is clearly misleading insofar that it hints that the mere presence of other pieces of evidence in the court dossier justifies a criminal conviction. The Strasbourg case law, in comparison, has repeatedly suggested that a conviction violates the Confrontation clause even when several items of evidence are present in the trial *dossier* or have been brought to the attention of the court or jury, if the prosecution case relied "mainly" on the anonymous evidence.

Even more complex problems of interpretation are posed by the phrasing of Article 706-58 of the Code, according to which 'anonymity may not be granted if, for the manner in which the offence has been perpetrated or the personality of the witness, knowledge of the declarant's identity is indispensable for the rights of the defence'. At first inspection, the provision seems to provide the accused person with an easy way to apply for judicial review against the decision to grant anonymity before the *Chambre de l'instruction*. Anonymity of accusers, in fact, poses an immediate threat to the adversariality of the proceeding and the fundamental right to confrontation. It remains to be seen, however, how the Supreme Court will read this provision and, subsequently, how extensively prosecutors, magistrates and courts will make use of anonymity.

3.4 Critical Assessments of National Laws

Chapter 2 argued that, although anonymity orders do not necessarily negate the concept of a fair trial, the use of anonymous evidence should be restricted to the most exceptional circumstances and counterbalanced by tangible advantages for the accused person. Witness intimidation has also been located as one of the few legitimate causes for the concealment of the accuser's identity from the defendant. Curtailment of the right to confrontation when declarants face immediate threats and risk of reprisals is based upon the competing fundamental rights of the accusers to freedom and security. In principle, these conclusions are shared by ECHR law, which allows a limited use of anonymous testimonies, subject to certain procedural countermeasures. Nevertheless, Chapter 3 has also shown that the rather vague test of corroboration has sometimes been adopted by ECHR law as a 'refuge' to unduly broaden the admissibility of anonymous testimonies.

It is also settled that the fairness of anonymity orders must necessarily be judged upon the facts in each and every case, and, therefore, the inclinations of the criminal courts are far more important than the state of statutory and codified legislation. The judgment concerning how seriously the personal security of the declarant will be at risk, in fact, invariably depends upon several case-sensitive factors, including the nature of the offence under investigation, the personality of the suspect, the environment surrounding the criminal offence and the related proceedings, and the effectiveness of alternative strategies of social control.

This being said, 'departures' from the 'confrontational paradigm' relating to anonymous witnesses have been found in all the jurisdictions under examination. These findings are not surprising, as anecdotal evidence suggests that intimidation of witnesses is a common occurrence in the three model countries. In England and Italy, case law and statutory provisions are clearly construed to restrict the admissibility of this type of evidence to highly exceptional circumstances in which the most serious offences are under prosecution and evidence of immediate danger to the life and personal security of witnesses has been gathered. On the other hand, the very structure of the French criminal process and a recent statutory reform give French courts numerous opportunities to base their decisions on evidence deriving from unknown sources.

As anticipated, no violation of the European Convention is likely to be found when Member States allow national courts to make use of anonymous testimonial evidence, provided that anonymity is employed as a last resort in the prosecution of the offences that pose extremely serious social concern. The Convention, however, only establishes a minimum standard of protection for the rights and freedoms of the accused person, and certainly does not prevent Member States from ensuring further protection to individual fundamental rights such as the right to confrontation. It is also true that States are under the positive obligation to protect other individuals involved in the criminal process, but this may be ensured through a variety of instruments available to governmental authorities, which do not necessarily involve such an extensive departure from the confrontational paradigm.

In addition, the oft-repeated claim that witness anonymity is absolutely necessary in the fight against organized crime can be dismissed by the English and Italian examples. The practice of English law suggests that, notwithstanding the absence of a specific exclusionary rule against anonymous testimonial evidence, the identity of the accusers has been screened from the defendant in a very limited number of proceedings concerning murder and the terrorist activities of the I.R.A., and it has been subject to penetrating judicial review.

In Italy, prominent successes against mafia have been achieved in recent years and still an almost absolute statutory ban applies against the use of evidence from anonymous informants. Only a minor exception applies in the case of identity change. The Italian witness and victims protection program,[108] in fact, specifically allows certain police informants to apply for a change of name.[109] In practice, only permanent informants in mafia crimes qualify for such change, since this measure is applicable only as a last resort, when any other means of protection (such as restraining orders, police escort, change of residence) is inadequate to confront the risks to the personal safety of the declarant. Once the identity change is finalised, concerned individuals are summoned to testify under their new identity. Although formally named, these declarants are anonymous for the purposes of this work, as the defence has no chance to trace their 'real' identities and prior instances of discreditable conduct. The examination of individuals who have changed their identities under the aforementioned program usually takes place through a video-link.[110] Although applicable only very rarely, these combined provisions certainly collide with the firmly established requirements of ECHR law. Firstly, no obligation is placed upon the prosecution to inform the defence of the identity change. Secondly, no guarantee is given to the defence that the character of the declarant had been fully investigated and reported to the court. As a matter of fact, the court itself may not even be aware of the said change. Last but not least, no corroboration test is required for this type of evidence.

In comparison, the present state of French law merits firm criticism. In line with the inquisitorial tradition of that jurisdiction, the French law-makers continue to be easily responsive to arguments of social defence and public interest, notwithstanding the high-sounding commitment to the equality of arms and the presumption of innocence. In the views of a Parliament Commission, the reinforcement of the guarantees of accused persons in the Law 516/

---

[108] The program was first established by Law No. 82, 15 March 1991 and later restructured by Law No 45, 13 February 2001. For a comprehensive comment see P.L. Vigna and R. Alfonso, *Lineamenti della Legge sui Collaboratori di Giustizia*, in P. Tonini (ed), *Giusto Processo: Nuove Norme sulla Formazione e Valutazione della Prova*, Cedam, Padova, 2001, 97-126.

[109] See Decree-Legisl. No. 119, 29 March 1993. Applications must be addressed to the Department of Home Affairs and the Department of Justice and are to be examined by a joint committee. A ministerial decree then establishes the terms and conditions of the identity change and provides for the related amendments in the birth certificate, other public records, and the issuing of new documents such as identity card, passport, national health care number and fiscal code.

[110] Art. 147bis(3)(a), supplementary provisions of the Code of Criminal Procedure.

2000 necessarily called for a series of counter-reforms aimed at the improvement of the 'efficiency' of the criminal process.[111] Amid the discomfort of those who denounced *sécurité quotidienne* as an attempt to curtail and circumvent constitutional rights and civil liberties, the statutory reform illustrated in section 3.3. restored anonymous accusations and testimonies as an institutionalised feature of French criminal procedure. The vast majority of French criminal offences are punishable by a penalty higher than three years imprisonment, which has been set as the threshold for the admissibility of the anonymous witness. In addition, no specific standard of proof appears to be required for the issuing of anonymity orders and only limited counterbalances are established to compensate the departure from the confrontational paradigm. Although designed to survive challenges before the European Court of Human Rights by reference to the test of corroboration, French legislation clashes with the theoretical assumptions of this work, according to which the fundamental nature of the Right to Confrontation require law makers and courts to exercise the highest level of restraint in allowing incursions against it.

4 The Evidence of the Vulnerable Witness

Certain special measures are established in the three model countries in an effort to ensure the taking of the 'best' evidence from the vulnerable accuser. Although it is commonly argued that measures of this type are 'likely to maximise the completeness, coherence and accuracy'[112] of her testimony and to ensure her overall welfare in the criminal process, it is open to debate whether national laws of evidence are designed so to minimise the related intrusions into the fundamental Right to Confrontation, as is imperative in accordance with the theoretical assumptions of this work. At the outset, it must be repeated that in the seclusion of over-protected environments a vulnerable person (such as a child) may feel sufficiently safe to be open and honest but, equally, an individual who is telling lies or hiding an important part of the story may also be encouraged to persist in such behaviour.

---

[111] In 2002, a Parliamentary Commission has been established in order to review the contents of the Law No. 516, 15 June 2000. In a report published on February 6, 2002 (available at www.senat.fr/rap/l01-208/l01-2081.pdf) the Commission denounced the little attention paid by the Act to the necessary 'balance of interests that criminal procedure ought to entail' and suggested that further reforms of the Code should be primarily concerned with the pursuance of a more efficient criminal procedure (§I(B)(3), page 11). Anonymity of witnesses was also explicitly praised as an essential step in that direction (at 12).

[112] L.C.H. Hoyano, *Striking a Balance between the Rights of Defendants and Vulnerable Witnesses: Will Special Measures Directions Contravenes Guarantees of a Fair Trial?*, [2001] Crim. L.R. 948, 949.

Justifiably, comprehensive statutory instruments had to be laid out in England, where the orthodox adversarial method of evidence collection and the misuse of aggressive cross-questioning could turn the examinations of children and certain weak adults into psychological traumas. In fact, some of the most significant changes to the common law trial, with its insistence on oral evidence from testifying witnesses present in the courtroom, have occurred in relation to the child victim of a sexual abuse. By comparison, the matter has only recently come to the attention of French law-makers and commentators, since the penetrating control on court procedures by the presiding judge had long represented the most effective safeguard against harmful face-to-face confrontations between the defence and the fragile accuser.

In the following sections, the categories of vulnerable witnesses established by national laws are illustrated, and some special measures available to criminal courts for the collection of their depositions are discussed, and compared. A separate section illustrates the extensive, and questionable, use of hearsay evidence as a refuge for the vulnerable witness.

4.1 Eligibility: The National Definitions of the Vulnerable Witness

The question to be answered here is which individuals qualify to be assisted by special measures based upon their alleged 'vulnerability' in French, Italian and English testimony law. No specific guidance on this point is provided by ECHR law.

Age and gateway offences are the sole parameters prescribed by French statutory law. Pursuant to Article 706-52 of the *Code de procedure pénale*, special measures for the collection of testimonies apply exclusively to those under the age of eighteen, in criminal proceedings for certain specified offences, most of which are sexual in nature.[113] Similarly, at the time of its coming into force in 1989, the Italian Code of criminal procedure afforded protective measures to the child witness alone. In 1997, however, the Italian Constitutional court extended the statutory protection to the 'mentally impaired adult'.[114] This phrase echoes the rule for the defence of insanity under the terms of Article 88 of the Criminal Code and, as a result, it only refers to a certified disease of mind, not instances of distress or fear. More recently, statutory amendments to the Italian Code of criminal procedure have also established additional guarantees for minors who were victims, or witnesses, of sexual offences.[115]

---

113 These offences are listed in Art. 706-47 F-CPP; they include rape (Art. 222-23 F-CP), sexual assault (Art. 222-27 F-CP) and mistreatment by family members and relatives of a minor (Art. 227-22 F-CP).

114 (I) Corte cost, judgment No. 283/1997, [1997] Giur. Cost. 2564.

115 Cf. Arts. 498(4bis) and 498(4ter) I-CPP, inserted by Law No. 269, 3 August 1998 (depositions taken outside the courtroom and, if necessary, at the place of residence of the concerned juvenile; use of one-way mirrors to screen the accused person from the vulnerable witness).

In comparison, a rather comprehensive and sophisticated definition of the vulnerable witness is to be found in England. In the report *Speaking up for Justice,*[116] several definitions were in fact illustrated and discussed. Models based on limited categories and listed individual characteristics were eventually rejected in favour of a combined approach, which took account of both personal qualities and 'situational factors' which made it likely that a declarant would suffer emotional traumas if unable to give evidence without special measures of protection. As a result, the option of an offence gateway was dismissed by the group who laudably reasoned that a witness was either vulnerable, or he was not.[117] Statutory reform largely followed these assumptions, and Sections 16 and 17 of *Y.J.C.E.A. 1999* laid down essentially three basic categories of eligibility, based on age, incapacity and fear or distress about testifying. A panoply of 'Special Measures Directions' may then be applied to (a) all witnesses under the age of seventeen; (b) witnesses with a mental or physical disorder or impairment of intelligence and social functioning which the court considers significant enough to affect the quality of their evidence; (c) witnesses likely to suffer from fear and distress in giving evidence to an extent that is above the ordinary apprehension and is expected to affect its quality.

This being said, it is apparent that, while the English criminal courts are legally required to assess multiple circumstantial and situational factors capable of making a person 'vulnerable', little if no margin of appreciation is left to their continental counterparts. This state of affairs is in line with the tradition of continental law, where eligibility criteria often take the form of inflexible parameters, intended to ensure an identical treatment of citizens and to prevent the establishment of eccentric practice by local criminal courts.

Rigidity in the eligibility criteria for the vulnerable witness may find some counterbalance in France, where the president of the court of Assize enjoys great discretion in the management of the trial hearings. Pursuant to Article 309 of the procedural Code, by way of illustration, he is entitled to interview each and every witness in person, thus preventing a face-to-face confrontation between the counsel and the testifying accusers. Rigidity is far more problematic in Italy, where non eligibility for any reason invariably results in the individual being cross-examined by the parties in a purely adversarial manner. It must also be said, however, that too loose a standard for eligibility could also result in a significant extension of the impact of the related 'departures' from the 'confron-

---

[116] Home Office, *Speaking Up for Justice, supra* note 71, 19. The report of the interdepartmental working group on the treatment of vulnerable or intimidated witnesses made 72 recommendations aimed at improving access to justice for vulnerable or intimidated witnesses, including children. Part II of the *Y.J.C.E.A. 1999* contains the legislative framework for implementing those measures requiring legislation.

[117] For discussion see L. Ellison, *The Adversarial Process and the Vulnerable Witness*, Oxford Univ. Press, Oxford, 2001, 36-37.

tational paradigm', with subsequent undue intrusions into the fundamental Right to Confrontation.

4.2 The Collection of the Evidence of the Vulnerable

It is not my intention to map each and every special measure relevant to the vulnerable witness under domestic law. Instead, patterns of deviation from the standard way of collecting court testimonies and out-of court depositions when the witness falls into this category will be outlined, and several 'confrontational' concerns will be subsequently raised.

4.2.1 Unsworn Courtroom Evidence

A large group of vulnerable witnesses, namely children, are under no legal obligation to tell the truth when they give evidence at the stage of the trial. As a consequence, they are not punishable for the offences of perjury or false testimony. In England, a child under the age of 14 is not even permitted to give sworn evidence under section 55(2) of the *Y.J.C.E.A. 1999*. The same rule also applies to any witness who lacks the appreciation of the solemnity of the occasion or the particular responsibility to tell the truth involved in taking an oath. In France, children under the age of 16[118] are not required to take an oath,[119] while in Italy the age threshold is set at 14.[120]

The jurisdictions under scrutiny attach little if no importance to the provisions concerning the administration of the oath in the case of the child witness, their priority being to ensure in any case the collection of his deposition. In fact, no test of competency exists in French law, while in Italy an expert finding of inability to testify is relevant to the evaluation of the witness' s deposition, not its admissibility.[121] The test of competency also bears limited selective value in England, where it is sufficient that the witness understands the questions put to him and is able to give answers which can be understood.[122] A violation of the rules concerning the oath does not amount to procedural nullity in France[123] and Italy, and cannot be an independent ground for appeal in England.[124] There, unsworn evidence is admissible despite the fact that the concerned witness had to take the oath or affirmation and, in fact, did not do so.

---

[118] Art. 335 F-CPP. The age limit refers the time of the deposition, not the time of the offence: (F) Cass. crim., 29 November 1989, *Bull. crim.* n°456, X.

[119] Their depositions technically qualify as *renseignements*, not testimonies, although this distinction has no significant impact on their evidentiary value.

[120] Art. 497(2) I-CPP.

[121] Art. 196 I-CPP.

[122] *Y.J.C.E.A. 1999*, s. 53; cf. also *R. v. D.*, [2003] Q.B. 90 (C.A.)

[123] (F) Cass. crim., 2 October 1990, *Bull. crim.* n°327, Hakkoum.

[124] *Y.J.C.E.A. 1999*, s. 56.

Furthermore, no statutory provision appear to be established so as to alert the criminal courts over the use of this unsworn evidence,[125] although it is somehow expected that the young age of the declarant would be a matter for serious consideration at the time of deliberation. In France, the testimony of the child witness may be freely appreciated by the court.[126] In Italy, although case law has established certain limited parameters (coherence, completeness, consistency over time)[127] to which the courts must refer in the assessment of the testimony of the vulnerable, no specific corroboration requirement applies. Requirements of corroborations have also been abolished in English law pursuant to *C.J.A. 1988*, s. 34 and *C.J.P.O. 1994*, s. 32.[128]

The state of domestic laws is in some conflict with the assumptions of this work, according to which the obligation of truth-telling is an essential component of the 'confrontational paradigm', for the reasons mentioned in Chapter 1. When a testifying witness is irresponsible in what he reports, and may suffer no consequences in the case of falsehood, the very scope and function of adverse-questioning is impaired. Although the obligation of truth telling may often be unenforceable for substantive reasons (agency,[129] capacity or mental disorder), more could be made to convey to the vulnerable witness the concept of an 'ethical' obligation to be sincere, due to the solemnity of the occasion and the gravity of the consequences for the accused person. This is even more important at a time in which, for psychological reasons, utter informality governs the taking of the depositions of the vulnerable. In all model countries, depositions may be taken in venues other than the courtroom,[130] in the absence of the public,[131] and traditional symbols of judicial solemnity may also be removed.[132]

In this specific area of testimony law, a lesson may be learned from the United States criminal justice system; there, F.R.E. 603 provides that all witnesses are required to declare that they will testify truthfully, by oath of

---

[125] In Italy, case law has established a number of parameters (coherence, completeness, consistency over time) to which reasons of the criminal courts must necessarily refer in the assessment of the testimony of the vulnerable although no corroboration requirement applies.

[126] T. Cretin, *La Preuve Impossible? De la Difficulté d'Administrer la Preuve des Infractions dont sont Victimes les Mineurs: Attentats à la Pudeur, Violences et Mauvais Traitements*, [1992] R.S.C. 53, 54.

[127] Cf. (I) Cass. crim., 16 October 1997, Vacca, [1998] Cass. Pen. 2090.

[128] For prior warnings to the jury in the case of mentally ill witnesses cf. *R. v. Spencer*, [1987] A.C. 128 (H.L.); *R. v. Bagshaw*, [1984] W.L.R. 477 (C.A.).

[129] The minimum age of criminal responsibility is 10 in England and Wales, 13 in France, 14 in Italy.

[130] For example, testimonies may be collected at the place of residence of minors in Italy, pursuant to Arts. 398(5bis) and 498(4bis) I-CPP.

[131] *Y.J.C.E.A. 1999*, s. 25, Art. 306 F-CPP, Art. 472 I-CPP.

[132] Removal of wigs and gown may be ordered in England under the terms of *Y.J.C.E.A. 1999*, s. 26. Reduction in the courtroom formalities was earlier recommended by J.R. Spencer and R. Flin, *The Evidence of Children: the Law and the Psychology*, 2nd edn., Blackstone, London, 1993, 116-118.

affirmation administered in a form calculated to awaken their conscience and impress their mind with the duty to do so. This does not necessarily mean that all juveniles will be later prosecuted, or punished, for perjury. Although F.R.E. 603 does not address the form of ceremony required for the administration of the oath or affirmation, it is still to be interpreted to call for an actual commitment on the part of the witness to tell the truth.[133] Children who testify in a U.S. criminal court must thus show their commitments to the truth, regardless of their age. The test for competency of the child witness 'depends on his capacity and intelligence, and his appreciation of the difference between truth and falsehood, as well as of his duty to tell the former'.[134] As a result, it has come to be the common practice for the criminal courts to hold a *voire dire* examination to determine the competency of a child before allowing him to enter the witness box.

This being said, however, it must also be acknowledged that no complaint for the mere absence of an obligation to tell the truth have so far been brought to the attention of the Strasbourg bodies. It is doubtful that this issue alone may ground a finding of violation of the Confrontation Clause of the Convention.

4.2.2 Interviewer and Mode of Examination

This section investigates who is entitled to question the vulnerable witness. Particular attention is paid here to court testimonies and other depositions that may stand as evidence at trial. Something is also said about the restrictions established under national law to the range of questions that the interviewer may pose to certain vulnerable witnesses.

A major difference among the model countries concerns the respective roles of the court and parties. While in France it is improbable that the president of the court would allow counsel directly to question a vulnerable witnesses pursuant to the discretionary powers of Article 312 of the procedural Code, in Italy a statutory rule requires that examinations of minor witnesses (or 'impaired adults') at trial or the *incidente probatorio* be conducted by the court, not the parties.[135] In theory, the rule is open to derogation: the court may allow the parties to examine and cross-examine the witness when it is satisfied that such course of procedure will not affect the 'serenity' of the witness. In practice, judges are reluctant to relinquish their powers. It is open to question, neverthe-

---

133 *U.S. v. Allen*, 127 F.3d 1292, 1295-1296 (10th Cir. 1997), in which 12-year old child said she 'understood she had promised to tell the truth', and 'knew difference between truth and lie and knew she was to tell the truth and would be punished if she lied'.

134 *U.S. v. Jones*, 482 F.2d 747, 752 (D.C. Cir. 1973).

135 Art. 498(4) I-CPP. The provision is praised by the majority of Italian commentators: D. Siracusano and others, *Diritto Processuale Penale*, 4th edn., Giuffrè, Milano, 2001, vol. II, 332.

less, whether an examination by an Italian judge can be at all effective,[136] since he comes fresh to the case and has little if no knowledge of the facts in issue.[137]

In spite of the theoretical flexibility of the Italian and French statutory provisions, rooted in their jurisprudence remains the idea that parties to the proceedings should be prevented from gaining too an extensive control over judicial procedures. The fear is that parties could use examinations, at best, to the detriment of the vulnerable interviewee and, at worst, as harmful truth-distorting weapons.[138] This claim overlooks that other statutory provisions give to Italian and French judges wide powers in order to ensure that trial examinations do not go beyond what a person should be asked to endure.[139] In addition, basic strategic considerations will normally lead parties to abstain from gladiatorial behaviours, since this may cast a bad light upon them, particularly in the eyes of the lay members of the Assize Court. This reluctance to allow the parties to directly question the vulnerable, however, is not likely to cause any disquiet at Strasbourg.[140]

In comparison, the special measures directions for vulnerable witnesses approved in England by virtue of the *Y.J.C.E.A. 1999* authorise cross-examination by the opposing parties, albeit not necessarily at the trial stage and not by the defendant in person. Major restrictions apply in England as to the *range of questions* that may be put to *certain* vulnerable witnesses, namely complainants in sexual cases. Restrictions of this type are absent in Italy or France, where the law sets no straitjacket upon the court with regard to the mode of the interrogation. Peculiar to the English approach is that not only 'procedural', but also 'substantive' concerns, are taken into account in the administration of the testimony of the vulnerable. This is in line with the common law's familiarity with 'substantive' exclusionary rules (*i.e.* rules that prevent certain questions to be asked to the witness, in the light of the information that they may elicit), while provisions of this kind are traditionally foreign to continental criminal procedures.[141]

The restrictions in question refer to the sexual history of the complainant, either with the defendant or third persons, and may be only briefly discussed

---

136 This critical view is endorsed by G. Frigo, *Sub Articolo 498*, in M. Chiavario (ed.), *Commento al Nuovo Codice di Procedura Penale*, Utet, Torino, 1991, vol. V, 252.

137 Findings of the preliminary investigations are collected in the prosecution dossier, which may not be disclosed to the court.

138 Adversarial examinations amount to a 'cruel scrutiny' of the declarant, according to F. Cordero, *Procedura Penale*, 7th edn., Giuffrè, Milano, 2003, 936.

139 Cf. Art. 499(6) I-CPP and Art. 309 F-CPP. See also, in France, Art. 339 F-CPP.

140 Art. 6(3)(d) of the Convention states that the defendant had a right to 'examine witnesses' or 'have them examined' on his behalf. The latter expression gives full legitimacy to the inquisitorial practice of examinations conducted by the court.

141 The distinction between 'substantive' and 'procedural' exclusionary rules has been outlined earlier, in Chapter 4.

here. In many cases at common law evidence of this type was tendered not in relation to any fact in issue (*e.g.* consent), but on the issue of the complainant's credit, a collateral matter on which the accused could cross-examine the witness but not adduce evidence of his own. Rules were first amended by *S.O.(A.)A. 1976* and later completely re-written by *Y.J.C.E.A. 1999*, s. 41. This provision introduced a general prohibition against evidence of prior sexual conduct between the complainant and the accused or other persons, although either may be admitted with the leave of the court upon certain specified conditions.[142] It is interesting to notice that the extent of the restrictions has caused some discomfort in the House of Lords, for which the crux of the matter is to ensure the right to 'crucial' evidence and, more specifically, the right of the accused to effectively examine and cross-examine witnesses under the terms of Article 6(3)(d) of the European Convention. In *R. v. A. (No. 2)*,[143] it was suggested that the many requirements provided for in Section 41 had to be re-interpreted[144] so as to ensure that relevant evidence which may affect the outcome of the case is not excluded. What is important here is to underline that the House of Lords referred to Article 6(3)(d) of the Convention despite the fact that ECHR discourse had always been short of announcements over the specific questions that defendants, or counsel, should expect to be entitled to pose to an adverse witness.

The process of interviewing vulnerable witnesses could also involve the attendance of an adult or some specialised intermediaries. Their presence at the time of the taking of depositions is equally welcomed by statutory provisions in England,[145] Italy[146] and France.[147] Nonetheless, nothing is said in any of the model countries about the extent and limits of their intervention. Ideally, the intermediary should be an expert in psychology or child care and his function should be strictly limited to communicate questions put to the witness and a

142 *Y.J.C.E.A. 1999*, s. 41(3) and (5).

143 [2002] 1 A.C. 45 (H.L.). The House of Lords was probably influenced to some extent by a decision of the Supreme Court of Canada (*R. v. Seaboyer*, [1991] 2 S.C.R. 577) in which a blanket exclusion of cross-examination of the complainant was unconstitutional for reasons similar to those invoked under Art. 6 of the European Convention. Early discussion of the impact of this case on the interpretation of *Y.J.C.E.A. 1999*, s. 41 is provided by D. Birch, *Rethinking Sexual History Evidence: Proposals for Fairer Trials*, [2002] Crim. L.R. 531.

144 It is recalled that *H.R.A. 1998*, s. 3(1) requires that an Act of Parliament be 'read and given effect to in a way which is compatible with the Convention rights'.

145 *Y.J.C.E.A. 1999*, s. 29 (only for children and witnesses suffering from disabilities or a significance impairment of intelligence and social functioning). The role of intermediaries had been approved of by prior case law: cf. *R. v. Duffy*, [1999] Q.B. 919 (C.A.) (evidence of an interview between a social worker and a witness with severe speech difficulties).

146 Art. 498(4) I-CPP.

147 Art. 706-53 F-CPP.

witness's replies and to explain both so far as is necessary to enable both to be understood.[148] Independent questioning by the intermediary cannot be regarded as a substitute for the 'adverse questioning' component of the confrontational paradigm, as it has been conceptualised in Chapter 1. No specific guidance on this point has been provided so far by ECHR law, while in the United States intermediaries have survived constitutional challenges only when they have acted as 'megaphones'[149] or translators of inaudible answers.[150]

Earlier in this work it has been argued that the role of intermediary for a vulnerable should not be played by those who are themselves witnesses for the prosecution or by those who may be reasonably suspected of bias against the accused. Italian and French law are unresponsive to such claim and deserve further criticism. There, statutory provisions explicitly[151] permit the appointment of a relative of the child as intermediary, even when the defendant is also a member of the family. In such cases, the intermediary will most often bear strong views about the offence, and may also have his or her own motive against the accused.[152]

4.2.3 Early Interviews

Although every person is less accurate and complete in his account after a long retention interval,[153] empirical research suggests that even a short delay may result in a dramatic deterioration of the eyewitness memory of children.[154] This arguably poses problems to criminal justice systems, since investigations require weeks if not months, and trials inevitably take place some

---

148 See L. Ellison, *Cross-Examination and the Intermediary: Bridging the Language Divide*, [2002] Crim. L.R. 114.

149 This expression is used by L. Hoyano, *Striking a Balance between the Rights of Defendants and Vulnerable Witnesses: Will Special Measures Directions Contravene Guarantees of a Fair Trial?* [2001] Crim. L.R. 948, at 964.

150 *U.S. v. Romey*, 32 M.J. 180 (Court of Mil. Appeals 1991) (Third-party whisper procedure of child victim whispering testimony to her mother who then repeated it complied with confrontation clause in court-martial for sodomy).

151 Art. 498(4) I-CPP; Art. 706-53 F-CPP.

152 In *U.S. v. Romey*, *supra* note 150, the presence of the witness' s mother at the time of the deposition was approved because, among other reasons, she acknowledged her absence from the home during the period the alleged crimes occurred, she did not provide substantive testimony for Government, and she did not engage in any extortious conduct toward accused.

153 See generally, E.F. Loftus, *Eyewitness Testimony*, Harvard Univ. Press, Cambridge, 1996.

154 See the findings of J.E.B. Myers, K.J. Saywitz and G.S. Goodman, *Psychological Research on Children as Witnesses: Practical Implications for Forensic Interviews and Courtroom Testimony*, (1996) 28 Pacific L.J. 3; R. Flin and others, *The Effect of a Five-Months Delay on Children's and Adults' Eyewitness Memory*, (1992) 83 British Journal of Psychology 323.

time after the offence has been allegedly perpetrated. Related to this problem is also the issue of the adverse effects of multiple interviewing, which may result in distorting the memory of the vulnerable witness, especially when leading questions were abused by the interviewer in prior occasions.[155] Considerations of this sort have inspired a recommendation of the Council of Europe, according to which vulnerable witnesses should be examined at the 'earliest stage of the criminal proceedings, as soon as possible after the facts have been reported'. Such examination should not be repeated. Also, statements made at the pre-trial stage should be 'recorded in order to avoid unnecessary repetitive examinations that may cause trauma'.[156]

Law-makers in the three model countries are sensitive to these matters. A common strategy of national jurisdictions is to stage an early interview of the vulnerable at a tailor-made pre-trial hearing, to be video-recorded and later played at trial, or included in the court dossier. Depositions of this kind stand as evidence at trial and may even substitute the courtroom testimony.[157] The crucial problem here is to assess whether these early interviews are 'confrontational' in nature. In other words, it is to be investigated what role can be played by the defence at such hearings and, further, whether an early timing of examination may in itself pose a threat to the Right to Confrontation.

To begin with some point of certainty, it is understood that the standards set by the Strasbourg judiciary require that all the evidence be produced in the presence of the accused 'with a view to adversarial argument', but it is not stipulated *when* a witness is to be available for examination by the defence. Although arguments that confrontational examinations should necessarily take place at trial may be treated sceptically at Strasbourg,[158] the matter still raises confrontational concerns in accordance with the assumptions of this work.

It is settled that in order for an early examination to be truly 'confrontational' certain minimal conditions must be met. The fact that defence counsel may hear and see what the witness is saying is by no means sufficient. This is precisely the state of the law in France, where counsel cannot play an active role in the hearings before the prosecutor or the *juge d'instruction*. Video recorded interviews of vulnerable witnesses pursuant to Art. 706-52 F-CPP must therefore be regarded as 'unilateral' takings of depositions and, should the witnesses fail to come to court, she must be regarded as an 'absent witness' for the purposes of this work. It may also not be entirely satisfying that counsel are entitled to put questions to the witness, under the same conditions as in courtroom

---

155 D.A. Poole and L.T. White, *Tell Me Again and Again – Stability and Change in the Repeated Testimonies*, in M.S. Zaragoza (ed.), *Memory and Testimony in the Child Witness*, Sage, Thousand Oaks, 1995, 24-43.

156 Recommendation No. 13/1997 of the Committee of Ministers of the Council of Europe, concerning intimidation of witnesses and the rights of the defence, §25-27.

157 See, for instance, *Y.J.C.E.A. 1999*, s. 28(5) which has not yet, however, come into force.

158 This view is subscribed to by L Hoyano, *Striking a Balance...*, *supra* note 149, at 959.

examinations. At the time of trial, in fact, counsel will have been given access to the whole findings of the preliminary investigations,[159] and will have been supplied with all the prior statements of the summoned witnesses.[160] Further, in Italy and England counsel will have also had the opportunity to perform private investigations to gather information relevant to the credit of the declarant and the reliability of her account. At an early stage of the investigation, with little to no information at disposal, counsel may have no knowledge of the facts at issue and, consequently, could fail to address any meaningful question to the prosecution informants.

Italian law provides a convincing solution to this problem. In Italy, a limited disclosure is always required on the part of the prosecution when a witness is heard at the *incidente probatorio*, since depositions collected at that stage stand as evidence at the subsequent trial.[161] Pursuant to Article 398(3) prosecutors are bound to disclose all prior statements of the relevant witness at least two days before the hearing takes place, so that the statements may be put to the witness under cross-examination. Instead, when the taking of evidence involves a person aged under 16 in prosecutions for certain specified sexual offences, a prominent exception applies: the *whole* findings of the investigations must be disclosed to the defence.[162] Failure to comply with disclosure provisions results in the non-usability of the depositions taken at that specific hearing. In comparison, no exception to the statutory duty of disclosure may be found in English law with regard to cross-examination under *Y.J.C.E.A. 1999*, s. 28, despite the fact that no court examination of the vulnerable would normally take place at all once this provision comes into force. Purely for the sake of speculation (since nobody

---

[159] In *Rowe and Davis v. U.K.*, [2000-II] RJD 287, (2000) 30 EHRR 1 at para. 60 the European Court stated that the right to a fair trial means that the prosecution authorities should disclose to the defence all material evidence in their possession for and against the accused. Although some restrictions are permitted under ECHR law, the satement seems to point to wider test of materiality then the more limited one implied under English statutory law. The formulation also seems to challenge the purported distinction between primary and secondary duty of disclosure, which has also been endorsed by *C.J.A. 2003*.

[160] In Italy, prior statements of witnesses are included in the prosecution dossier, which is disclosed to the defence by virtue of Art. 415bis of the Code of Criminal Procedure. In England, the prosecution duty to disclose covers all prior statements of witnesses. Most if not all of the testimonial evidence favourable to the prosecution will in fact have been disclosed at committal proceedings. Duty of disclosure also applies to prior statements that 'might reasonably be considered capable of undermining' the prosecution case' (*C.P.I.A. 1996*, s. 3(1)(a) as amended by *C.J.A. 2003*, s. 32) and that may therefore be put in cross-examination to a courtroom accuser by counsel as prior inconsistent statements, if the declarant gives evidence against the accused.

[161] It must be noted, however, that the examination at the *incidente probatorio* does not prevent the parties from summoning the witness for the courtroom testimony.

[162] Art. 398(3bis) I-CPP.

knows whether and when *Y.J.C.E.A. 1999* s. 28 will ever come into force) one may wonder whether such virtual cross-examination would amount to a proper challenge 'with a view to adversarial argument' in the terms of ECHR law.

4.2.4 Audio-visual Technology

A cursory glance at contemporary European legislation suggests that audiovisual technology is considered the 'way ahead' for the taking of the evidence of the vulnerable. Rules for live video-links via closed-circuit televisions and videotaped pre-trial depositions may now be found in English, Italian and, more limitedly, French statutory law. It should also be noted that none of the jurisdictions in question subscribe to the view that video taped and closed-circuit testimony should only be made available *after* a witness has been confronted with the accused in open court and rendered speechless as a result.

In England, video recordings of investigative interviews have been admissible in lieu of examinations-in-chief in proceedings concerning sexual offences since October 1992, when *C.J.A. 1988*, s. 32(a) was implemented.[163] *C.J.A. 1988*, s. 32 also introduced provisions for live video-links. The rules were later replaced in a much extended form, to cover any vulnerable and intimidated witnesses, by *Y.J.C.E.A. 1999*.[164] When video taped interview are played at trial the jury is provided with a transcript of it, when it is necessary to follow the evidence.[165] In Italy, tape recorded examinations-in-chief and cross-examinations of children at the *incidente probatorio* may be played at trial and may stand there as evidence. Live audio links can also be employed to screen the accused from the sight of a child witness under the age of 16, by virtue of Article 498(4ter) of the Code of criminal procedure. In France, rules for the video-taping of child's depositions in sexual cases before the *juge d'instruction* and prosecutor may be found in Article 706-53 of the *Code de procedure pénale.* No statutory provisions for trial video-links exist, while a much more radical option can be pursued by the president of a criminal court under the discretionary powers of Article 339 of the Code. This provision authorises the removal of the accused from the courtroom when a witness or codefendant[166] gives evidence, if only the president deems it appropriate in the interests of justice. Regrettably, such decisions are not subject to judicial review, despite their impact on the confrontational paradigm and, consequently, on the fundamental Right to Confrontation.

---

[163] *C.J.A. 1991*, s. 54.

[164] Live video links are now available at trials on indictment for the collection of the evidence of any witness (other than the defendant) pursuant to *C.J.A. 2003*, 51(1), and subject to the conditions enumerated under s. 51(4).

[165] Transcripts are withdrawn before retirement: *R. v. Welstead*, [1996] 1 Cr. App. R. 59 (C.A.).

[166] (F) Cass. crim., 12 January 1977, *Bull. crim.* n°17, Bindewald.

A question remains as to whether 'virtual' testimonies may breach the guarantees of a fair trial, and more importantly, whether national laws of evidence may abuse of this means despite the openly announced commitment to the fundamental Right to Confrontation. Earlier in this work, doubts have been cast over the idea that audio-visual technology is a *panacea* for the problems concerning the vulnerable witness. Instead, it may also be seen as a silent bypass of the 'most terrifying nightmare' of prosecutors; that is, the live collection of her evidence. Certainly, technology serves sensible purposes insofar as it ensures the scrutiny of the conditions upon which out-of-court statements were collected by judicial authorities or it screens the vulnerable accused from the sight of the fearful accuser. Nevertheless, the related provisions may also detract from the immediacy of 'live' testimony in the courtroom and, as a result, from the requirements of the 'confrontational paradigm', as described in Chapter 1.

While only little authority is provided on the collection of the evidence of the vulnerable in ECHR law, debate is intense in national jurisprudence. While, as a tendency, judges and prosecutors across Europe welcome the use of equipment in the courtroom,[167] counsel often argue that live television links alter the manner in which evidence is given and make it impossible to pose real challenges to the declarant. In England and Italy especially, the use of audiovisual technology has been subject to sharp contention, although different are the reasons invoked by commentators and, it must be said, no 'constitutional' or 'Human Rights' challenges to statutory law have yet been successful.[168]

In England, it is agreed that the use of pre-recorded testimony and video-link has involved a major change in the working practices of the criminal justice systems. For a start, video interviews are often in the narrative, a feature that makes these testimonies similar to those collected in inquisitorial proceedings. As a consequence, the engrained opposition *fluency v. interruption* no longer applies here. A second line of argument concerns the so called 'risk of prejudice', according to which the very presence of a physical barrier in the courtroom may stigmatise the latter.[169] This claim has been endorsed by the English Court of Appeal[170] and *Y.J.C.E.A. 1999*, s. 32, which calls for a 'counterbalance', in the form of a discretionary tailor-made warning of caution to the jury. It is also

167 For a Scottish survey of the judges' reaction to the new technology cf. K. Murray, *Live Television Link: An Evaluation of Its Use by Child Witnesses in Scottish Criminal Trials*, The Scottish Office, Edinburgh, 1995, 168.

168 In the United States, taking of evidence through video link in sexual cases does not amount to a violation of the Confrontation Clause of the Sixth Amendment, see Chapter 1.

169 For a comprehensive discussion of this claim see T.M. Massaro, *The Dignity Value of Face-to-Face Confrontations*, (1988) 40 U. Flo. L.R. 863, at 903.

170 In *R. v. Foster*, [1995] Crim. L.R. 333 (C.A.); *R. v. Cooper and Schaub*, [1994] Crim. L.R. 531 (C.A.). In *R. v. Ghani*, 25 October 1999 (C.A.), unreported it was said that it would normally be appropriate to direct the jury not to draw any adverse inference against the accused from the use of a screen.

claimed that live links cause a diminution of demeanour evidence, although the evidentiary value of non verbal behaviour remains highly contested.

In comparison, in Italy the debate on the new technology has concentrated on statutory provisions concerning mafia crimes.[171] Conclusions reached in that regard also apply to the collection of the 'virtual' evidence of the vulnerable. Commentators have discussed the practical features of new technologies and the consequences of connection failures.[172] Bad quality in the reception of long-distance links, for instance, has led to describe video examinations as 'artificial cartoon copies'[173] of live confrontations. The Constitutional Court, however, plainly dismissed the claim that video links may conflict with adversarial principles[174] and took the view that the employment of state of the art technology makes remote locations into an 'extended space' of the courtroom.

Beyond speculation, a case-by-case assessment is necessary to measure the impact of televised examinations on any of the components of the 'confrontational paradigm', as described earlier in this work. On the one hand, the court must be prepared to substitute live testimony when the quality of the technology is exceedingly poor. On the other hand, attention must be paid to the actual mode of examination. While hearing and seeing the witness distinctively through a video camera is an essential pre-condition of fairness, nevertheless the crucial matter is whether 'simultaneous adverse questioning' is permitted. This appears to be the case in Italy and England. There, parties are not expected to disclose their questions in advance and live televised examinations allow the adjustment of the parties' strategy to the course of evidence. This is not to deny that technology may still interfere with the spontaneity of the declarant deposition; yet, in such conditions the intrusions into the accused' s Right to Confrontation should be reasonably perceived as minimal, and justifiable according to the theoretical foundations of this work.[175]

---

171 Law No. 11, 7 January 1998 introduced trial video-conferences and video-examinations for certain organized crime trials, in order to keep certain dangerous defendants and witnesses in remote locations (mainly tailor-made conference rooms in State prisons), which are linked by cable to most courtrooms of the Italian tribunals and Courts of Appeal. While in 1998 provisions were passed as temporary emergency measures, they are now permanent pursuant to Art. 3, Law No. 279/2002.

172 G.P. Voena, *La Legge sulle Videoconferenze e sull'Esame a Distanza nel Processo Penale*, in G. Conso and V. Grevi (eds), *Profili del Nuovo Codice di Procedura Penale – Appendice di aggiornamento*, 4th edn., Cedam, Padova, 1998, 25.

173 G. Frigo, *L'Eccezione che Diventa la Regola*, [2003] Dir. Pen. Proc. 412, 413.

174 (I) Corte cost, judgment No. 342/1999, [1999] Giur. Cost. 2692.

175 Intrusions into fundamental rights are to be accepted when the values protected by such right are at stake 'only in some attenuated form': cf. Chapter 1, s. 1.3.

4.3 A Common Strategy: Hearsay as a Refuge for the Vulnerable Witness

The most pressing threat to confrontation is posed by the 'absent vulnerable witness'. The present section discloses that all the national jurisdictions under scrutiny[176] employ hearsay techniques as a 'refuge' for the vulnerable witness who had never been confronted with the accused or counsel. Earlier in this work, it was argued that 'absence' may only be tolerated when, despite the effort of the prosecution, it has been truly *impossible* to ensure the courtroom presence of the accuser (*e.g.* because of death, serious illness, residence in a Country in which evidence on commission cannot be taken). Absence, in other words, ought not be the automatic judicial response to the condition of 'vulnerability' of the declarant. A panoply of measures may well ensure, at least, a protected examination with limited participation of the defence. This alone may be said to comply with the assumption of this work, according to which 'departures' from the 'confrontational paradigm' are legitimate insofar as they are kept to a minimum.

As explained earlier, hearsay is routinely admissible in French law. Firstly, prior depositions of informants and witnesses before the *juge d'instruction* must be assembled in the court dossier and are admissible as evidence of the fact stated therein. The general rule is that prior statements are to be read in court only *after* the witness has taken the stand. Nevertheless, this rule only applies when a court examination takes place. Instead, if the witness is 'unavailable' to testify, those prior depositions purely substitute oral evidence. The test of unavailability has been broadly construed by the French courts, as to include all the cases in which the collection of the evidence is not useful for the discovery of the truth. In practice, this certainly includes the evidence of children and other individuals who may suffer traumas as a result of a court testimony. A statement by a G.P. would usually satisfy the court of their unfitness to give evidence. Secondly, it must also be recalled that hearsay statements of court declarants may not be objected by the parties. Testimonial evidence may thus be brought in evidence in the form of the indirect account of a family member, social worker, doctor or other person to which the alleged victims had reported facts relevant to the offence under prosecution. In both scenarios, the defendant would have no chance to confront his accusers. This state of affairs may cause some discomfort at Strasbourg, since no requirement of corroboration is prescribed in French statutory law.

---

176 Similar considerations also apply in the United States. In the leading case *White v. Illinois*, 502 U.S. 346, 112 S. Ct. 736 (1992) (for discussion see above, Chapter 1) the statements of a sexually abused child to her babysitter, mother, and a police officer were admitted in evidence under the spontaneous declaration (F.R.E. 803(2)) and medical examination (F.R.E. 803(4)) exceptions to the hearsay rule.

In England, the rule against hearsay has been virtually abolished in criminal proceedings since *C.J.A. 2003*, s. 114 came into force on April 5, 2005. While it is too early to assess what types of hearsay the courts will be prepared to admit under the conditions listed thereat, it is interesting to outline that, even under the more restrictive prior regime, hearsay evidence could already serve as a 'refuge' for the vulnerable witness.[177] Discussion hereinafter is limited to documentary hearsay (ie prior 'depositions' of the vulnerable) although testimonial statements of a vulnerable could also be admitted as part of the *res gestae* exception to the hearsay rule.[178]

As for documents *C.J.A. 1988*, s. 23(2)(a), dealing with first hand hearsay, requires that the maker of the statement be shown to be unavailable for reasons including unfitness to attend by reason of 'bodily or mental conditions'. This could certainly include a state of vulnerability due to a certified mental illness,[179] or even anxiety alone.[180] When the out-of-court statements in question were collected for the purposes of pending or contemplated proceedings the leave of the judge is required to admit them in evidence, by virtue of Section 26. Statements to the police, therefore, would come within the terms of Section 26 so that leave is necessary, but, it was argued, a child's statement to a social worker investigating sexual abuse would not, if the object of the enquiry was purely to protect the child.[181] In such a case the trial judge would have only to consider how to exercise his residual discretion to exclude the evidence under *CJA 1988*, s. 25(1), and the presumption in fact is that hearsay evidence should be admitted, unless the 'interests of justice' called for its exclusion. The only limited counterbalance in favour of the accused derives from the need to warn the jury that statements had not been subject to cross-examinations and this element had to be taken into account in deciding how far they can safely rely on them.[182]

In Italy, the courts have acted as the guarantor of public interest in this specific area of the law. For more than a decade, the Constitutional Court and the *Corte di cassazione* attempted to circumvent statutory exclusionary rules of

---

177 Even before the coming into force of *C.J.A. 1988*, this matter has raised the interest of English commentators: cf., among others, J.R. Spencer and P.G. Tucker, *The Evidence of Absent Children*, [1987] N.L.J. 816.

178 Under this heading it would be possible to lead evidence that a child had said 'I'm scared of Daddy' in order to show that she was afraid of her father; this example is given by H.L. Westcott and G.M. Davies and J.R. Spencer, *Protecting The Child Witness: Hearsay Techniques and Other Innovations: Children, Hearsay, and the Courts: A Perspective From the United Kingdom*, (1999) 5 Psych. P.P.& L. 282, 286.

179 *R. v. Duffy, supra* note 145.

180 *R. v. Setz-Dempsey*, (1994) 98 Cr. App. R. 23 (C.A.).

181 J. McEwan, *Documentary Hearsay Evidence-Refuge for the Vulnerable Witness?*, [1989] Crim. L.R. 629, 639.

182 Wording of the direction should have been tailor-made to the circumstances of the case: *R. v. Hardwick*, The Times, 28 February 2001 (C.A.).

evidence so to allow non-confronted depositions from a vulnerable declarant to be used, to the obvious benefit of the prosecution. In particular, case law has broadly construed certain legal concepts, relevant to the rules governing a) prior depositions of absent witnesses and b) hearsay statements of court witnesses.

On the one hand, prior depositions – which are assembled in the prosecution dossier – may only be read out when 'unpredictable' circumstances make a court examination of the concerned witness impossible (Article 512 Italian Code of Criminal Procedure. Strict legal reasoning should have led to conclude that, whenever a vulnerable witness is involved, the 'unpredictability' requirement cannot be satisfied, since multiple elements (sudden decrease of memory, emotional shock, distress) pose a foreseeable risk of some future difficulties to bring the witness to the stand. This is why the prosecution is given the opportunity to collect early evidence at the *incidente probatorio*. Nonetheless, the courts argued that unpredictability is a subjective requirement and, therefore, that it applies to a vulnerable as to any other witness.[183] On the other hand, hearsay statements of testifying witnesses are only admissible in Italy when the direct source of evidence is 'dead', 'infirm' or 'untraceable' (Article 195 Italian Code of Criminal Procedure). Here, the concept of 'infirmity' has been expanded so to include not only certified mental illnesses, but also instances of distress and anxiety that may cause the court deposition to be 'worthless',[184] especially in cases of children of a very young age and other handicapped persons. 'Infirmity' has also been interpreted as to cover the mere risk that a *future* illness may develop as a consequence of the court depositions.[185]

One would expect that this state of affairs could be easily challenged as a violation of the Confrontation Clause, now embedded in Article 111(3) of the Italian Constitution. Indeed, some commentators[186] have argued that such readings of statutory provisions circumvent the stringent exclusionary rules of evidence established by the law in 2001 for the pre-trial depositions of an informant. Admitting this type of hearsay, this reasoning goes, opens the doors of the adjudication process to testimonial evidence that is functionally equivalent to the 'statements taken unilaterally by the police or prosecutors'.[187] At present, however, prior case law trends have not been reversed and no challenge has yet been brought before the Constitutional Court.

---

[183] (I) Cass. crim., 25 September 2000, Galliera, [2002] Cass. Pen. 616.

[184] (I) Corte cost., judgment No. 20/1995, [1995] Giur. Cost. 232.

[185] (I) Cass. crim., 25 September 2000, Galliera, *supra* note 183.

[186] S. Maffei, *Il Diritto al Confronto con l'Accusatore*, CELT, Piacenza, 2003, 372-374; G. Di Paolo, *L'Acquisizione nel Processo Penale delle 'Dichiarazioni a Contenuto Testimoniale' del Minorenne*, [2003] Cass. Pen. 1672.

[187] G. Di Paolo, *L'Acquisizione nel Processo Penale...*, *supra* note 186, 1673.

5 Conclusion

This chapter has discussed the evidence of absent, anonymous and vulnerable witnesses in the three European model Countries. Despite the announced commitment of each of them to the principle of the supremacy of oral evidence, this is everywhere intermingled with restrictions, exceptions and derogations. Research has shown that none of the jurisdictions under scrutiny is yet perfectly aligned to ECHR law, despite the fact that the Strasbourg Court only sets a minimum standard for the protection of the Right to Confrontation.

As expected in the light of the considerations made in Chapter 2, the evidence of absent witnesses is admissible in multiple circumstances in all the Countries under investigation. Yet, it is rather surprising to discover that the corroboration requirement – indispensable under ECHR law, as discussed in Chapter 3 – finds almost no implementation at domestic level. Research has also registered a tendency towards the gradual loosening of procedural rules in the examination of alleged vulnerable witnesses: the European trend is clearly based upon the idea that their evidence should be promptly secured – sometimes even informally or in the form of hearsay. Early interviews and audiovisual technology, however, are employed in all model Countries to minimise the impact into the Right to confrontation

Further, the research carried out in this chapter has found certain areas of national law that afford an additional protection to the defendant (compared to ECHR law) and may thus give a meaningful contribution to a general theory of confrontation. Italian and English criminal trials, for instance, are almost impermeable to anonymous evidence. Even in the prosecution of most serious crimes and most dangerous offenders, counsel and defendants are informed of the real identity of the prosecution witness and may effectively attack his or her credibility. In comparison, the present state of French law merits firm criticism in respect with anonymous witnesses. In line with the inquisitorial tradition of that jurisdiction, the French law-makers continue to be easily responsive to arguments of social defence and public interest, notwithstanding the high-sounding commitment to the equality of arms and the presumption of innocence.

CHAPTER 7

Conclusion

ECHR law, national and international laws afford some degree of protection to the right of the defendant to confront adverse witnesses. Analysis of such protection has been the focus of this work, under the assumption that a 'Human Rights' approach is the ideal lens for investigating the process of adjudication in criminal trials.

The Right to Confrontation has been treated as 'fundamental', given its standing in national constitutional law and in many international treaties for the protection of the individuals subject to a criminal prosecution. First and foremost, a theoretical framework has been established upon principles of natural justice, in an attempt to outline the significance of the 'confrontational paradigm' for a process of adjudication that can sensibly claim to be fair to the defendant. It was argued that criminal jurisdictions must ensure the priority of the Right to Confrontation, being a fundamental right, over arguments of procedural efficiency and public interest. A serious commitment to confrontation, however, yields substantial costs for society. Such costs may include the exclusion from evidence of the depositions gathered unilaterally by judicial authorities (police, prosecutors, examining magistrate) when the declarant fails to come to court, as well as the establishment of guarantees to ensure the participation of the defence in the protected examinations of the vulnerable and anonymous witness.

A truly European discourse on the Right to Confrontation cannot overlook the jurisprudence on Article 6(3)(d) of the European Convention on Human Rights. In the last twenty years, successful challenges to national rules of evidence and procedure have been brought before the Strasbourg organs by convicted persons in allegedly unfair domestic proceedings. Many lessons have been learned from ECHR law. Firstly, the Confrontation Clause of the Convention can be invoked against the use in evidence of the out-of-court statements of police and prosecution informants. This draws a clear line between the European and U.S. constitutional discourse on the Right to Confrontation: in the U.S., the admissibility of the evidence of an absent witness is governed almost exclusively by the statutory law of hearsay. Secondly, although anonymous testimony is tolerated as a legitimate tool in the prosecution of certain serious crimes, the defence must be given an opportunity to play a part in the examination, while the court must also be aware of the identity of the witness. On far too many occasions, nevertheless, the claim that unchallenged testimonial evidence was neither the only nor the main piece of evidence against the defendant led the Strasbourg Court to approve of domestic proceedings that would have deserved much firmer scrutiny.

The concepts of 'testimonial evidence' and 'confrontational paradigm' served also as functional equivalents, in the assessment of the contribution of three European countries to a general theory of confrontation. Italy, France and England (and Wales) were chosen for their diverging traditions – based on the adherence to either the adversarial or the inquisitorial model of procedure – as well as for the similar crime rates that their systems of justice are facing. It has been said that multidirectional changes characterise the present state of domestic laws of evidence and procedure due to the ongoing effort of super-active legislators. Although a fair criminal trial is the openly announced objective of all movements of criminal justice reforms, fairness is pursued in considerably different manners. Italy directly amended its Constitution, while France inserted a preliminary article in the Code of criminal procedure. In England, *H.R.A. 1998* advocated the urgent alignment of domestic law to ECHR law. Not even the most preserved sanctuary of nationhood (such as the law of hearsay in England, and the leading role of the judge in the examination of witnesses in France) have been left untouched by the recent upheavals of national procedures.

Each model country follows its own peculiar style for the court examination of witnesses. Although, in broad terms, the taking of the evidence of prosecution witnesses conforms to the 'confrontational paradigm', considerable variants have been found in the practice of domestic litigation. In England – and increasingly more frequently in Italy – court examinations consist of sharp, and repeatedly interrupted, sequences of questions and answers, while in France testimonies unfold as spontaneous narrative recollections of the declarant's memories. Prior inconsistent statements can be used only for impeachment in Italy, while they are admissible evidence in France and also in England and Wales. In England, a co-accused who takes the stand has an obligation to answer questions and state the truth, while in Italy and France he or she enjoys a statutory right to lie. These variants epitomise the beauty of diversity in this area of the law across Europe.

Although each model country is said to be inspired by the principle of the supremacy of oral evidence, this is everywhere intermingled with restrictions, exceptions and derogations. Research has shown that none of the jurisdictions under scrutiny is yet perfectly aligned to ECHR law, despite the fact that the Strasbourg Court only sets a minimum standard for the protection of the Right to Confrontation. Major inconsistencies have been found in French law: while the deposition of an absent witness is routinely admissible and does not require supportive evidence, anonymity can be granted to prosecution witnesses in virtually all proceedings for offences of an intermediate gravity. In Italy and England, the evidence of an absent witness can sometimes be brought to the court's attention as oral hearsay or a document, and no corroboration tests apply in such cases. Also, hearsay evidence serves as refuge for the evidence of a vulnerable witness.

This is not to deny that certain areas of national law afford an additional protection to the defendant and may thus give a meaningful contribution to a general theory of confrontation. Italian and English criminal trials, for instance, are almost impermeable to anonymous evidence. Even in the prosecution of most serious crimes and most dangerous offenders, counsel and defendants are informed of the real identity of the prosecution witness and may effectively attack his or her credibility. Other means (namely, tailor-made Witness Protection Programs) may serve the purpose to protect the life and security of the informant, while simultaneously ensuring a face-to-face confrontation between the accused and the accuser. Valuable findings have been made with regard to the national treatment of police informants who are summoned by the prosecution and fail to attend the trial. English and French law are construed around the concept of 'witness unavailability' so that reading of prior allegations is acceptable whenever it is proved that public authorities made a reasonable effort to secure his or her attendance. In comparison, Italian law has recently abandoned any reference to such effort: absence is *in itself* considered as an attempt of the declarant to avoid public confrontation with the defendant in person. The burden of proving that the declarant was absent because he or she was kept away against his or her will rightly lies with the prosecution. National laws and court practices have also deployed a panoply of protective measures to ensure the participation of the defence in the collection of the evidence of the vulnerable witness, either at trial or in dedicated pre-trial hearings.

This being said, the Right to Confrontation should now gain a special claim on the attention of European evidence scholars. Its spirit and corollaries can no longer be regarded as the 'soft law' of an International Court, since they are in fact deeply infused into domestic discourse. Of course, announcing serious commitment to a fundamental right is a great deal easier than bringing it about in practice. Further, several other claims may still be recognised at the European level as no less fundamental than the call for confrontation. This is, in effect, the reason why the evidence of absent, anonymous and vulnerable witnesses is so often admissible against a defendant. Yet, rules of evidence and procedure should be construed and interpreted, so to give to the Right to Confrontation the standing and consideration that this work has shown – it is hoped – that it deserves.

Bibliography

P. Alldridge, *Reform Movements in Criminal Procedure and the Protection of Human Rights in England*, 64 (1993) R.I.D.P. 1115

J.A. Allison and L.S. Wrightsman, *Rape-The Misunderstood Crime*, Sage, Newbury Park, 1993

A.R. Amar, *Confrontation Clause First Principles: A Reply to Professor Friedman*, (1998) 86 Geo. Law Journal 1045

A.R. Amar, *The Constitution and Criminal Procedure: First Principles*, Yale Univ. Press, New Haven, 1997

E. Amodio, *Giusto Processo, Diritto al Silenzio e Obblighi di Verità dell'Imputato sul Fatto Altrui*, [2001] Cass. Pen. 3587

E. Amodio, *Libero Convincimento e Tassatività dei Mezzi di Prova: un Approccio Comparativo*, [1999] R.I.D.P.P. 3

E. Amodio and E. Selvaggi, *An Accusatorial System in a Civil Law Country: the 1988 Italian Code of Criminal Procedure*, (1989) 62 Temple L.R. 1211

H. Angevin, *Incidences de la Convention Européenne des Droits de l'Homme sur la Procédure Pénale Française et Plus Spécialement sur celle de la Cour d'Assises*, [1991-7] Droit Pénal 3

A. Ashworth, *Human Rights, Serious Crime and Criminal Procedure*, Sweet & Maxwell, London, 2002

Auld L.J., *Review of the Criminal Courts of England and Wales, Report*, Stationery Office, London, 2001

K. Auromaa, *Trends in Criminality*, in *Crime and Criminal Justice in Europe*, Council of Europe Publishing, Strasbourg, 2001

J.L. Austin, *How to Do Things with Words*, Oxford Univ. Press, Oxford, 1962

G.M. Baccari, *La Testimonianza del Prossimo Congiunto dell'Imputato*, Cedam, Padova, 2003

I. Bacik, C. Maunsell and S. Gogan *The Legal Process and Victims of Rape*, Dublin Rape Crisis Centre, Dublin, 1998

C. Bagley and K. Mallick (eds), *Child Sexual Abuse and Adult Offenders: New Theory and Research*, Ashgate, Aldershot, 1999

H. de Balzac, *La Comedie Humaine – Splendeurs et Misères de Courtisanes – III*, Paris, 1840

M. Bargis, *Incompatibilità a Testimoniare e Connessione di Reati*, Giuffrè, Milano, 1980

N.H. Baughan, *The Confrontation Clause and the Supreme Court's Preference for Out-of-Court Statements*, (1993) 46 Vanderbilt L.R. 235

C. Beccaria, *Dei Delitti e delle Pene, con Commentari di Varii Insigni Scrittori*, Masi, Livorno, 1824

D.J. Beck, *Nature of Legal Malpractice*, (1991) 43 Baylor L.R. 43

P.W. Bennet, *After White v. Illinois: Fundamental Guarantees to a Hollow Right to Confront Witnesses*, (1993) 40 Wayne L.R. 159

J. Bentham, *Traité des Preuves Judiciaires*, Paris, 1823

J. Bentham, *Traité des Preuves Judiciaires*, 2nd edn., Paris, 1830

J. Bentham, *Rationale of Judicial Evidence, Specially Applied to English Practice*, Hunt and Clarke, London, 1827

R. Bernhardt, *Thoughts on the Interpretation of Human Rights Treaties*, in F. Matscher and H. Petzold (eds), *Protecting Human Rights: The European Dimension*, Heymanns, Köln, 1988, 65

W.M. Best, *The Principles of the Law of Evidence*, 12th edn., Sweet & Maxwell, London, 1922

Bingham L.J., *A Criminal Code: Must We Wait Forever?*, [1998] Crim. L.R. 694

D. Birch, *Rethinking Sexual History Evidence: Proposals for Fairer Trials*, [2002] Crim. L.R. 531
D. Birch, *The Criminal Justice Act 1988-The Evidence Provisions*, [1989] Crim. L.R. 15
J.A. Blumenthal, *A Wipe of the Hands, a Lick of the Lips; the Validity of Demeanor Evidence in Assessing Witness Credibility*, (1993) 72 Nebraska L.R. 1157
B. Bouloc, G. Levasseur and G. Stefani, *Procédure Pènale*, 17th edn., Dalloz, Paris, 2000
M. Bourmanne, *L'Audition des Témoins Lors du Procés Pénal dans la Jurisprudencee des Organes de la Convention Européenne des Droits de l'Homme*, [1995] R.T.D.H. 45
C.M. Bradley, *The Convergence of the Continental and the Common Law Model of Criminal Procedure*, (1996) 7 Crim. Law Forum 472
L.C. Brannon, *The Trauma of Testifying in Court for Child Victims of Sexual Assault v. the Accused's Right to Confrontation*, (1994) 18 Law & Psychol. Rev. 442
C. Brants, N. Jörg and S. Field, *Are Inquisitorial and Adversarial Systems Converging?*, in P. Fennell and others (eds.), *Criminal Justice in Europe: A Comparative Study*, Clarendon, Oxford, 1995, 41
A. Braunschweig, *La Procédure Pénale en Droit Français*, 64 (1993) R.I.D.P. 1089
S. Bronitt, *Entrapment, Human Rights and Criminal Justice: A Licence to Deviate?*, (1999) 29 Hong Kong L.J. 216
The Bureau of Justice Statistics – U.S. Department of Justice, *Felony Sentences in State Courts – 1998*, (2001)
T. Campbell, K.D. Ewing and A. Tomkins, *Sceptical Essays on Human Rights*, Oxford Univ. Press, Oxford, 2001
F. Casorla, *La Preuve en Procédure Pénale Comparée – Le Droit Français*, (1992) 63 R.I.D.P. 183
H. Causse, *Le Principe de Sûreté et le Droit à la Sécurité*, [2001] Gaz. Pal. Doct. 2007
D. Cheney, *Criminal Justice and the Human Rights Act 1998*, 2nd edn., Jordans, Bristol, 2001
J.Y. Chevallier, *La Preuve en Procédure Pénale Comparée – Rapport de Synthèse pour les Pays d'Europe Continentale*, (1992) 63 R.I.D.P. 43
M. Chiavario (ed.), *Commento al Nuovo Codice di Procedura Penale*, Utet, Torino, 1991, vol. V
M. Chiavario, *Les Mouvements de Réforme du Procès Pénal et la Protection des Droits de l'Homme en Italie*, 64 (1993) R.I.D.P. 1193
M Chiavario, *Limites en Matière de Preuve dans la Nouvelle Procédure Pénale Italienne*, [1992] R.S.C. 30
M. Chiavario, *Procedura Penale – Un Codice tra Storia e Cronaca*, Giappichelli, Torino, 1994
A.L.T. Choo, *Hearsay and Confrontation in Criminal Trials*, Clarendon, Oxford, 1996
E. Coke, *Institutes of the Laws of England – Part III*, Clarke, London, 1809
G.F. Cole, S. Frankowsky and M.G. Gertz, *Major Criminal Justice Systems: a Comparative Survey*, 2nd edn., Sage, Newbury Park, 1987
Commission Justice Pénale et Droits de l'Homme, *La Mise en Etat des Affaires Pénales. Rapports*, La Documentation Française, Paris, 1991
L.J. Constantinesco, *Traité de Droit Comparé*, Paris, 1972
P. Conte and P Maistre Du Chambon, *Procédure Pénale*, 3rd edn., Dalloz, Paris, 2001
F. Cordero, *Procedura Penale*, 7th edn., Giuffrè, Milano, 2003
P. Corso, *La Preuve en Procédure Pénale Comparée – Le Droit Italien*, (1992) 63 R.I.D.P. 205
J.A. Coutts, *Written Statements of Witnesses Abroad*, (1998) 62 J. Crim. L. 68
T. Cretin, *La Preuve Impossible? De la Difficulté d'Administrer la Preuve des Infractions dont sont Victimes les Mineurs: Attentats à la Pudeur, Violences et Mauvais Traitements*, [1992] R.S.C. 53

M.R. Damaška, *Evidence Law Adrift*, Yale Univ. Press, New Haven, 1997

M.R. Damaška, *Evidentiary Barriers to Conviction and Two Models of Criminal Procedure: a Comparative Study*, (1973) 121 U. Penn. L.R. 506

M.R. Damaška, *Negotiated Justice in International Criminal Courts*, (2004) 2 Journal Intl. Crim. Justice 1018

M.R. Damaška, *Of Hearsay and its Analogues*, (1992) 76 Minnesota Law Rev. 425

M.R. Damaška, *Presentation of Evidence and Fact-finding Precision*, (1975) 123 Univ. Pa. L.R. 1083

M.R. Damaška, *Structures of Authority and Comparative Criminal Procedure*, (1975) 84 Yale L.J. 480

M.R. Damaška, *The Faces of Justice and State Authority: a Comparative Approach to the Legal Process*, Yale Univ. Press, New Haven, 1986

M. Daniele, *La Testimonianza 'Assistita' e l'Esame degli Imputati in Procedimenti Connessi*, in R.E. Kostoris (ed.), *Il Giusto Processo tra Contraddittorio e Diritto al Silenzio*, Giappichelli, Torino, 2002, 196

F.G. Davies, *Preserving the Anonymity of Witnesses*, (1997) 161 J.P.&L.G.L. 351

L. De Cataldo Neuberger, *Chiamata in Correità e Psicologia del Pentitismo nel Nuovo Processo Penale*, Cedam, Padova, 1992

B. De Smet, *La Défense Face aux Témoin Anonymes et les Exigences d'un Procés Equitable dans la Jurisprudence de la Cour Européenne des Droits de l'Homme'* (1999) 70 R.I.D.P. 761

A. De Tocqueville, *De la Démocratie en Amérique*, 17th edn., Lévy, Paris, 1888

G. Delaloy, *La Cour de Cassation et la Statut Pénal du President de la République*, [2002-1] Droit Pénal 1

B. Deleuze and J.R. Spencer and D. Vorms, *La Preuve: Une Question Inclassable*, (1993) 15 Arch. Pol. Crim. 37

M. Delmas Marty, *Une Nouvelle Procédure Pénale – Présentation*, [2001] R.S.C. 3

M. Delmas-Marty and J.R. Spencer (eds), *European Criminal Procedures*, Cambrige Univ. Press, Cambridge, 2002

I.H. Dennis, *The Law of Evidence*, 2nd edn., Sweet & Maxwell, London, 2002

H. Dent and R. Flin, *Children as Witnesses*, Wiley, Chichester, 1992

V. Dervieux, *The French System*, in M. Delmas-Marty and J.R. Spencer (eds.), *European Criminal Procedures*, Cambrige Univ. Press, Cambridge, 2002, 218

G. Di Chiara, *La 'Nuova' Istruttoria Dibattimentale: Attuazione del 'Giusto Processo', Metodo del Contraddittorio e Prova Rappresentativa*, [2001-V] Foro Ital. 295

G. Di Chiara, *Le Linee Prospettiche del 'Difendersi Cercando': Luci e Ombre delle 'Nuove' Investigazioni Difensive*, [2002] Leg. Pen. 1

G Di Chiara, *L'Inquisizione come "Eterno Rimedio": Tecnica delle Contestazioni ed Usi Dibattimentali delle Indagini a Seguito della Sentenza 255/92 della Corte Costituzionale*, [1992-I] Foro Ital. 2013

C. Di Martino, *Prova Testimoniale (Diritto Processuale Penale)*, in *Enciclopedia Giuridica Treccani*, Treccani, Roma, 1991, vol. XXV, 1

G. Di Paolo, *L'Acquisizione nel Processo Penale delle 'Dichiarazioni a Contenuto Testimoniale' del Minorenne*, [2003] Cass. Pen. 1672

C. Dickens, *The Pickwick Papers*, London, 1836-37

O. Dominioni, *Un Nuovo Idolum Theatri: il Principio di non Dispersione Probatoria*, [1997] R.I.D.P.P. 736
F. Doroy, *Le Réexamen d'une Décision Pénale Consécutif au Pronuncé d'un Arrêt de Condamnation de la CEDH Mise en œuvre de la Réforme du 15 Juin 2000: Questions Juridiques et Problèmes Pratiques*, [2003-6] Droit Penal n°18
J.G. Douglas, *Beyond Admissibility: Real Confrontation, Virtual Cross-Examination and the Right to Confront Hearsay*, (1999) 67 Geo. Wash. L.R. 191
J.G. Douglas, *Virtual Cross-Examination: The Art of Impeaching Hearsay*, (2003) 34 Journal Mar. Law & Com. 149
R.M. Dworkin, *Taking Rights Seriously*, Duckworth, London, 1977
J. Elliot, *The Debates in the Several State Conventions on the Adoption of the Federal Constitution*, 2nd edn., Lippincott, Philadelphia, 1836
L. Ellison, *Cross-Examination and the Intermediary: Bridging the Language Divide*, [2002] Crim. L.R. 114
L. Ellison, *The Adversarial Process and the Vulnerable Witness*, Oxford Univ. Press, Oxford, 2001
B. Emmerson and A. Ashworth, *Human Rights and Criminal Justice*, Sweet & Maxwell, London, 2001
S. Enright, *The Anonymous Witness*, [1996] N.L.J. 1032
E. Fairchild and H.R. Dammer, *Comparative Criminal Justice Systems*, 2nd edn., Wadsworth, Belmont, 2001
L.J. Fassler, *The Italian Penal Procedure Code: An Adversarial System of Criminal Procedure in Continental Europe*, (1991) 29 Colum. J.T.L. 245
P. Fennell and others (eds.), *Criminal Justice in Europe: A Comparative Study*, Clarendon, Oxford, 1995
P. Ferrua, *Una Garanzia 'Finale' a Tutela del Contraddittorio: il Nuovo Art. 526 comma 1bis CPP*, in P. Tonini (ed.), *Giusto Processo: Nuove Norme sulla Formazione e Valutazione della Prova*, Cedam, Padova, 2001, 522
M. Findlay, *Synthesis in Trial Procedures? The Experience of International Criminal Tribunals*, (2001) 50 I.C.L.Q. 26
P. Fiorelli, *La Tortura Giudiziaria nel Diritto Comune*, Giuffrè, Milano, 1953
R. Flin, *Children's Testimony. Psychology on Trial*, in M.S. Zaragoza, *Memory and Testimony in the Child Witness*, Sage, Thousand Oaks, 1995, 240
R. Flin and others, *The Effect of a Five-Months Delay on Children's and Adults' Eyewitness Memory*, (1992) 83 British Journal of Psychology 323
E. Florian, *Delle Prove Penali*, Vallardi, Milano, 1924
J. Frank, *Courts on Trial. Myth and Reality in American Justice*, Princeton Univ. Press., Princeton, 1949
R.D. Friedman, *Adjusting To Crawford: High Court Decision Restores Confrontation Clause* Protection, (2004) 19 Criminal Justice 4
R.D. Friedman, *Anchors and Flotsam: Is Evidence Law "Adrift"?*, (1988) 107 Yale L.J. 1921
R.D. Friedman, *Confrontation: The Search for Basic Principles*, (1998) 86 Geo L.J. 1011
R.D. Friedman, *Thoughts from across the Water on Hearsay and Confrontation*, [1998] Crim. L.R. 697
G. Frigo, *Dalla Tutela Penale della Prova alla Tutela Penale dell'Indagine*, [1995-3] Crit. Dir. 210

G. Frigo, *L'Eccezione che Diventa la Regola*, [2003] Dir. Pen. Proc. 412
G. Frigo, *Sub Articolo 498*, in M. Chiavario (ed.), *Commento al Nuovo Codice di Procedura Penale*, Utet, Torino, 1991, vol. V, 252
J.A. Frowein and W.P. Peukert, *EMRK-Kommentar*, 2nd edn., Engel, Kehl, 1996
M. Garçon, *L'Avocat et la Morale*, Bouchet-Chastel, Paris, 1963
R. Garraud, *Traité Théorique et Pratique d'Instruction Criminelle et de Procédure Pénale*, Larose & Tenin, Paris, 1907
A. Giarda, *La 'precaria' facoltà di non testimoniare dei prossimi congiunti dell'imputato*, [1994] Corr. Giur. 963
G.S. Goodman and others, *Testifying in Criminal Court*, Chicago Univ. Press, Chicago, 1992
M.H. Graham, *Witness Intimidation. The Law's Response*, Quorum Books, Westport, 1985
E. Grande, *Italian Criminal Justice: Borrowing and Resistance*, (2000) 48 Am. J. Comp. Law 227
V. Grevi, *Le Dichiarazioni Rese dal Coimputato nel Nuovo Codice di Procedura Penale*, in L. De Cataldo Neuberger, *Chiamata in Correità e Psicologia del Pentitismo nel Nuovo Processo Penale*, Cedam, Padova, 1992, 7
B. Grossfeld, *The Strength and Weakness of Comparative Law*, Clarendon, Oxford, 1990
M. Guerrin, *Le Témoignage Anonyme au Regard de la Jurisprudence de la Cour Européenne des Droits de l'Homme*, (2002) R.T.D.H. 45
H.C. Gutteridge, *Comparative Law*, 2nd edn., Cambridge Univ. Press, Cambridge, 1949
H.M. Harlan, *White v. Illinois and the "Hearsay Clause" of the Sixth Amendment*, (1993) 54 Luisiana L.R. 177
L.A. Harper, *The English Navigation Laws: A Seventeenth-Century Experiment in Social Engineering*, Columbia Univ. press, New York, 1939
D.J. Harris, M. O'Boyle and C. Warbrick, *Law of the European Convention on Human Rights*, Butterworths, London, 1995
A.W. Hasselbach, *Placing a Child Victim of Sexual Abuse Behind a Screen During Courtroom Testimony as Violation of Sixth Amendment Confrontation Clause*, (1989) 57 Univ. Cincinnati L.R. 1537
J. Hatchard, B. Huber and R.A. Vogler, *Comparative Criminal Procedure*, British Institute of Intl. & Comp. Law, London, 1996
F. Helie, *Traité de l'instruction Criminelle*, Hingray, Paris, 1845
Home Office, *Criminal Statistics England and Wales 1998 (Cm. 4649)*, London, Stationery Office, 1998
Home Office, *Report of the Commission to Consider Legal Procedures to Deal with Terrorist Activities in Northern Ireland (Cm. 5185)*, London, Stationery Office, 1972
Home Office, *Rights Brought Home: The Human Rights Bill (Cm. 3782)*, London, Stationery Office, 1997
Home Office, *Speaking Up for Justice: Report of the Interdepartmental Working Group on the Treatment of Vulnerable or Intimidated Witnesses in the Criminal Justice System*, London, Stationery Office, 1998
T.B. Howell, *A Complete Collection of State Trials and Proceedings for High Treason and Other Crimes and Misdemeanors from the Earliest Period to the Year 1783*, London, 1816
L. Hoyano, *Striking a Balance between the Rights of Defendants and Vulnerable Witnesses: Will Special Measures Directions Contravene Guarantees of a Fair Trial?* [2001] Crim. L.R. 948

G. Illuminati, *Il Nuovo Dibattimento: l'Assunzione Diretta delle Prove*, [1988-V] Foro Ital. 355
H. Institoris and J Sprenger, *Malleus Maleficarum*, Nuremberg, 1519
R. Iraola, *The Sixth Amendment Right to Confrontation a Witness in Federal Criminal Trials About his True Name, Address, and Place of Employment*, (2002) 38 Crim. L.B. 396
Irvine L.J, *The Development of Human Rights in Britain under an Incorporated Convention on Human Rights*, [1998] Public Law 221
J.D. Jackson, *Two Models of Proof in Criminal Procedure*, (1988) 51 Modern L.R. 549
A. Jennings, A. Ashworth and B Emmerson, *Silence and Safety: The Impact of Human Rights Law*, [2000] Crim. L.R. 879
R.N. Jonakait, *The Origins of the Confrontation Clause: An Alternative History*, (1995) 27 Rutgers L.J. 77
R.N. Jonakait, *Restoring the Confrontation Clause to the Sixth Amendment*, (1988) 35 U.C.L.A. L.R. 557
D. Jousse, *Nouveau Commentaire sur l'Ordonnance Criminelle du Mois d'Août 1670*, Paris, 1756
D. Kennedy, *The International Human Rights Movement: Part of the Problem?*, [2001] European Human Right Law Review 245
S. Kines, *Why Suppress the Truth? U.S., Canadian and English Approaches to the Exclusion of Illegally Obtained Real Evidence in Criminal Cases*, [1996-2] R.P. 147
R.W. Kirst, *Hearsay and the Right to Confrontation in the European Court of Human Rights*, (2003) 21 Q.L.R. 777
R.E. Kostoris (ed.), *Il Giusto Processo tra Contraddittorio e Diritto al Silenzio*, Giappichelli, Torino, 2002
E. Lambert, *Les Effects des Arrêts de la Cour Européenne des Droits de l'Homme: Contribution à une Approche Pluraliste du Droit Européen des Droits de l'Homme*, Bruylant, Bruxelles, 1999
J.H. Langbein *Torture and the Law of Proof: Europe and England in the Ancien Régime*, Chicago Univ. Press, Chicago, 1977
G. Lattanzi, *La Formazione della Prova nel Dibattimento*, [1989] Cass. Pen. 2298
Law Commission, *Corroboration of Evidence in Criminal Trials*, Law Com. No. 115, 1990
Law Commission, *Evidence in Criminal Proceedings: Hearsay and Related Topics*, Law Com. No. 245, 1997
Law Commission, *The Hearsay Rule in Civil Proceedings* (Law Com. No. 216, 1993)
H. Leclerc, *Les Limites de la Liberté de la Preuve – Aspects Actuels en France*, [1992] R.S.C. 17
R. Legeais, *L'Utilisation de Témoignages sous Forme Anonyme ou Déguisée dans la Procédure des Juridictions Répréssives*, (1998) R.I.D.C. 711
P. Legrand (ed.), *Common Law d'un Siecle à l'Autre*, Blais, Cowansville, 1992
M. Leigh, *The Yugoslav Tribunal: Use of Unnamed Witnesses against Accused*, (1996) 90 American Journal Intl. Law 235
M. Leigh, *Witness Anonymity Is Inconsistent with Due Process*, (1997) 91 American Journal Intl. Law 80
M. Lemonde, *La Protection des Témoins devant les Tribunaux Français*, [1996] R.S.C. 815
R.O. Lempert and S.A. Saltzburg, *A Modern Approach to Evidence. Text, Problems, Transcripts and Cases*, 2nd edn., West, St. Paul, 1982
S. Levmore, *Law, Economics, & Norms: The Anonymity Tool*, (1996) 144 Univ. Penn. L.R. 2191
E.A. Lind J. Thibaut and L. Walker, *Discovery and Presentation of Evidence in Adversary and Non Adversary Proceedings*, (1973) 71 Mich. L.R. 1129

E.F. Loftus, *Eyewitness Testimony*, Harvard Univ. Press, Cambridge, 1996

F. Lombard, *Les Jurés: Justice Représentative et Représentation de la Justice*, L'Harmattan, Paris, 1993

S. Maffei (tr), *Il Codice di Procedura Penale Francese*, CELT, Piacenza, 2002

S. Maffei, *Il Diritto al Confronto con l'Accusatore*, CELT, Piacenza, 2003

S. Maffei, *Le Testimonianze Anonime nella Giurisprudenza della Corte Europea dei Diritti dell'Uomo*, [2003] Cass. Pen. 1700

S. Maffei, *Negotiations 'on Evidence' and Negotiations 'on Sentence': Adversarial Experiments in Italian Criminal Procedure*, [2004] Journal Intl. Crim. Just. 1050

S. Maffei, *Prova d'Accusa e Dichiarazioni di Testimoni "Assenti" in una Recente Sentenza della Corte Europea dei Diritti dell'Uomo*, [2001] Cass. Pen. 2836

S. Maffei, *Un Caso in Tema di Dichiarazioni Testimoniali d'Accusa "Ritrattate" nella Giurisprudenza della Corte Europea dei Diritti dell'Uomo*, [2002] Cass. Pen. 1818

K.F. O'Malley, J.E. Grenig and W.C. Lee, *Federal Jury Practice and Instructions – Criminal*, 5th edn., West, St. Paul, 2000

L. Marafioti, *L'Art 507 CPP al Vaglio delle Sezioni Unite: un Addio al Processo Accusatorio e all'Imparzialità del Giudice Dibattimentale*, [1993] R.I.D.P.P. 829

G. Marcus, *Secret Witnesses*, [1990] P.L. 207

A. Maron, *'Principales Dispositions du Décret du 16 Mai 2003, Relatif à la Protection des Témoins et à l'Utilisation de Moyens de Télécommunication*, [2003-7/8] Droit Pénal n°23

T.M. Massaro, *The Dignity Value of Face-to-Face Confrontations*, (1988) 40 U. Flo. L.R. 863

F. Matscher and H. Petzold (eds.), *Protecting Human Rights: The European Dimension*, Heymanns, Köln, 1988

R. May, *Criminal Evidence*, 4th edn., Sweet & Maxwell, London, 1999

J. McEwan, *Documentary Hearsay Evidence-Refuge for the Vulnerable Witness?*, [1989] Crim. L.R. 629

J. McEwan, *Evidence and the Adversarial Process*, 2nd edn., Hart Publishing, Oxford, 1998

R.E. Megarry, *Lawyer and Litigant in England*, Stevens, London, 1962

A Melchionda, *Prova (Diritto Processuale Penale)*, in *Enciclopedia del Diritto*, Giuffrè, Milano, 1988, vol. XXXVII, 650

R. Merle and A. Vitu, *Traité De Droit Criminel – Procèdure Pénale*, 5th edn., Cujas, Paris, 2001

P. Mirfield, *Silence, Confessions and Improperly Obtained Evidence*, Clarendon, Oxford, 1997

K.J.A. Mittermaier, *Das Englische, Schottische und Nordamerikanische Strafverfahren*, Enke, Erlangen, 1851

K.J.A. Mittermaier, *Erfahrungen über die Wirksamkeit der Schwurgerichte in Europa und Amerika über ihre Vorzüge, Mängel und Abhülfe*, Enke, Erlangen, 1865

K.J.A. Mittermaier, *Teoria della Prova nel Processo Penale*, F. Ambrosoli Italian Translation, Sanvito, Milano, 1858

M. Momeni, *Balancing the Procedural Rights of the Accused against a Mandate to Protect Victims and Witnesses: An Examination of the Anonymity Rules of the International Criminal Tribunal for the Former Yugoslavia*, (1997) 41 Howard L.J. 155

T. Mommsen, *Römisches Strafrecht*, Duncker & Humblot, Leipzig, 1899

E.M. Morgan, *Hearsay and Non–Hearsay*, (1935) 48 Harvard L.R. 1138

E.M. Morgan, *The Jury and the Exclusionary Rules of Evidence*, (1937) 4 Univ. Chicago L.R. 247

C.B. Mueller and L.C. Kirkpatrick, *Evidence*, 2nd edn., Aspen Law & Business, Gaithersburg, 1999

C.B. Mueller and L.C. Kirkpatrick, *Evidence under the Rules*, 4th edn., Aspen Law & Business, Gaithersburg, 2000

R. Munday, *Inferences from Silence and European Human Rights Law*, [1996] Crim. L.R. 370

R. Munday, *Réflexions Historiques et Comparatives sur le Procès par Jury*, in P. Legrand (ed.), *Common Law d'un Siecle à l'Autre*, Blais, Cowansville, 1992, 493

P. Murphy (ed.), *Blackstone's Criminal Practice 2004*, Oxford Univ. Press, Oxford, 2003

P. Murphy, *Evidence*, 8th edn., Oxford Univ. Press., Oxford, 2003

K. Murray, *Live Television Link: An Evaluation of Its Use by Child Witnesses in Scottish Criminal Trials*, The Scottish Office, Edinburgh, 1995

T.J. Murray, *Videotaped Depositions: Putting Absent Witnesses in Court*, (1982) 68 A.B.A.J. 1402

J.E.B. Myers, K.J. Saywitz and G.S. Goodman, *Psychological Research on Children as Witnesses: Practical Implications for Forensic Interviews and Courtroom Testimony*, (1996) 28 Pacific L.J. 3

D.A. Nance, *The Best Evidence Principle*, (1988) 73 Iowa L.R. 229

A. Nappi, *Guida al Codice di Procedura Penale*, 7th edn., Giuffrè, Milano, 2000

M. Newark, *The Hostile Witness and the Adversary System*, [1986] Crim. L.R. 441

P. Nicolopoulos, *La Procédure devant les Juridictions Répressives et le Principe du Contradictoire*, [1989] R.S.C. 1

J.F. Nijboer, *Children and Young Persons in the Criminal Justice System: The Council of Europe Recommendation on Witness Protection and Rights of the Defence*, (1999) 10 Criminal Law Forum 443

M. Nobili, *Giusto Processo e Indagini Difensive: Verso Una Nuova Procedura Penale?*, [2001] Dir. Pen. Proc. 5

M. Nobili, *Il Nuovo "Diritto delle Prove" ed un Rinnovato Concetto di Prova*, [1989] Leg. Pen. 395

M. Nobili, *Il Principio del Libero Convincimento del Giudice*, Giuffrè, Milano, 1974

R.G. Nuce, *Child Sexual Abuse: A New Decade for the Protection of Our Children?*, (1990) 39 Emory L.J. 581

J.L. O'Brian, *National Security and Individual Freedom*, Harvard Univ. Press, Cambridge, 1955

C. Osborne, *Hearsay and the European Court of Human Rights*, [1993] Crim. L.R. 255

C. Ovey and R.C.A. White, *European Convention on Human Rights*, 3rd edn. Oxford univ. Press, Oxford, 2002

R. Pattenden, *The Hostile Witness*, (1992) 56 Journal Crim. Law 414

P.P. Paulesu, *Giudice e Parti nella 'Dialettica' della Prova Testimoniale*, Giappichelli, Torino, 2002

A. Perrodet, *The Italian System*, in M. Delmas-Marty and J.R. Spencer (eds.), *European Criminal Procedures*, Cambrige Univ. Press, Cambridge, 2002, 348

M.E. Pipe and G.S. Goodman, *Elements of Secrecy: Implications for Children's Testimony*, (1991) 9 Behav. Science & Law 33

W.T. Pizzi, *Trials without Truth: Why Our System of Criminal Trials Has Become an Expensive Failure and What We Need to Do to Rebuild It*, N.Y. Univ. Press, New York, 1999

W.T. Pizzi and L. Marafioti, *The New Italian Code of Criminal Procedure: The Difficulties of Binding an Adversarial Trial System on a Civil Law Foundation*, (1992) 17 Yale J. Intl. Law, 1

D.H. Pollitt, *The Right of Confrontation: Its History and Modern Dress*, (1959) 8 Journal of Public Law 381

D.A. Poole and L.T. White, *Tell Me Again and Again-Stability and Change in the Repeated Testimonies*, in M.S. Zaragoza, *Memory and Testimony in the Child Witness*, Sage, Thousand Oaks, 1995, 24

R. Pound, *The Causes of Popular Dissatisfaction with the Administration of Justice*, (1964) 35 Federal Rules Decisions 273

J. Pradel, *Inquisitoire-Accusatoire: une Redoutable Complexité*, (1997) 68 R.I.D.P. 213

J. Pradel, *La Notion de Procés Equitable en Droit Pénal Européen*, (1997) 27 Revue Général de Droit 505

J. Pradel, *La Preuve en Procédure Pénale Comparée – Rapport Général*, (1992) 63 R.I.D.P. 13

J. Pradel, *L'Appel contre les Arrêt d'Assises: un Apport Heureux de la Loi du 15 Juin 2000*, [2001] D. Chron. 1964

J. Pradel, *Presentation du Code Français de Procedure Penale*, in S. Maffei (tr), *Il Codice di Procedura Penale Francese*, CELT, Piacenza, 2002, 7

G. Radbruch, *Zur Einführung in die Carolina*, in Die Peinliche Gerichtsordnung Kaiser Karls V von 1532 *(*Carolina*)*, 5th edn., Reclam, Stuttgart, 1996

L. Raison Rebufat, *Le Principe de Loyauté en Droit de la Preuve*, [2002] Gaz. Pal. Doct. 1195

M.L. Rassat, *Traité de Procédure Pénale*, PUF, Paris, 2001

P.L. Reichel, *Comparative Criminal Justice Systems – A Topical Approach*, 2nd edn., Prentice Hall, Upper Saddle River, 1999

J.C. Reitz, *How to Do Comparative Law*, (1998) 46 Am. J. Comp. Law 621

R.W. Renton and H.H. Brown, *Criminal Procedure According to the Law of Scotland*, 6th edn., Green-Sweet & Maxwell, Edinburgh, 1996

P.J. Richardson (ed.), *Archbold Criminal Pleading, Evidence and Practice 2004*, Sweet & Maxwell, London, 2004

G. Robertson, *Freedom, the Individual and the Law*, 7th edn., Penguin, Harmondsworth, 1993, 282

W. Roumier, *Pour en Finir avec un Réforme Inachevée: à Propos de l'Appel des Décisions en Matière Criminelle*, [2003-10] Droit Penal n°28

A. Samuels, *Reading the Statement of the Witness Absent through Fear*, (1999) 163 J.P.&L.G.L. 50

A. Saunders and R. Young, *Criminal Justice*, 2nd edn., Butterworths, London, 2000

K.J. Saywitz, *Improving Children's Testimony: the Question, the Answer and the Environment*, in M.S. Zaragoza, *Memory and Testimony, supra* note 27, at 113-140

S.J. Schulhofer, F Greenberg and B.J. Greenberg, *La Preuve en Procédure Pénale Comparée – Rapport de Synthèse pour les Pays de Common Law*, (1992) 63 R.I.D.P. 33

R Screvens, *Le Statut du Témoin et sa Protection Avant, Pendant et Après le Procès Pénal*, [1989] R.D.P.C. 3

M.L. Seigel, *Rationalising Hearsay: A Proposal for a Best Evidence Hearsay Rule*, (1992) 72 Boston Univ. L.R. 907

B.J. Shapiro, *'Beyond Reasonable Doubt' and 'Probable Cause': Historical Perspectives on the Anglo-American Law of Evidence*, Univ. California Press, Berkeley, 1991

L.H. Shiffman, *Sectarian Law in the Dead Sea Scrolls: Courts, Testimony and the Penal Code*, Chico Scholars, California, 1983

J.A. Simpson and E.S.C. Weiner, *The Oxford English Dictionary*, 2nd edn., Clarendon Oxford, 1989, vol. XX

D. Siracusano and others, *Diritto Processuale Penale,* 4th edn., Giuffrè, Milano, 2001
J.R. Spencer, *Introduction,* in M. Delmas-Marty and J.R. Spencer (eds.), *European Criminal Procedures,* Cambrige Univ. Press, Cambridge, 2002, 1
J.R. Spencer, *Evidence,* in M. Delmas-Marty and J.R. Spencer (eds.), *European Criminal Procedures,* Cambrige Univ. Press, Cambridge, 2002, 594
J.R. Spencer, *La Preuve en Procédure Pénale Comparée – Le Droit Anglais,* (1992) 63 R.I.D.P. 83
J.R. Spencer, *Les Limites en Matière de Preuve – Aspects actuels,* [1992] R.S.C. 42
J.R. Spencer, *Orality and the Evidence of Absent Witnesses,* [1994] Crim. L.R. 628
J.R. Spencer, *The Case for a Code of Criminal Procedure,* [2000] Crim. L.R. 519
J.R. Spencer, *The English System,* in M. Delmas-Marty and J.R. Spencer (eds.), *European Criminal Procedures,* Cambrige Univ. Press, Cambridge, 2002, 142
J.R. Spencer and R. Flin, *The Evidence of Children: the Law and the Psychology,* 2nd edn., Blackstone, London, 1993
J.R. Spencer and P.G. Tucker, *The Evidence of Absent Children,* [1987] N.L.J. 816
S. Stavros, *The Guarantees for Accused Persons under Article 6 of the European Convention on Human Rights: an Analysis of the Application of the Convention and a Comparison with Other Instruments,* Martinus Nijhoff, London, 1993
H.L. Stephen, *The Trial of Sir Walter Raleigh,* (1919) 2 Trans. Royal Hist. Soc. (4th Series) 172
J.F. Stephen, *Criminal Procedure from the Thirteen to the Eighteenth Century,* in *Select Essays in Anglo-American Legal History,* Little Brown, Boston, 1908
R.H. Stier, *Revisiting the Missing Witness Inference. Quieting the Loud Voice from the Empty Chair,* (1985) 44 Maryland L.R. 137
M. Stone, *Instant Lie Detection? Demeanour and Credibility in Criminal Trials,* [1991] Crim. L.R. 822
J.W. Strong *McCormick on Evidence,* 5th edn. West, St. Paul, 1999
F. Sudre *Droit International et Européen des Droits de l'Homme,* 5th edn., P.U.F., Paris, 2001
F. Sudre (ed.), *L'Interprétation de la Convention Européenne des Droits de l'Homme,* Bruylant, Bruxelles, 1998
J. Susini, *Le Témoin, le Témoignage et la Police,* [1980] R.S.C. 499
C. Tapper, *Cross and Tapper on Evidence,* 9th edn., Butterworths, London, 1999
J.P. Taylor, *A Treatise on the Law of Evidence as Administered in England and Ireland: with Illustrations from the American and Other Foreign Laws,* Maxwell & son., London, 1848
H. Temime, *L'Appel des Arrêt d'Assises,* [2001] R.S.C. 53
S.C. Thaman, *The Lay Participation in the Criminal Trial in the XXIst Century,* (2001) 72 R.I.D.P. 19
J.B. Thayer, *A Preliminary Treatise on Evidence at the Common Law,* Sweet and Maxwell, London, 1898
P. Thornton, *The Prejudiced Defendant: Unfairness Suffered by a Defendant in a Joint Trial,* [2003] Crim. L.R. 433
P Tonini (ed.), *Giusto Processo: Nuove Norme sulla Formazione e Valutazione della Prova,* Cedam, Padova, 2001
P. Tonini, *La Prova Penale,* 4th edn., Cedam, Padova, 2000
P. Tonini and P. Ferrua, *Testimonianza Volontaria dell'Imputato e Diritto al Contraddittorio. Progetto di Modifica del Codice di Procedura Penale,* [2000] Cass. Pen. 2868

G. Ubertis, *Principi di Procedura Penale Europea*, Cortina, Milano, 2000

M. Van de Kerchove, *La Preuve en Matière Pénale dans la Jurisprudence de la Cour et de la Commission Européennes des Droits de l'Homme*, [1992] R.S.C. 1

C. Van den Wyngaert (ed.), *Criminal Procedure Systems in the European Community*, Butterworths, London, 1993

P. Van Dijk and G.J.H. Van Hoof, *Theory and Practice of the European Convention on Human Rights*, 3rd edn., Kluwer, The Hague, 1998

S. Van Drooghenbroeck, *La Proportionnalité dans le Droit de la Convention Européenne des Droits de l'Homme: Prendre l'Idée Simple au Sérieux*, Bruylant, Bruxelles, 2001

G. van Kessel, *European Perspectives on the Accused as a Source of Testimonial Evidence*, (1998) 100 W. Virginia L.R. 799

P.L. Vigna and R. Alfonso, *Lineamenti della Legge sui Collaboratori di Giustizia*, in P. Tonini (ed), *Giusto Processo: Nuove Norme sulla Formazione e Valutazione della Prova*, Cedam, Padova, 2002, 97-126

G.P. Voena, *La Legge sulle Videoconferenze e sull'Esame a Distanza nel Processo Penale*, in G. Conso and V. Grevi (eds), *Profili del Nuovo Codice di Procedura Penale – Appendice di aggiornamento*, 4th edn., Cedam, Padova, 1998, 25

M. Vogliotti, *La Logica Floue della Corte Europea dei Diritti dell'Uomo tra Tutela del Testimone e Salvaguardia del Contraddittorio: il Caso delle Testimonianze Anonime*' [1998] Giur. Ital. 851

Voltaire, *Commentario sopra il Libro dei Delitti e delle Pene*, 1767

Voltaire, *Prix de la Justice et de l'Humanité*, Ferney, 1778

R. Vouin, *L'Application du Code de Procédure Pénale et le Malheur des Temps*, [1962] R.S.C. 65

W. Wade, *Constitutional Fundamentals*, Stevens, London, 1989

O.G. Wellborn, *Demeanor*, (1991) 76 Cornell L.R. 1075

H.L. Westcott and G.M. Davies and J.R. Spencer, *Protecting The Child Witness: Hearsay Techniques and Other Innovations: Children, Hearsay, and the Courts: A Perspective From the United Kingdom*, (1999) 5 Psych. P.P.& L. 282

J.H. Wigmore, *Evidence in Trials at Common Law*, J.H. Chadbourn Rev., Little Brown, Boston, 1974

G. Williams, *The Proof of Guilt*, 3rd edn., Stevens, London, 1969

F.J. Wrottesley, *The Examination of Witnesses in Court*, 3rd edn., Sweet and Maxwell, London, 1961

J. F. Yetter, *Wrestling with Crawford v. Washington And The New Constitutional Law of Confrontation*, (2004) 28 Florida Bar Journal 26

I. Younger, M. Goldsmith and D.A. Sonenshein, *Principles of Evidence*, 4th edn., Anderson, Cincinnati, 2000

H.C. Yourov, *The Margin of Appreciation Doctrine in the Dynamics of European Human Rights Jurisprudence*, Kluwer, The Hague, 1996

E. Zappalà, *Le Procès Pénal Italien entre Système Inquisitoire et Système Accusatoire*, (1997) 68 R.I.D.P. 111

S. Zappalà, *Human Rights in International Criminal Proceedings*, Oxford Univ. Press, Oxford, 2003

M.S. Zaragoza, *Memory and Testimony in the Child Witness*, Sage, Thousand Oaks, 1995

A.A.S. Zuckerman, *The Principles of Criminal Evidence*, Clarendon, Oxford, 1989

M. Zuckerman, B.M. Depaulo and R. Rosenthal, *Verbal and Nonverbal Communication of Deception*, (1981) 14 Advanced Exper. Soc. Psychol. 1

K. Zweigert and H. Kötz, *Introduction to Comparative Law*, 3rd edn., Clarendon, Oxford, 1998

Table of Cases

EHCR Cases

Before the Court

United Kingdom

Other Courts

Italy

Constitutional Court

Supreme Court

Other Courts

USA

Australia

Canada

Table of Legislation

United Kingdom

Abbreviations

A.B.A.J.	American Bar Association Journal
Arch. Nuova Proc. Pen.	Archivio della Nuova Procedura Penale (Italian Law Journal)
Behav Sc & L	Behavioral Sciences and the Law
Bull. crim.	Bulletin des arrêts de la Cour de Cassation – Chambre Criminelle
Cass. Pen.	Cassazione penale (Italian Law Journal)
C.C.A.	Court of Criminal Appeal
CD	Collection of Decisions of the European Commission of Human Rights
C.L.R.	Commonwealth Law Reports
Corr. Giur.	Corriere Giuridico (Italian Law Journal)
Crit. Dir.	Critica del Diritto (Italian Law Journal)
D.	Revue Dalloz Sirey
Digest Strasbourg	Digest of Strasbourg Case-Law relating to the European Convention on Human Rights
Dir. Pen. Proc.	Diritto Penale e Processo (Italian Law Journal)
DR	European Commission of Human Rights Decisions and Reports
ECHR	European Convention for the Protection of Human Rights and Fundamental Freedoms
EHRR	European Human Rights Reports
EHRR CD	European Human Rights Reports – Commission Decisions
(F) Cass crim	Cour de Cassation – Chambre Criminelle (France)
F-CP	French Criminal Code
Foro Ital.	Il Foro italiano (Italian Law Journal)
Gaz. Pal. Doct.	Gazette du Palais – Doctrine (French Law Journal)
Giur. Cost.	Giurisprudenza Costituzionale (Italian Law Journal)
Giur Ital.	Giurisprudenza italiana (Italian Law Journal)
H.L.	House of Lords
(I) Cass. crim.	Corte di Cassazione-sezione penale (Italy)
(I) Corte cost.	Constitutional Court (Italy)
I-CP	Italian Criminal Code
I-CPP	Italian Code of Criminal Procedure
F-CPP	French Code of Criminal Procedure
I.C.C.	International Criminal Court
J.C.P.	La Semaine Juridique (French Law Journal)
J.P.&L.G.L.	Justice of the Peace and Local Government Law
Leg. Pen.	Legislazione penale (Italian Law Journal)
L.J.	Law Journal
L.R.	Law Review
N.L.R.	New Law Journal
P.L.	Public Law (British Law Journal)
Psych. P.P.&L.	Psychology, Public Policy and Law
Q.B.D.	Queens Bench Division

Q.L.R.	Quinnipiac Law Review
R.D.P.C.	Revue de droit pénal et de criminologie
R.G.D.	Revue général de droit
R.I.D.C.	Revue internationale de droit comparé
R.I.D.P.	Revue internationale de droit pénal
R.I.D.P.P.	Rivista italiana di diritto e procedura penale (Italian Law Journal)
RJD	European Court of Human Rights: Reports of Judgments and Decisions
R.P.	Res publica
R.S.C.	Revue de science criminelle et de droit pénal comparé
R.T.D.H.	Revue trimestrielle des droits de l'homme
S.C.R.	Supreme Court Reports (Canada)
Trans. Royal Hist. Soc.	Transactions of the Royal Historical Society
U.C.L.A. L.R.	University of Los Angeles California Law Review
U.N. Sec. Council Res.	Resolution of the United Nations Security Council
U.N. Ybk.	United Nations Yearbook
U.S.C.	United States Code
W.L.R.	Weekly Law Reports
Y.B.	Yearbook of the European Convention on Human Rights

Index